Implementing Auditing Procedures

Combined text

NVQ Accounting Unit 17
AAT Diploma Pathway Unit 17

John Taylor

Jo Osborne

osborne
BOOKS

Published by Osborne Books Limited
Unit 1B Everoak Estate
Bromyard Road
Worcester WR2 5HP
Tel 01905 748071
Email books@osbornebooks.co.uk
Website www.osbornebooks.co.uk

Design by Richard Holt
Cover image from Getty Images

Printed by the Bath Press, Bath

British Library Cataloguing in Publication Data
A catalogue record for this book is available from the British Library

ISBN 1 872962 98 X

Contents

Acknowledgements

The authors wish to thank the following for their help with the production of the book: Mike Gilbert, Rosemarie Griffiths and Jenny Clarke. Thanks must also go to Trish Sayer of McKnights of Worcester for advising on current auditing practice and for providing standard letters used in the auditing process.

The publisher would like to thank Tesco PLC and the Auditing Practices Board for the reproduction of extracts from published accounts, audit reports and International Standards on Auditing.

Lastly, the publisher is indebted to the Association of Accounting Technicians for permission for the reproduction of extracts from the Unit specifications and the sample simulation, DJ's Limited.

Authors

John Taylor is a Chartered Accountant who spent many years in professional practice, advising small and medium-sized businesses before becoming the Financial Director of a Leeds based public limited company. In 2004 John joined the staff of Leeds Metropolitan University, where he specialises in teaching management accounting and auditing on a range of professional courses, including the AAT qualifications.

Jo Osborne is a Chartered Accountant who trained with Ernst & Young in their London office. She then moved to Cable & Wireless where she spent two years in their internal audit department before moving into an investment appraisal role. Jo has taught AAT at Hillingdon College and more recently at Worcester College of Technology where she teaches on all levels of the AAT qualification.

Introduction

Implementing Auditing Procedures has been written to cover the requirements of Unit 17 'Implementing Auditing Procedures'.

Implementing Auditing Procedures is a very practical book designed for use by students who do not necessarily work in an auditing environment but who need a guide to the subject which covers both theory and practice.

Implementing Auditing Procedures has been written within the theoretical framework of the relatively new International Standards on Auditing (ISAs), available on www.apb.org.uk

Implementing Auditing Procedures is a 'combined text' which contains two main sections:

- A **tutorial section** containing seven chapters covering the Unit 17 performance criteria and 'knowledge and understanding' requirements. The chapters contain:
  - a clear text with Case Studies
  - a chapter summary and key terms to help with revision
  - student activities – the answers to a selection of which are to be found for download at www.osbornebooks.co.uk
- A **practice simulation** section containing two full length simulations, one of which is the AAT guidance simulation – DJ's Limited – published when the New Standards were first introduced in 2003.

A note to tutors – Tutor Packs

The answers to simulations and selected student activities are available in a separate paper-based *Tutor Pack*. This data – together with the answers to the remaining student activities – is also available electronically on a CD. Please contact the Osborne Books Customer Services on 01905 748071 for details of how to obtain this tutor support material.

Osborne website

The Osborne Books website has proved popular for its free downloads and multiple choice quizzes. As noted above, the answers to some of the student activities in this book can be downloaded from www.osbornebooks.co.uk

1 Introduction to auditing

The aim of this chapter is to give you an introduction to auditing. We will cover the detailed aspects of auditing later, but in this introductory chapter we explain what an audit is, why auditors are needed, who can and cannot be an auditor, and outline the process of auditing. We also look at the difference between internal and external auditors.

This chapter covers:

- what an audit is

- who needs to be audited

- who can do an audit

- appointment of auditors

- the audit process

- the auditor's report

- internal auditors

- the expectation gap – what people think auditors do and what they actually do

PERFORMANCE CRITERIA COVERED

unit 17 IMPLEMENTING AUDITING PROCEDURES

This chapter introduces the background to auditing and covers some of the underpinning Knowledge and Understanding that is common to all three elements of Unit 17. Specifically it covers aspects of:

1   A general understanding of the legal duties of auditors; the content of reports; the definition of proper records

4   Types of audit: relationship between internal and external auditors

AUDITING IN CONTEXT

It is quite likely that, if you work in an accounts environment, you will have come into contact with auditors. You may even be involved in audit work if you work for a firm of Chartered or Chartered Certified accountants.

Auditors seem to arrive once or twice a year, ask a lot of questions, look at accounting records and go away again. What are they doing, what purpose does it serve and why is it important?

The role of the auditor is often misunderstood. Quite often people who come into contact with auditors, or even staff actually involved in auditing, only see part of the process. They are quizzed by auditors or they carry out audit tests but rarely see the whole process through from beginning to end.

This book explains the whole audit process from start to finish so that you will better understand why auditors are there, the job they have to do and the reasons why they to ask so many questions.

WHAT IS AN AUDIT?

Firstly we need a description of what an audit is.

An audit is a process by which an independent, qualified third party expresses an opinion as to whether a set of financial statements of a company represent a true and fair view of its financial affairs for an accounting period.

What does this mean? It means that the annual accounts of a company are reviewed by an independent, qualified accountant who signs a report to say that they properly reflect the financial position of the company for the financial year just ended.

Not all businesses have to be audited. Sole traders, partnerships and small companies are not required to have an audit, but larger companies and some public bodies like local authorities or parts of the NHS are.

We examine the issue of who is and is not required to have an audit in more detail later in this chapter.

WHY DO WE NEED AUDITS?

Why do most companies have to be audited when, for example, a business, which is run as a partnership, does not?

Consider the situation of a company and the way in which it operates.

You will be aware from your studies that a company is a legal entity, separate from its owners and managers. Once this principle was established in law it became necessary for the interests of the owners of the business to be safeguarded. In all but the smallest businesses, the shareholders were simply investors who were not normally involved in the day-to-day running of the business.

Consequently, they needed reassurance that the professional managers (the directors) whom they employed to run the business had been doing so properly. Who better to give the shareholders that reassurance than professionally qualified accountants who were independent of the business and who had their own code of ethics and professional competence? The shareholders employed accountants to provide them with a report on the accuracy of the financial statements, and so the auditing profession came into being.

It is important for you to understand the distinction between shareholders (sometimes referred to as '**members**') who own a company and directors who manage the business on behalf of the shareholders.

In small companies these may be the same individuals, but in larger companies shareholders and directors are more likely to be completely different people. Study the diagram below.

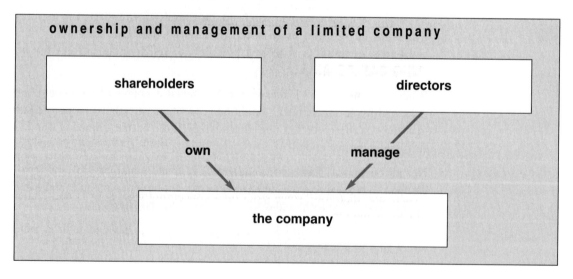

ownership and management of a limited company

| shareholders | directors |

own   manage

the company

In Chapter 2 we will examine in detail the legal framework within which auditors and directors must operate. This is based on the **Companies Act 1985.** It is this Act that forms the basis of the legal relationship between the auditors, the shareholders, the directors and the company itself.

Companies Act
1985

WHO NEEDS TO BE AUDITED?

All limited companies, except small companies, are required to have an audit. In this respect the law makes no distinction between a private family-run limited company and a large company such as Tesco plc. Both are equally required by law to have their financial statements audited and auditors must make a report to the owners of the business.

In addition to companies, some public bodies also have to be audited but these fall outside the scope of Unit 17 and this book.

Sole traders and partnerships do not require an audit and small companies satisfying certain criteria are also exempt. How is a small company defined?

The official definitions, which you do need to remember, are:

■ **small companies** – private limited companies, which are not part of a larger group, and are not banking or insurance companies. Their turnover must be £5.6m or less, their balance sheet totals £2.8m or less and they should employ fewer than 50 people.

■ **small charities that are companies** – these are charities which are companies with a gross income of £250,000 or less and a balance sheet total of £1.4m or less

■ **dormant companies** (ie companies which have not carried out any transactions in the financial period)

WHO CAN DO AN AUDIT?

Because of the role they play in the financial community auditors should have specific qualities. They must be technically proficient accountants with a strong code of ethics. They must also be independent of both the company they are auditing and the shareholders they are reporting to.

There are, therefore, some strict rules concerning who is, or is not, eligible to be an auditor.

One point it is important to make clear is that the person who signs the auditor's report must be qualified to do so.

When we refer to an 'auditor' therefore, we are referring to a person who is qualified to sign an audit report. The staff who work for the auditor, despite the fact they will carry out most of the detailed checking work, may not have the necessary qualification, although, of course, they may be studying for it.

eligibility to be an auditor

The Companies Act states that auditors must be a member of a **Recognised Supervisory Body (RSB)**.

recognised supervisory bodies (RSBs)

RSBs are organisations which have the responsibility of overseeing the regulation of the auditing profession in the UK and the maintenance of professional standards.

Their rules say that persons eligible for appointment must either hold an appropriate qualification or be firms controlled by suitably qualified individuals.

These are the Recognised Supervisory Bodies:

- Institute of Chartered Accountants in England & Wales (ICAEW)
- Institute of Chartered Accountants in Scotland (ICAS)
- Institute Of Chartered Accountants in Ireland (ICAI)
- Association Of Chartered Certified Accountants (ACCA)
- Association of Authorised Public Accountants (AAPA)

The AAT is not an RSB, so members of the AAT cannot act as auditors unless they are also a member of one of these qualifying bodies. However, AAT members often form part of an audit team.

An individual who holds a similar overseas qualification may be eligible to practice as an auditor in the UK but his/her status would have to be confirmed prior to them commencing work.

The RSB's role is to monitor and inspect their members on a regular basis to ensure that professional standards are being maintained.

who may and may not be an auditor

The Companies Act (Section 27) states that a person may **not** be an auditor if he/she is:

- an officer or employee of the company being audited
- any person in business partnership with an officer or employee of the company being audited

This is clearly to ensure that the auditor remains independent. It also implies that the following **may** be appointed as an auditor of a company:

- a shareholder of the client company
- a debtor or creditor of the client company

The Recognised Supervisory Bodies have stricter policies on independence than the law. In practice, an individual who is, for example, the wife of a director of a business, will not be able to accept the appointment as auditor to that business, even though the law does not specifically prohibit it.

APPOINTMENT OF AUDITORS

When a company first requires an audit the directors appoint the auditors. Their appointment lasts until the end of the first Annual General Meeting (AGM) of the company. If the shareholders wish to they can re-elect the auditors to serve for another year until the end of the next AGM, and again at the AGM of each subsequent year, if they are happy with the auditors.

If the shareholders do not re-elect the auditors, another firm can be appointed to act as auditors in their place.

Before accepting an appointment an auditor should carry out a certain amount of preliminary investigative work. We will look at this in more detail in Chapter 3.

We will now use a Case Study to show how the relationship between the auditors and shareholders works.

Case Study

TASHA: THE ROLE OF THE AUDITOR

situation

Tasha has shares in a company that operates a small chain of restaurants and shops in the South of England.

Henry, who is Tasha's brother, and his assistant Hugo, are the directors and manage the business on a daily basis. Tasha is not a director as she initially only invested in the company to help her brother get started.

The company is growing quickly because Henry has worked hard to expand the business.

Tasha is concerned that, as the business grows, she will lose touch with it and that Henry and Hugo could, together, do what they want without telling her.

She is also concerned that if it goes wrong her investment may be lost.

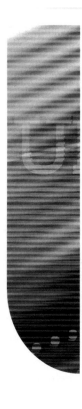

required

You are the auditor to the company. Explain to Tasha the role of the auditor in this situation.

solution

The main points that would help reassure Tasha would be as follows:

■   the company must prepare accounts that have to be audited and sent to the shareholders

■   the auditor has to be professionally qualified and independent of the company and the directors

■   the role of the auditors is to express an opinion as to the truth and fairness of the accounts sent to the shareholders

■   a company has to comply with the requirements of the Companies Act 1985 which has quite specific requirements about how the company must be managed and what books and records it must keep.

■   Tasha has the right, as a shareholder, not only to receive an audited set of accounts but also to come to the Annual General Meeting where they would be formally presented

THE AUDIT PROCESS

We will now examine the way in which an audit process works.

The steps which an auditor will go through, from being asked to take up an appointment to signing the auditor's report, are normally as follows:

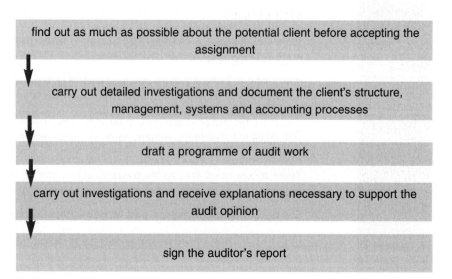

find out as much as possible about the potential client before accepting the assignment

carry out detailed investigations and document the client's structure, management, systems and accounting processes

draft a programme of audit work

carry out investigations and receive explanations necessary to support the audit opinion

sign the auditor's report

The separate elements of this process will be dealt with in more detail, step by step, in subsequent chapters in this book.

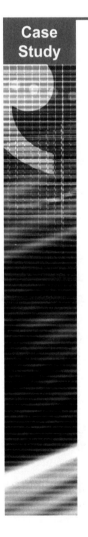

There is another important factor to consider and that is the **timescale** of this process.

There are deadlines for companies to file accounts with the Registrar of Companies which we will consider further in Chapter 2, and there is also a deadline for sending accounts to shareholders. Shareholders must receive a copy of the final audited accounts not less than 21 days before the date of the Annual General Meeting so once a date for that has been set, the timescale for the work has to be based on that deadline.

In reality, most companies will want to finalise their accounts within a few months of the year end, so in most cases final audits are carried out then. The Case Study that follows illustrates the way in which these timescales work.

Case Study

TIMPANI LTD: TIMESCALE OF THE AUDIT

situation

Auditors Crash & Co have been approached to be the first auditors of Timpani Ltd and have accepted. The financial year end is 31 December and they have been told that the AGM will be held on 21 April.

It is now early September and the audit has to be completed in time to send the accounts to the shareholders.

required

You are the audit manager and have been told to draw up an outline plan of how the audit assignment will be arranged. This will form the basis of detailed planning later.

solution

Your approach is to identify the key tasks and decide how much time will be needed to carry out each one.

You know that the accounts have to be sent to the shareholders 21 days before the date of the AGM and so your real deadline is 31 March.

The duration of each task is based on your estimate of how much work there is to be done and how long you think it will take based on your experience.

As this is the first audit Timpani Ltd has had, the tasks may take more or less time and the plan should allow for this.

You draw up a basic plan which is shown on the next page.

Task	Duration	Date
Visit Timpani for an introductory meeting to explain the role of the auditor and the auditing process. Also to discuss what will be expected of Timpani in terms of preparing accounts and making information available to the auditors	1 day	Immediate
Planning visit by audit team to document Timpani's accounting system	1 week	late September
Plan a programme of audit work and meet with Timpani's staff to agree timings	1 day	by early October
First audit visit	1 week	early November
Year end work – eg stocktaking etc	1 day	31 December
Final audit visit	2 weeks	late February
Review final accounts by auditors and discussion with management	1 day	mid March
Sign auditor's report	1 day	by 31 March

This plan depends upon Timpani's accounts staff having the accounts and supporting schedules ready on time. This is why preliminary discussions with their staff are important so that everybody knows what they have to do, and by what date.

THE AUDITOR'S REPORT

We will deal with the precise wording of auditors' reports in Chapter 7. At this stage you need only be aware that it is the job of the auditor to report on the company's financial statements for an accounting period.

What auditors have to decide, based on the evidence they have collected during their audit work, is whether the accounts show a true and fair view of the profit and loss account and the balance sheet for the financial period.

They also have to confirm that the company has maintained proper books and records. We will examine what this means in practice in Chapter 7.

After it has been signed, copies of the auditor's report must be sent to

- the shareholders
- the Registrar of Companies

What happens in practice is that the report is included with the statutory accounts when these are sent out to the shareholders and when the accounts are sent to Companies House to be filed on the public record.

INTERNAL AUDITORS

We will now look at the difference between **internal** and **external** auditors.

Internal auditors play a different role to the auditors we have been dealing with so far, who are often known as external auditors.

Internal auditors are part of the company's management system. They are employed by the company and often have a role in quality or cost control as well as in checking financial records.

Internal and external auditors have completely different roles and duties.

The table below summarises the differences between the two types.

	Internal auditors	External auditors
Independence	Part of management control system	Independent of the company
Report to	Management	Shareholders
Responsibilities	Decided by management	Statutory (in law)
Scope	As instructed by management	To express an opinion on the accounts and the underlying books and records
Qualifications	No requirement to be a qualified accountant	Must be suitably qualified

THE EXPECTATION GAP

Expectation Gap

The **expectation gap** is the name given to the difference between what the public thinks auditors do and what they actually do.

When large organisations are seen to fail, whether through poor management or fraud, auditors are often criticised in the press or at shareholder meetings for failing to meet the expectations of the public. These are often unrealistic demands and do not form part of auditors' duties.

The result is often criticism of the auditing profession, loss of confidence in the audit function and legal action taken against individual audit firms.

Research has discovered that the general public thinks that auditors:

- check every single transaction
- prepare the financial statements
- guarantee that the financial statements are correct
- are responsible for finding and reporting frauds, however small
- are responsible for detecting illegal acts by directors

The truth in the real world is, of course, very different.

auditors and fraud

One important legal principle was decided in the courts in 1896 in the Kingston Cotton Mill case.

WATCHDOG & NOT A BLOODHOUND !

The judge in that case established that the auditors' role was similar to that of a '**watchdog not a bloodhound**'. This has become a famous phrase to describe the auditors' function.

The judge went on to say that what an auditor had to do was use 'reasonable skill and judgement appropriate to the circumstances'.

The auditor was not expected to investigate every transaction but should use his or her professional abilities to support the opinion given in the auditor's report.

This judgement established that the auditors' role is to express an opinion on the financial statements presented to them by the directors. Auditors are not expected to hunt for what has *not* been included in the accounts.

However, as we will see in later chapters, it is the job of auditors to ensure that they carry out enough testing work to support their audit opinion and be alert to the possibility of fraud. If, during this work, they do discover errors, omissions or frauds, then they must wherever possible, investigate them and must also report them.

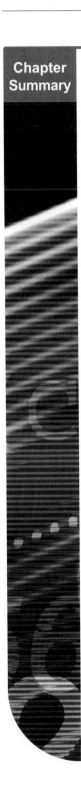

■ An audit is a process in which a suitably qualified third party expresses an opinion as to whether a set of accounts prepared for shareholders represents a true and fair view of the company's financial position at the period end.

■ Shareholders are not always involved in the day-to-day running of the business, so it is the duty of auditors to report to them on the financial position of the company in which they have an ownership stake.

■ All companies need to be audited except small charities, dormant companies, and companies with a turnover of £5.6m or less.

■ Auditors have to be members of a Recognised Supervisory Body. They should not be closely connected with the audit client and must be able to demonstrate that they are independent of the company they are auditing.

■ The audit process is a series of steps the auditor will go through from investigations prior to accepting an appointment to reporting on control weaknesses.

■ The directors appoint the first auditors who hold office until the end of the first Annual General Meeting.

■ Auditors are re-appointed at the Annual General Meeting, or if they are not re-appointed, a new audit firm is appointed until the end of the next Annual General Meeting.

■ The form of the audit report is laid down in the Companies Act 1985. It requires the auditors to report whether, in their opinion, the financial statements present a true and fair view of the company's financial position.

■ Internal auditors are part of the management team and fulfil a completely different function to external auditors.

■ There is a gap, called the expectation gap, between what the public thinks auditors do and what their role actually is.

<table>
</table>

Key Terms

audit   a process by which a suitably qualified third party expresses an opinion as to whether a set of accounts prepared for shareholders represents a true and fair view of the company's financial position at the period end

true and fair   the opinion required by the Companies Act 1985 to be given by the auditors on the company's financial statements

accounting period   the period for which accounts are prepared, normally one year

members   an alternative word for shareholders – the people who own the company

annual general meeting   the meeting at which the directors account to the shareholders for their running of the company during the accounting period – the accounts are presented at this meeting and the auditors can attend to present their report

Companies Act 1985   the statute which sets out the responsibilities of directors and auditors and governs the conduct of company affairs

Recognised Supervisory Body (RSB)   one of the main accountancy bodies recognised for the regulation and supervision of auditors – all auditors must be a member or work for a firm controlled by members of such bodies

Registrar of Companies   the Government official with whom annual accounts and other statutory documents must be filed – documents kept by the Registrar are available to the general public

internal auditors   employees of the company whose role it is to check that internal financial procedures are being complied with and who also often have a role in quality and cost issues

Student Activities

answers to the asterisked (*) questions are to be found in the Student Resources Section of www.osbornebooks.co.uk

1.1* The following statements have been made by a trainee auditor. Decide whether you think that they are true or false and write down your reasons for your decision.

(a) If there is a fraud within a company the auditor will be in trouble if he/she has not found it.

(b) The main legislation which relates to auditing is the Companies Act 1985 and associated regulations.

(c) Auditors are responsible to the directors who appoint them.

(d) All companies have to have auditors but partnerships and sole traders do not.

(e) It is primarily the responsibility of the auditors to prepare the accounts and ensure that they comply with the legislation.

(f) You can be an auditor if you have a professional accounting qualification.

(g) The directors run the business on behalf of the shareholders and the auditor is there to comment on the company's accounts.

(h) Internal auditors have a role which is defined by the management of a company.

1.2* The previous auditors of Kirog Ltd have resigned and your firm has been appointed. There are no problems connected with the resignation. However it is now 2 March and the year end is 31 March. The directors expect to have accounts available by 15 May and they want to hold the AGM as soon as possible after that. Work out a timetable to enable the audit to be carried out within the timescale. Detail the steps to be taken.

1.3* Your local newspaper has asked you to comment on a major financial scandal. The journalist is under the impression that the auditors could have prevented the scandal involving two senior directors conspiring in a huge fraud. He believes that the auditors check everything and also prepare the accounts. What would you tell him to change that opinion?

1.4 You have recently taken over the audit of a motor dealership. At your first meeting with the client after having accepted the role the managing director hands you a pile of internal audit reports and says 'Well that's your work done for the year.'

He tells you that the previous auditors used these reports as the basis of their audit and then just checked the accounts for arithmetical accuracy and with control totals from the accounting records. In this way they were able to keep the audit fee to a minimum.

Describe what you would say to the managing director to explain that you might well adopt a different approach to this year's audit.

2 Auditing – the legal framework

this chapter covers . . .

This chapter describes the legal framework which governs the work of auditors and directors of a company. It explains the duty of care owed by auditors to shareholders and the responsibility they have to third parties. It describes the principles which govern the professional behaviour and personal qualities that are expected of an auditor when dealing with client information and client staff.

The chapter covers:

■ the responsibility of directors in maintaining financial records and preparing financial accounts

■ the responsibility of auditors to shareholders and third parties

■ the legal framework governing the work of auditors

- in statute law (particularly the Companies Act 1985)

- International Standards on Auditing (ISAs)

- Case law (court decisions relating to auditing)

■ the issue of professional ethics - the responsible way in which auditors deal with clients and keep confidentiality

PERFORMANCE CRITERIA COVERED

unit 17 IMPLEMENTING AUDITING PROCEDURES

This chapter introduces the background to auditing and covers some of the underpinning Knowledge and Understanding that is common to all three elements of Unit 17. Specifically it covers the following items:

1   A general understanding of the legal duties of auditors: the content of reports; the definition of proper records

2   A general understanding of the liability of auditors under contract and negligence including liability to third parties

3   Relevant legislation, relevant Statements of Auditing Standards*

*now replaced by the International Standards on Auditing

OVERVIEW OF THE LEGAL FRAMEWORK

Companies are required by the Companies Act 1985 to prepare annual financial statements and to have these statements audited. The directors and auditors have separate responsibilities in the process. The fact that directors and auditors have an ultimate responsibility to the shareholders of the company means that these responsibilities will inevitably be linked.

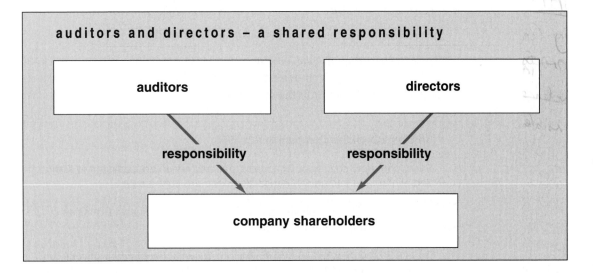

auditors and directors – a shared responsibility

auditors

directors

responsibility

responsibility

company shareholders

a shared responsibility

Directors have a primary responsibility to prepare the accounts and report to the shareholders, who own the business, telling them how well the company has performed financially in the accounting period.

The **auditors'** responsibility follows on: they must check these accounts and report to the same shareholders whether or not the directors have accounted fairly and truthfully.

who is audited?

All companies that need to be audited, whether they are private limited companies or public limited companies are dealt with in the same way. Auditors have the same duty to the shareholders in a small family company as they do to the shareholders of a multinational public limited company.

Remember:

■ companies that qualify as small companies will be exempt altogether from the requirement for an audit (see page 5)

■ sole traders and partnerships do not require an audit

RESPONSIBILITIES OF DIRECTORS

The Companies Act 1985 states that the directors of the company are responsible for:

■ maintaining proper financial records

■ preparing financial statements in the prescribed format

We are now going to look at each of these responsibilities in turn.

maintaining proper financial records

The exact wording in the Companies Act is set out below. Whilst it is useful for you to read this, you don't have to remember it word for word and will not be required to refer to the section number.

Section 221 of the Companies Act 1985

Every company shall keep accounting records which are sufficient to show and explain the company's transactions and are such as to:

(a) disclose with reasonable accuracy at any time, the financial position of the company at that time, and

(b) enable the directors to ensure that any balance sheet and profit and loss account prepared under this part complies with the requirements of this Act.

To put this more simply, the directors of the company have a legal responsibility to keep the books of account of the business up-to-date and in sufficient detail so that reasonably accurate financial statements can be produced at any time. They must also make sure that the company keeps hold of all related information that was used to produce them.

In practice, this means that documentation relating to the day-to-day financial transactions of the business such as sales and purchase invoices, credits notes, bank statements etc, must be kept by the company even when they have been recorded in the accounts.

In addition, directors must ensure that they keep financial information in such a way that the requirements for disclosure of information in accounts as required by the Companies Act, can be met.

The Companies Act specifies the minimum requirement for accounting records that it expects a business to keep. Set out on the next page is an interpretation of what this means in real terms for a company.

Companies Act requirement	Books and records required
A record of payments and receipts:	Cashbook Petty cash book
A record of assets and liabilities:	Asset register Debtors ledger Creditors ledger
If the company deals in goods:	A record of stock Stock lists at the period end All statements of stock taking from which the stock listings have been prepared, ie the stock count sheets

Note that where the company is not engaged in a normal retail trade it must also keep records of goods sold and purchased in enough detail so that sellers and buyers can be identified.

The records must be kept at the office registered with the Registrar of Companies, known as the Registered Office, or at some other location the directors consider to be suitable. Smaller businesses often choose to have their accountant's office as their Registered Office but keep all the accounting records at their business premises.

These regulations must be complied with – if the directors of a company are found to have failed to keep records in sufficient detail they are guilty of an offence under the Companies Act and can be imprisoned or fined.

preparing financial statements

We will now examine the legal requirement to prepare financial statements. This may touch on some of the points you cover in Unit 11 (Drafting Financial Statements) which deals with the formats for preparing annual accounts. You should be aware from your studies that these formats are now increasingly regulated by International Accounting Standards (IAS).

So what do we mean by the term 'financial statements'?

The Companies Act specifically refers to the preparation of:

■ the balance sheet

■ the profit and loss account or other form of income statement

- the statement of cash flows and total recognised gains and losses
- the notes to these statements and notes of the accounting policies adopted

The Companies Act also sets out some specific duties for the directors when preparing the financial statements. These should be familiar to you from your Financial Accounting studies. The directors must:

- prepare the financial statements on a going concern basis, unless they consider that the business will not be able to continue for the foreseeable future
- select suitable accounting policies and apply them consistently
- make judgements and estimates that are reasonable and prudent where revenues and potential costs or losses are not known with certainty
- state whether the relevant accounting standards have been followed
- explain any reasons why accounting standards have not been followed

As you can see from the points above, the legal requirements of the directors regarding the maintenance of financial records and the preparation of financial statements are both strict and detailed.

In addition to all of this the directors have a responsibility to allow the auditors access at all times to the books and records of the business. This leads us into the next section on the rights and responsibilities of the auditors.

AUDITORS' RESPONSIBILITIES

the legal framework

Over the years the rights and responsibilities of auditors have been established in three different ways:

- **statute law** – particularly the Companies Act 1985
- – and more recently by **International Standards on Auditing** (ISAs), which are replacing the UK **Statements of Auditing Standards** (SASs) (for audits for accounting periods commencing on or after 14 December 2004)
- **case law** – where decisions relating to auditing have been decided in court

These three legal influences have created a framework of rights and responsibilities within which auditors operate. They work broadly along the lines of the flowchart shown at the top of the next page.

Statute law: the legal rights of auditors and their basic responsibilities are defined in the Companies Act.

The auditors' rights and responsibilities are then further defined in the **International Standards on Auditing** (ISAs), which are issued by the Auditing Practices Board (visit www.apb.org.uk). The two main functions of ISAs are:

1   they expand on the wording of auditing legislation and set out in detail what is expected of auditors and what rights and duties they have

2   they tell auditors how to deal with specific sets of circumstances and give examples and guidance on how audit work should be carried out

Case law gives auditors guidance as to how the court decisions have interpreted the law and the ISAs under certain circumstances. It also helps to define the extent of auditors' responsibilities.

AUDITORS' RESPONSIBILITIES TO SHAREHOLDERS

To SHAREHOLDERS

Auditors' primary responsibilities, set out by the Companies Act, can be summarised as:

■ to give an opinion to the shareholders as to the truth and fairness of the financial statements

■ to give an opinion as to whether the financial statements have been properly prepared in accordance with the Companies Act

They must also include in their report reference to:

■ whether proper books and records have been kept

■ whether proper information has been supplied to them from any branches of the business they have not visited

■ whether the accounts agree to the underlying financial records and supporting information

■ whether the contents of the Directors Report is consistent with the accounts

■ a statement of the separate responsibilities of auditors and directors

This is obviously a comprehensive list of requirements regarding the content of the audit report. We will look in more detail at the form and content of these reports in Chapter 7.

Fundamentally, the auditors' role is to report to the shareholders, who are the owners of the business, on the truth and fairness of the financial statements prepared by the directors and to confirm that proper records have been kept and full explanations received where necessary. It is important to appreciate that the auditors act for the shareholders collectively – as one body. They are not responsible to any one individual shareholder.

To 3RD PARTIES

auditors' responsibilities to third parties

As we have seen, the primary responsibility of the auditors is to report to the shareholders. But what about other readers of the accounts?

Because they are appointed by the shareholders the law says that auditors owe a duty of care to shareholders to carry out their work in a professional and thorough way.

This duty of care means that, if auditors fail to do their work properly, the shareholders have the right to take them to court to recover any losses that the auditors' negligence has caused them.

Is this same duty of care extended to other users of the accounts? In short, can the auditors be held liable to any one at all if they get it wrong?

If any person decided to sue the auditors in court because they had suffered some loss, they would have to show that the auditors:

■ owed a duty of care to the person who suffered the loss and

■ failed to carry out their audit work using reasonable skill and care

Once this had been established, the person bringing the court action against the auditors would have to prove:

■ the auditors were negligent in the way they carried out their work (ie they failed in their duty of care)

■ the person bringing the action suffered a loss

■ the loss arose as a result of the auditors' negligence

If all of this can be proved then the auditors are likely to be found guilty by the court of negligence and ordered to pay damages and compensation.

This could amount to a considerable sum – in the past, such claims have resulted in audit partners being made bankrupt and the audit firms ceasing to exist. It is no surprise that the partners in audit firms are naturally very interested in the law on responsibility to third parties!

One court case that has become very important in clarifying the extent of the duty of care of auditors is the Caparo decision, which is explained below. You do not have to remember all the facts of this case for your studies, but it is important that you understand how the principle it established affects the auditing profession.

---

the Caparo case

the facts . . .

In 1990 Caparo Industries sued audit firm Touche Ross for negligence in their audit of Fidelity plc, a company that Caparo had subsequently purchased.

Caparo stated that they had relied on the audited accounts to value Fidelity plc. It emerged that the asset value of Fidelity was substantially less than the audited accounts had shown. Caparo said that had they known the true position they would not have bought Fidelity.

the decision . . .

The judge in this case decided:

– that the auditors did not have a duty of care to third parties, unless

– they knew that these accounts were going to be relied upon for the purposes of making an investment.

Much to the relief of the auditors, Touche Ross, this was not found to be the case here.

WHAT GOVERNS THE AUDIT?

So far we have covered the responsibilities of the directors and the responsibilities of the auditors. We will now examine the legal rights that the auditors have which allow them to carry out their audit work effectively.

As we have seen, the work of the auditors is regulated in three ways:

■ through the Companies Act 1985

■ through International Standards on Auditing (ISAs)

■ through legal decisions made in individual cases in the courts

We will now look at these three areas in turn.

auditors' rights under the Companies Act 1985

Just as the Companies Act establishes the responsibilities of the directors, it also sets out the legal framework within which auditors function. In order to help the auditors carry out their audit work the Companies Act gives them certain specific rights, which are set out in the table below.

Auditors have the right to . . .	
the records	Auditors have a right of access at all times to the company's books, accounting records and vouchers.
information and explanations	The auditors have the right to all explanations and information from the company's officers that they consider necessary for their audit.
attend meetings	The auditors have the right to receive notice of all meetings which a shareholder can attend, and the right to attend those meetings.
speak at general meetings	The auditors have a right to speak at any general meeting of the company on any part of it which concerns them as auditors.
written resolutions	The auditors must be sent copies of any written resolution proposed.
require presentation of accounts	Auditors have the right to give notice in writing requiring that the company holds a general meeting for the purpose of laying the accounts before the shareholders.

In conclusion, the auditors basically have the right to access all the company's books and records and to ask any questions of the directors (and their staff) that they feel necessary to complete the audit. In addition to this they are entitled to attend company meetings and to speak to the shareholders at these meetings on any points that relate to their position as auditors.

It should be pointed out that in most cases the audit client is happy to provide the auditor with the information that is needed and will not obstruct them from addressing company meetings.

International Standards on Auditing (ISAs)

Accounting and auditing within the UK is regulated by the Financial Reporting Council. Within this body the **Auditing Practices Board (APB)** is responsible for issuing auditing standards, which set out, in detail, the role and conduct of auditors in certain circumstances. All auditors carrying out statutory audits in the UK are governed by these standards. Visit www.asb.org.uk for further information.

As auditing standards are being harmonised worldwide the APB is adopting the **International Standards on Auditing** (ISAs) which have been developed by the International Auditing and Assurance Standards Board (IAASB). These ISAs replace (for accounting periods commencing after 14 December 2004) the **Statement of Auditing Standards** (SASs) which traditionally regulated the auditing profession.

To put this into the context of your financial accounting studies, the work of the auditor is governed by ISAs in the same way as the financial statements prepared by the directors are governed by SSAPs, FRSs and, more recently, by International Accounting Standards (IASs). ISAs exist to support, advise and regulate auditors and to give guidance on specific situations.

AAT 'core' ISAs

The AAT has issued guidance stating which of these international standards it considers to be relevant to Unit 17. It has stated that it considers some of these ISAs to be 'core' statements, fundamental to carrying out a proper audit. You must be aware of these statements, although you will not be asked to quote them in your assessments. The 'core' ISAs are:

ISA 240	The auditors' responsibility to consider fraud in an audit of financial statements.
ISA 300	Planning the audit.
ISA 315	Obtaining an understanding of the entity and its environment and assessing the risks of a material misstatement.
ISA 330	The auditors' procedures in response to assessed risk.
ISA 500	Audit evidence.

In addition to these, the AAT also stresses the importance of an International Standard on Quality Control (ISQC) 'Quality control for firms that perform audits and reviews of historical financial information and other assurance and related service engagements'.

ISAs affecting the way audits are carried out

Following the replacement over time of the old Statements of Auditing Standards (SASs) with the new International Standards on Auditing (ISAs), the ISAs that are likely to have the greatest impact on the way audits are carried out are are shown below.

key regulations affecting audit implementation	
ISA 220	Quality control for audits of historical financial information.
ISA 240	The auditors' responsibility to consider fraud in an audit of financial statements.
ISA 300	Planning an audit of financial statements.
ISA 315	Obtaining an understanding of the entity and its environment and assessing the risks of a material misstatement.
ISA 330	The auditors' procedures in response to assessed risk.
ISA 500	Audit evidence.

Under the new ISAs, the issues of risk assessment and fraud have become more central to the planning of the audit, thus the evidence requirements are increased and audit planning has to take account of this new emphasis.

There is also a new requirement for audit firms to introduce quality control procedures into their own firm's working practices to ensure that audit work is carried out to the highest standard.

Throughout this book we will refer to relevant ISAs as we cover the different topics. Although we may quote some of the relevant paragraphs so that you can be aware of the precise wording of the key ISA, you are not expected to remember either the precise wording or the ISA number.

case law

A ruling in a previous decision made in the courts forms an important element of the legal framework affecting the work of auditors. The outcome of these cases and the comments of the judges have provided valuable guidance for auditors as to how to carry out their work (or in some cases how not to!). An example relating to auditors' responsibility to third parties has already been given on page 23. Over the years many firms of auditors have been sued for negligence – ie where a 'duty of care' has been neglected.

You are not expected to remember the names of cases or the exact words used by judges. They are quoted in this text to help to give you an impression of what is expected of auditors and how they should approach their work and dealing with clients.

PROFESSIONAL ETHICS

As we have seen, the rights and responsibilities of auditors are set out in several ways – by statute law, through ISAs and by case law. In addition to adopting the ISAs, the Auditing Practices Board (APB) also sets the standards expected of auditors with regard to their personal behaviour. This is known as the **ethical framework**.

Rather than setting out a large number of detailed rules on the behaviour of the auditors, the professional bodies have decided that it would be simpler to list the personal qualities that they expect a professional auditor to have. These are set out in International Standard on Auditing 200 'Objectives and general principles governing an audit of financial statements'.

This states that two of the most important personal qualities an auditor should have are:

- **integrity** – this means honesty, truthfulness and openness in dealing with clients' affairs
- **objectivity** – this means that auditors must not get too closely involved with their client

In addition to these two key areas we will also examine other aspects of behaviour and professional capability expected of the auditors in relation to the points below:

- independence
- professional competence
- reasonable skill and judgement

independence

The role of the auditors is such that they must take great care to ensure that their independence is not compromised in any way. They must be independent and must be 'seen to be independent'. At no point must their opinion on the truth and fairness of the client's financial statements be influenced either by their client or by anyone else.

Guidelines have been issued by the Recognised Supervisory Bodies (RSBs) as to what might compromise an auditor's independence. A summary of these guidelines is detailed here.

Auditors are not allowed to:

- have one single client that represents a high proportion of an auditor's total business – this is usually defined as having one client whose fee is more than 15% of the auditors' total fee income
- have family or close relatives working in the senior management of the client – for example, it would be unacceptable for the audit manager to be married to the financial controller of one of his clients
- hold shares in the client, either directly or indirectly
- accept loans from clients or lend clients money
- accept gifts or corporate hospitality – unless this is quite minimal
- provide accountancy services other than audit services to the client

Professional judgement must be exercised in all of these cases. If the audit is being performed on a major UK bank, for example, it is acceptable for members of the audit team to have mortgages with this bank. It is not, however, acceptable for the audit partner to have a substantial personal loan from the bank at a preferential rate. On the other hand no one would be very concerned if the audit client provided all the audit team with a free diary. However, it would be inappropriate for members of the audit team to be taken by the client on an all expenses paid trip to Aintree for the Grand National weekend.

professional competence

We have now established that the auditors must maintain independence at all times. We will now discuss the area of professional competence. It sounds obvious, but the auditors need to know what they are doing. This means that auditors should:

- be familiar with the principles of auditing which we have described in this book
- be aware of what the Companies Act 1985 says about how financial statements should be prepared and the disclosure requirements

You will already be familiar with this from your studies 'Drafting Financial Statements'. The fact that auditors must be members of Recognised Supervisory Bodies (RSBs) should ensure that they are also fully aware of these requirements.

In the area of professional competence case law goes some way to giving us a definition. Specifically, the judge in the **Kingston Cotton Mill** case defined what 'professional competence' actually means. The judge said:

> *'It is the duty of an auditor to bring to bear on the work he has to perform that skill, care and caution which a reasonably competent, careful and cautious auditor would use. What is reasonable skill, care and caution must depend on the particular circumstances of each case.'*

What the judge meant in this case was that the auditors had to use 'reasonable skill and care' in carrying out their audit work and that, as long as they did this, their duty to their client was fulfilled.

To summarise:

To summarise:

- the auditors owe a duty of care to the shareholders who appoint them
- as professionals, auditors are expected to carry out the work they have to do in a professionally competent way; but they are not expected to be all seeing and all knowing

During the course of their audit work the auditors have a professional duty to:

- make reasonable enquiries
- carry out sufficient work to support the audit opinion they are signing as to the truth and fairness of the accounts

DEALING WITH CLIENTS

This section of this chapter will examine the manner in which auditors approach their audit work.

Auditors are expected to behave in a professional manner at all times. This is particularly relevant when, at various points during the audit, they spend time at clients' premises and come into daily contact with management and staff. A well-briefed client team will appreciate that they must assist the auditors in any way that they can to ensure a smooth audit visit. However, in addition to providing the auditors with all the necessary information that they require, they still have to carry out their day-to-day duties as usual.

With this in mind the audit staff are expected to be:

■ courteous and polite

■ discreet – not getting involved in gossip or office politics

■ aware of the time commitments of clients' staff – they may have deadlines to meet

■ aware of the rule of confidentiality (see below)

In practical terms when dealing with client staff the auditors should:

■ avoid making unreasonable requests for information

■ deal with several queries at a meeting rather than pestering staff with a continuous stream of questions when they are trying to work

■ bear in mind client deadlines – for example, month-end routines should not be disturbed by demands from the auditors

For example, an audit junior may be very keen to obtain answers to all her queries on a particular audit test and in her enthusiasm she may bombard the client's finance staff with questions every time she finds an error. The audit supervisor, however, should encourage the junior to gather up a number of questions and arrange a meeting with client staff members to discuss the issues on a single occasion.

Although the auditors have a significant level of legal authority, insisting on exercising this authority should be avoided if at all possible. It should only be resorted to in exceptional circumstances when the auditors feel that they are being deliberately prevented from accessing information.

The auditors must remember that it is in their interest to maintain a good working relationship with a client's staff at all times and at all levels to allow for the smooth running of the audit and ensure minimal disruption to the client's day-to-day operations.

CONFIDENTIALITY

Finally we will look at the importance of **confidentiality**. During the course of their audit work the auditors discover a great deal of information about their client, some of which might be commercially sensitive and much of which will be confidential.

Confidentiality is, therefore, seen as being a very important aspect of auditors' responsibilities.

The fundamental rule is that auditors must not reveal any information that they have learned about a client to unauthorised third parties except in the most exceptional circumstances.

confidentiality – the exceptions

The Recognised Supervisory Bodies (RSBs) have established certain circumstances in which auditors are permitted to reveal information about their client to a third party.

These circumstances are:

Give Permission .

- when the **client gives permission**

- when **required to by law** – for example, under money laundering regulations, if the auditor suspects the client's involvement in this kind of activity they have a duty to disclose this; similarly if they suspect the client is involved in treason or terrorist activities this should be reported to the relevant authorities

- when there is a **professional duty to disclose** – for example if the auditor is giving evidence at a trial

- when it is **in the public interest** – for example if the client is guilty of serious environmental pollution or is selling a product which might prove to be a danger to the general public the auditor is permitted to give relevant information to third parties

In all instances the auditors must think carefully before revealing any information about their clients' affairs to a third party. If in doubt they should obtain legal advice or the advice of their professional body.

confidentiality – security of information

Security of Info :

A final practical issue regarding client confidentiality is in relation to security of information. The auditor will hold a substantial amount of client information in their audit files. Auditors must ensure the security of this information at all times:

- audit files should be kept locked away whenever they are left unattended

- audit files should never be left in vulnerable locations, for example in the boot of your car

- audit working papers should not be taken away from the auditor's office or the client premises unless absolutely necessary

- auditors should not discuss confidential client details in public places or with any unrelated third party even if it is a 'trustworthy family member'!

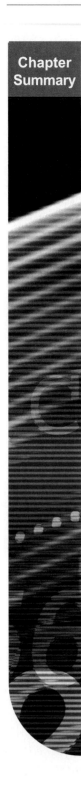

Chapter Summary

- The responsibilities of directors and auditors of limited companies are set out in the Companies Act 1985.

- It is the responsibility of the directors of a company to prepare the accounts and to provide all the information and explanations the auditors need.

- The content of the financial statements of a limited company is defined in the Companies Act 1985.

- The Companies Act 1985 sets out specific requirements for the books and records which have to be maintained by a limited company and it is the specific responsibility of the directors to ensure that proper books and records are maintained.

- The accounting records must be sufficient to be able to show the company's financial position at any time – they must be sufficient to enable the directors to prepare a profit and loss account and balance sheet in accordance with the Companies Act.

- Auditors are also regulated by International Standards on Auditing (ISAs) which set out detailed rules as to how audits should be conducted.

- Auditors owe a duty of care to the shareholders as a body not to individual shareholders.

- Auditors should use reasonable skill and care in carrying out their work.

- The Caparo case decided that auditors are not liable to third parties (outsiders) unless the auditors were aware of their interest in the client (eg buying the client) at the time of the audit.

- Auditors must ensure that they maintain their independence from their client.

- Auditors should behave in a professional manner at all times and treat clients' staff with courtesy and consideration.

- Auditors must treat all the information they discover about their client as confidential except in certain specific circumstances.

Companies Act 1985	the statute which sets out the responsibilities of directors and auditors and governs the conduct of company affairs
Registrar of Companies	the Government official with whom annual accounts and other statutory documents must be filed – documents kept by the Registrar (at Companies House) are available to the general public
Auditing Practices Board (APB)	a body responsible for developing and issuing professional standards for auditors in the UK
International Standards on Auditing (ISAs)	internationally accepted auditing standards which influence the conduct of auditors and audits within the UK; they are issued by the Auditing Practices Board (APB)
auditing case law	court decisions and judgements relating to auditing which establish rulings for the conduct of auditors and audits
duty of care	an obligation on auditors to act with reasonable skill and judgement in all circumstances; where there is a direct relationship the auditors owe more than a general duty and must act specifically in the best interest of their client
ethical framework	a set of principles, set out in Auditing Standards, which define the skills an auditor should have and the standard of behaviour expected of them in dealing with clients and their financial affairs
confidentiality	the principle that auditors must not reveal any information that they have learned about a client to unauthorised third parties except in exceptional circumstances

Student Activities

answers to the asterisked (*) questions are to be found in the Student Resources Section of www.osbornebooks.co.uk

2.1* Which of the following statements are not correct, and why?

(a)   Auditors can be sued by a client if the client has suffered a loss.

(b)   Auditors owe a duty of care to all the shareholders collectively.

(c)   The Caparo decision means that auditors cannot be sued by third parties.

(d)   Directors have to ensure that their company keeps proper books and records.

(e)   If auditors work for a client who has been money laundering they must tell the authorities.

(f)   Auditors can own shares in client companies.

(g)   If a firm of auditors receives a bottle of whisky from a client during the festive season, they must return it.

2.2* Your firm are the auditors of Guzzlers Ltd who own a chain of cafes and restaurants. You have acted for them for many years.

Describe the ethical issues raised by the following two situations and explain how you would deal with them.

(a)   A local bank lending officer contacts you and says the directors of Guzzlers Limited have approached the bank for a loan. The directors have sent her a copy of the accounts and suggests that she contacts you if there are any queries or if she needs more information.

(b)   Andy Nose is employed by your firm and has been the manager of the audit for several years. He comes to you and says that he has been asked by Guzzlers Limited to carry out some financial consultancy work for them.

2.3* The directors of Bigboy.com, a new start-up hi-tech company, have approached your accounting firm Columbus & Co, asking you to become their financial advisor and auditor.

The directors own 20% of Bigboy.com, the remainder of the shares being held by an investment company which provided start-up funding.

Bigboy.com has been operating for about a year in a totally computerised environment using the Internet. The company does not have much in the way of paper-based systems.

The attitude of the directors is that they consider administration to be a nuisance and do not want to have to spend much time on book-keeping. Most of their financial transactions are processed electronically and their view is that all they need is access to their bank account so they can see how much money they have – that is all that they have time for.

You are due to meet the directors tomorrow. Write a memo setting out the key points you want to make to them regarding:

(a)   the problems this attitude might create for them as directors

(b)   the problems this creates for your firm as auditors

2.4 You are the new auditor of Jojo Limited and have discovered that for the last three years the directors have deliberately overstated the valuation of stocks. Jojo is a family company but not all the directors are shareholders.

The directors have told you that they did it to keep the company trading in the short term as the bank would have called in the overdraft if the profits had not continued to rise. They ask you informally to turn a blind eye to this year's valuation as the company will cease to trade if the true position is revealed and as a result all the shareholders will lose their money.

If the company can carry on trading it stands a good chance of survival.

You are to write a letter to the managing director setting out your position as auditor.

2.5 You are the auditor of a business which comprises a small chain of supermarkets. The business has recently collapsed, owing the bank over £250,000. Investigations have revealed that one of the directors has been systematically defrauding the business over a number of years.

The director had access to the computerised accounting records and was able to take money from the business and alter stock and purchases records to cover the fraud. You have raised internal control concerns with the directors over the last few years and made several recommendations none of which were acted upon.

The bank have written to you as auditor alleging that as you were responsible for checking the transactions you should have discovered the fraud and therefore they intend suing you for recovery of their loss.

Write briefing notes for a meeting, setting out the main points relevant to the situation.

Planning the audit assignment

In this chapter we describe the procedures auditors should carry out before they accept a new audit client, and how they assess audit risk. We explain how auditors document their clients' financial systems and how they identify internal controls.

The chapter covers:

- accepting appointment as an auditor

- the engagement letter, which formally appoints the auditors

- knowledge of the client's business

- assessing audit risk

- documenting the systems

- the internal control systems of the client

- internal control questionnaires drawn up by the auditor

PERFORMANCE CRITERIA COVERED

unit 17 IMPLEMENTING AUDITING PROCEDURES

element 17.1

contribute to the planning of an audit assignment

A   ascertain accounting systems under review and record them clearly in appropriate working papers

B   identify control objectives correctly

C   assess risks accurately

D   record significant weaknesses in control correctly

H   follow confidentiality and security procedures

I   formulate the proposed audit plan clearly in consultation with the appropriate personnel

J   submit the proposed audit plan to the appropriate person for approval

ACCEPTING AN APPOINTMENT

Accepting an appointment as auditor is a serious step and one which should not be taken without a full consideration of all of the issues involved.

ISA 220 'Quality control for audits of historical financial information' states:

> *'Acceptance ... of client relationships and specific audit engagements includes considering*
>
> - *the integrity of the principal owners, key management and those charged with governance of the entity (ie the directors)*
> - *whether the engagement team is competent to perform the audit engagement and has sufficient time and resources*
> - *whether the firm and the engagement team can comply with ethical requirements'*

The process that the auditors need to go through before they can accept the appointment is best described by a series of steps as illustrated on the diagram on page 39.

We will discuss each step separately in detail.

[handwritten marginalia: efore Accept Appointment]
[handwritten marginalia: (1) legal + ethical probs]
[handwritten marginalia: (2) practical probs]
[handwritten marginalia: (3) contact existing auditors]
[handwritten marginalia: (4) investigate the client]

step 1 – legal and ethical problems

Before accepting any audit assignment the auditors have to decide whether there are any legal or ethical problems which might prevent them from accepting the assignment. We looked at these in some detail in Chapter 2. To remind you, the main considerations are:

- does anyone in the audit firm hold shares in the potential client?
- does anyone in the audit firm have a close relative in a senior position at the potential client?
- is the potential fee so large that it would be more than 15% of total practice income?

step 2 – practical problems

Providing there are no legal or ethical problems preventing their appointment, auditors should then consider whether they have adequate resources and sufficient expertise to carry out the proposed audit successfully.

For example:

- the potential client may have branches and departments located in different parts of the country, which all need to be visited at the same time the auditors must be sure that they have sufficient staff with the appropriate ability to carry out the work

- the potential client might operate a highly complex IT-based business requiring sophisticated computer-based auditing tools and technically skilled staff in order to carry out their audit work satisfactorily

Providing the auditors are satisfied that there are no practical problems which might prevent them from carrying out their work, they are free to move to the next step on the appointment ladder.

step 3 – contact existing auditors

The ethical rules state that incoming auditors must write to any outgoing auditors to:

- inform them of the proposed change

- ask them if there are any reasons why the appointment should not be accepted

This gives the outgoing auditors a chance to notify potential new auditors of any issues they have had with the audit or any problem they have had with the client.

Before any information is exchanged the client must give permission to:

- the incoming auditors to contact the outgoing auditors

- the outgoing auditors to discuss the client's affairs freely with the incoming auditors

Failure on the part of the client to give permission for either of the above to happen would mean that the incoming auditors should refuse to accept the appointment.

If the exchange of information does take place then the incoming auditors must decide if anything they are told will prevent them from accepting the audit engagement.

This is best illustrated by a Case Study, which follows on page 40.

The explanation of Step 4 then follows on page 41.

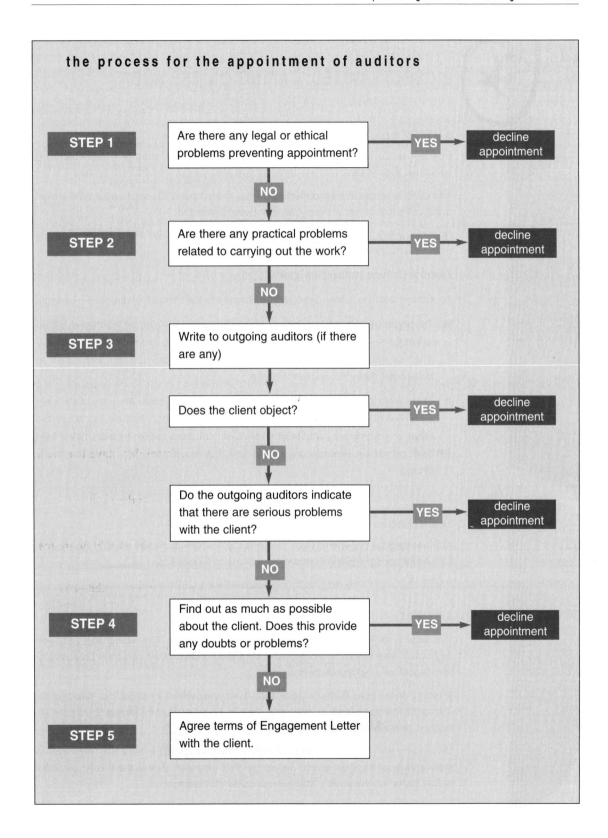

the process for the appointment of auditors

STEP 1 — Are there any legal or ethical problems preventing appointment? → **YES** → decline appointment

↓ **NO**

STEP 2 — Are there any practical problems related to carrying out the work? → **YES** → decline appointment

↓ **NO**

STEP 3 — Write to outgoing auditors (if there are any)

↓

Does the client object? → **YES** → decline appointment

↓ **NO**

Do the outgoing auditors indicate that there are serious problems with the client? → **YES** → decline appointment

↓ **NO**

STEP 4 — Find out as much as possible about the client. Does this provide any doubts or problems? → **YES** → decline appointment

↓ **NO**

STEP 5 — Agree terms of Engagement Letter with the client.

BIGBOLT LIMITED: TAKING ON THE AUDIT

situation

Stamper & Co have been approached to take over the audit of a manufacturing company, Bigbolt Ltd.

The client is similar in size to existing clients of Stamper & Co and there are no ethical problems which might prevent Stamper being appointed.

Stamper writes to the outgoing auditors Blotter & Co to ask them if there are any reasons why they should not accept the appointment.

Blotter & Co have written back saying:

- On two occasions they were refused access to the minutes of directors meetings.

- The financial statements originally included a large provision for 'damages'. When asked for evidence to justify this provision the managing director refused to supply it. It was eventually excluded from the accounts after the auditors 'threatened' to include details in their auditor's report.

- There were many problems surrounding the stock valuation. After the stock take, a number of count sheets went missing, and the auditors had doubts about the value of a significant number of items. Some of these problems were never fully dealt with but it was not considered that they would materially affect the stock figures.

required

After reading the comments from Blotter & Co, you are to decide whether Stamper & Co should accept the appointment as auditors to Bigbolt Ltd.

answer

The letter from Blotter & Co is clearly a cause for concern. The relationship between Bigbolt Ltd and Blotter has obviously completely broken down, which is presumably why Bigbolt are looking for new auditors.

It would seem from Blotter's letter that the management of Bigbolt is reluctant to disclose information and, in one case, had to be pressured by Blotter to remove or justify a provision in the accounts.

On the face of it, the management of Bigbolt does not appear to have very high ethical standards and the best advice would be that Stamper should think very carefully before taking on the audit – and even consider not taking it on.

step 4 – investigate the client

Assuming that the letter from the outgoing auditors does not show up any significant problem areas, the next step is for the audit firm to find out as much as they can about their potential client from as many sources as possible. Sources of information could include:

- the latest financial statements - which should be reviewed to find out if there could be any particular problem areas involved in the audit
- discussions with third parties such as bankers, legal advisors or members of the business community who might have knowledge of the prospective client – there clearly might be issues of confidentiality here which the prospective auditors and the other professionals will have to bear in mind
- relevant database searches or the internet for additional information about the client
- the client's own publicity material or other information which they are able or willing to provide

The whole point of this process is to help the auditor to find out as much as they possibly can about the client and its management **before** they accept the appointment.

When all these steps have been completed and the auditors have decided to accept, they need to formalise their appointment as auditors. This is done by sending an **engagement letter** to the client.

THE ENGAGEMENT LETTER

ISA 210

ISA 210 'Terms of audit engagements' states:

> '*It is in the interest of both client and auditor that the auditor sends an engagement letter, preferably before the commencement of the engagement, to help in avoid misunderstandings with respect to the engagement.*
>
> *The engagement letter documents and confirms the auditors' acceptance of the appointment, the objective and scope of the audit , the extent of the auditors' responsibilities to the client and the form of any reports*'.

The legal basis of the auditors' relationship with their client is written down in a formal document known as an **engagement letter**.

This is an extremely important document because:

- it confirms the auditors' acceptance of the appointment, and
- it sets out the responsibilities of each of the parties involved to ensure that there is no misunderstanding between the auditor and the client

The engagement letter forms a legally binding contract between the auditor and the client.

You should look at the sample engagement letter in the Appendix on pages 306-310. You are not expected to remember the contents in detail, but you should have a broad idea of what the engagement letter contains.

contents of an engagement letter

The engagement letter is an agreement between the directors and the auditors that each of them will play their part in preparing and auditing the financial statements.

As a minimum requirement it should include the following:

1   The directors agree to be responsible for:

  - maintaining proper accounting records

  - preparing the financial statements which must comply with the appropriate legislation and Accounting Standards

  - making all the books and records available to the auditors as they need them

  - giving any explanations and providing any additional information the auditors need

2   The auditors agree to:

  - express an opinion on the financial statements

  - conduct the audit in accordance with the appropriate Auditing Standards

3   The letter will give a general indication of the nature and extent of the audit work to be carried out. This might include:

  - confirmation that the auditors will visit branches or subsidiaries

  - confirmation that they will attend stock counts

  - the use of specialist software to evaluate computer systems

4   The letter will also give an indication:

  - if any other firms of auditors are to be involved in a secondary role, eg auditing remote branches or subsidiaries

  - whether independent experts, eg expert valuers, are to be used

5 The letter should also confirm that the responsibility for detecting fraud and for safeguarding the client's assets is the responsibility of the company management and not the auditors.

In addition to these key points the letter is likely to include:

■ a statement to the effect that any weaknesses in controls identified during the audit will be reported to management

■ arrangements regarding fees

■ the nature and scope of any additional work to be carried out, eg taxation calculations

At this point the auditors should also ensure that their appointment has been agreed by the directors. They do this by obtaining a copy of the signed minutes of the directors' meeting at which their appointment was confirmed and putting it on their Permanent File. (We will look in more detail at the Permanent File later in this chapter.)

When auditors have accepted the audit and have been officially appointed, their real audit work can begin.

KNOWLEDGE OF THE BUSINESS

We have already said that the auditors must find out as much as possible about a potential client before they can accept the appointment as auditors. When they have been appointed, they must take this a stage further and find out as much detailed information as they can about their new client, its management and staff, and the business environment in which it operates.

ISA 315 'Understanding the entity and its environment and assessing the risks of material misstatement' states:

> *'The auditor should obtain an understanding of the entity and its environment, including its internal control, sufficient to identify and assess the risk of material misstatement of the financial statements whether they are due to fraud or error, and sufficient to design and perform further audit procedures.'*

the business environment

During the course of the relationship with the client, the auditor should constantly gather information about the business environment in which the client operates. This will include:

■ information about the client's position and reputation within its industry sector

- the general economic conditions within the industry sector, including the level of competitiveness and political or economic factors

- the possible effect of technological change or environmental factors

- any cyclical or seasonal aspects of the business or any vulnerability to factors such as changes in fashion

- any major legislative or regulatory impacts which might affect the client

- economic conditions such as interest rates or inflation

Information can be gathered from a variety of sources including:

- industry specific publications, trade journals and websites

- previous experience of other clients in the same industry

- discussions with previous auditors

- government publications, statistics, surveys

- financial journals

the business, its management and staff

Auditors cannot begin to carry out any work on verifying the financial statements unless they have a complete understanding of the following:

- the structure of the organisation – its divisions, departments or subsidiaries

- the management structure

- the products and processes

- the financial systems

This type of information can only be successfully obtained by direct contact with the client's management and staff. They are the only real source of the detailed information that will allow the auditors to fully understand the 'who', 'what', 'why', 'where' and 'when' of the client's day-to-day activities.

The auditors should have a clear understanding of:

- the client

- the client's business activities

- the internal and external environments in which the client operates

The auditors will then be in a position to decide what audit work is required to ensure that the correct audit opinion is reached.

ASSESSING AUDIT RISK

The correct assessment of audit risk is vital, and is probably one of the most important aspects of audit that you have to study.

The whole approach that the auditors take to their audit work is based on how they assess the level of risk that their audit client represents. Basically, if the auditors think that the client represents a high level of risk they will need to carry out much more detailed audit work than if they assess it as being low risk.

We will now look at what we mean by risk in the context of auditing.

Audit Risk.

what is audit risk?

Audit risk is the risk that after carrying out all the audit work the auditors give the wrong opinion of the client's accounts.

They may say that the accounts do not give a true and fair view when in fact they do. Or conversely, more worryingly, they may say that the accounts do give a true and fair view when they do not. In either case, the auditors do not want to get it wrong – in the worst scenario the matter could end up in the courts with serious legal consequences.

audit risk and fraud

One thing that must be stressed is that audit risk has nothing directly to do with fraud. It is not the auditors' job to set out to detect fraud. As we have seen, they are not 'bloodhounds' but 'watchdogs'. Therefore, when auditors are assessing risk they are not assessing the risk that they might fail to detect a fraud.

ISA 240

Note, however, that **ISA 240 'The Auditors' responsibility to consider fraud in an audit of financial statements'** requires auditors to approach any audit assignment with a degree of professional scepticism and says that they must bear the possibility of fraud in mind when planning audit work. This means that auditors should identify areas where the company's assets are at greatest risk or where its controls are weakest.

risk assessment

ISA 315

ISA 315 'Obtaining an understanding of the entity and its environment and assessing the risks of material misstatement' requires auditors to identify and document areas of significant audit risk where they consider there could be a material misstatement, for example:

- in the financial statements as a whole
- for individual disclosures within the financial statements

Auditors have to understand and identify risk arising both out of the company's operations and from its systems of internal control by carrying out a **risk assessment**.

[handwritten margin note: Risk Assessment]

This is done by a combination of:

- analytical review procedures, ie identifying inconsistencies in the figures being audited (see Chapter 4)
- discussions with management and other relevant people in the company
- observation and inspection of the company's procedures and controls

A quick planning meeting with the financial director is not sufficient!

When the risks have been identified, the auditors have to design audit procedures so that these risks are reduced to an acceptable level. Auditors also have to identify whether there are risks which are so great that they deserve special audit consideration, ie so significant that normal audit testing processes will not be sufficient to validate the disclosures in the financial statements.

Auditors must fully document all the steps in their risk assessment.

One important point which ISA 315 stresses is that the risk assessment must be communicated and discussed with the whole audit team so that everyone on the assignment is aware of potential areas of risk.

categories of risk

Auditors will **measure** the levels of audit risk so that they can estimate how likely it is that they will give a wrong audit opinion. They therefore find it easier to break the audit risk down into different types – ie 'categories' – of risk.

There are three main categories of risk:

[handwritten margin note: Risk. • inherent • control • detection]

- **inherent** risk – the risk is in the nature of the business or the item or system being investigated
- **control** risk – the internal control system of the company may have weaknesses
- **detection** risk – the auditors may not pick up a significant error or misstatement

The combination of these three types of risk will determine the **overall** level of audit risk and allow the auditors to assess how much audit testing they will need to do.

THE AUDIT RISK MODEL

Audit Risk Model

The formula that links the three aspects of audit risk – inherent, control and detection – is known as the **audit risk model** and is the only audit formula that you have to remember:

audit risk = inherent risk x control risk x detection risk

As we will see below, the items in the formula are not normally given numerical values, but a risk rating of high or low.

It is clear that the auditors will want to ensure that the overall level of audit risk is as low as possible so that they will be able to come to the correct opinion. We will first explain in detail the three types of risk and show how the auditors can assess them and the extent to which they can control them.

inherent risk

Inherent risk is the risk that an item or items in the accounts will contain a material error or misstatement, simply because of the characteristics of the company or the characteristics of the particular item.

The following tables show the key signs of inherent risk that the auditors will look out for and the effect those factors may have.

INHERENT RISK	
management & ownership of the business	
potential risk areas	*the effect*
domineering owner or director	may influence the attitude of other directors and senior management towards disclosure in the financial statements or in the operation of the business
relationships between managers	direct relationships (eg in family companies) between managers or directors could reduce the effectiveness of the internal controls
level of management expertise	inexperienced or unqualified management may not appreciate the likelihood of error
expectations of stakeholders	expected levels of dividends by shareholders guarantees about profit levels given to lenders when applying for credit

the business	
potential risk areas	*the effect*
nature of the business	over-dependence on a single customer, product or supplier
	business operating a trade which involves cash or goods which are easy to steal
	products which are out of fashion or obsolete (this can give problems with finished goods stock valuations)
industry factors	a highly competitive trading environment
	regulatory requirements which result in substantial cost to the business
theft of assets	stock or other assets which could be easily stolen and converted into cash, eg computers, alcohol and cigarettes
	large amounts of cash held in the business
information technology	lack of computer systems documentation
	reliance on a few key experts
	security issues
staffing	constant staff changes
	low staff morale
	little or no training

the accounts of the business	
potential risk areas	*the effect*
complex accounts	complex financial structures involving subsidiary or associated businesses
	companies engaged in complex trade eg foreign currency or share trading, freight forwarding, high tech businesses
items relying on judgement	this requires objectivity on the part of the client staff making the judgements (eg high levels of provisions at the year end)
cash transactions	tracing cash transactions is always more difficult than tracing credit transactions

There are, of course, many more inherent risks unique to specific companies. As auditors it is important to remember that if some aspect of the business appears unusual or poses a significant inherent risk, then it must be considered when assessing the level of audit risk.

If a company has several areas of inherent risk, the auditor is likely to grade the level of inherent risk as high. Read the Case Study that follows.

Case Study

INHERENT RISK – MUCKERS LIMITED

situation

You have been approached to be the new auditors of Muckers Limited

Muckers Ltd is a construction company engaged in the construction of housing projects, small office complexes and factory units.

Its main trade is in acquiring disused or derelict land and buildings ('brownfield' sites) at a low cost and building developments which they then sell to businesses looking for premises. They have been quite successful as the Development Director, Roger Random, has been able to find attractive sites which the company can acquire quite cheaply. They also build new housing developments, mostly on 'greenfield' sites in development areas on the edge of town.

The Development Director, Roger Random, has recently handed in his notice as he is leaving to join a larger construction firm.

Muckers is owned and run by the Mucker family. Cyril Mucker, Chairman and Chief Executive, owns 60% of the shares. The only other director, apart from Roger Random, is Cyril's brother, Hugo Mucker, who is responsible for overseeing the building contracts.

The financial accounting section is run by Paula Poppett (who is not a qualified accountant) and produces a set of management accounts quarterly. There are no budgets or management accounts as Cyril Mucker believes that watching the bank balance is the way to run the business.

The company has recently had some difficulty with two of its sites. On the 'brownfield' site inspectors have discovered contamination from an old asbestos factory and have forbidden any further development until it is decontaminated by specialist contractors. Muckers will have to pay for this. On a 'greenfield' housing project Muckers built twelve houses but have only sold two, as there are rumours that the local authority have decided to put in plans to central government for a dual carriageway bypass next to the new development.

The company employs a large number of temporary casual staff who are paid weekly in cash.

required

Before you take on this client what would be your assessment of inherent risk?

solution

The inherent risk involved in this client is high for a number of reasons, including:

■ The company is under the control of a very small group of shareholders all of whom are related. One of them, Cyril Mucker, is a major shareholder.

■ Cyril is also the chairman and chief executive, so this makes him a dominant force in the company.

■ There is a very weak finance function, with no representative at director level. It seems unlikely that Paula Poppett could stand up to Cyril Mucker if there was any dispute about the figures.

■ There is no proper management accounting system or budgeting.

■ They have recently lost a key employee, Roger Random, who was responsible for much of the company's success in the past.

■ They have problems with two of their building developments. It is not known what the financial effect might be, but it is likely to be substantial. The business might then come under financial pressure.

■ The business trades in a highly-regulated environment, particularly with regard to planning constraints, Health & Safety and environmental rules about disposal of materials. This requires constant monitoring to ensure that the company complies with all the appropriate statutory regulations.

■ A large number of staff are paid in cash, which results in a higher risk of theft.

control risk

Control risk – the second element of audit risk – is the risk that the internal controls of the company being audited are not operating properly and so do not prevent or detect material errors or misstatements. This could mean:

■ a significant error may pass through the system undetected

■ transactions may be missed out completely

■ transactions may be wrongly recorded

Internal controls are the safeguards that the client has built into the systems and processes to minimise risk or error. This will include procedures such as matching invoices to orders and delivery notes before the invoice is processed and authorising the invoice before it is paid.

A key part of the auditors' preliminary work is to evaluate these internal controls. Later in this chapter we will see how auditors go about doing this.

If the auditors are satisfied that the internal controls are working well, then they may be able to assess the control risk as low.

Significant weaknesses in the internal controls would lead to the auditors assessing the control risk as high.

detection risk

Detection risk is the risk that the auditors' own tests will fail to detect material errors or misstatements in the financial statements.

If we think about inherent and control risk, neither of these can be influenced by the auditors. Detection risk is different in that it is the only element of audit risk which is within the auditors' control.

If we go back to the audit risk model . . .

audit risk = inherent risk x control risk x detection risk

Suppose that, after carrying out their assessment, the auditors set the value of inherent risk and control risk as follows:

> inherent risk = high   control risk = high

In order to make the level of audit risk acceptable, the auditors will have to do a large amount of audit testing in order to make the detection risk low.

So, in this case:

audit risk =	inherent risk	x	control risk	x	detection risk
acceptable =	high	x	high	x	low

On the other hand, if, after carrying out their risk assessment, the auditors judge inherent and control risk to be low, they will be able to reduce their audit work to an acceptable level, making the detection risk high.

numerical scoring of risk

As accountants you are used to attaching numerical values to things, so you may well look at this system of risk assessment and think it is a bit vague. Auditors sometimes use a **numerical scoring system** for each of the categories of risk in order to arrive at an overall estimate. Remember that in every case the evaluation of risk ultimately requires skill and judgement on the part of the auditor which is gained through training, qualification and experience. Read the following Case Study:

Case Study

AUDIT RISK MODEL – IMPORTERS LIMITED

situation

You work for an auditing firm which has taken on a new client, Importers Limited. This company imports and sells electronic toys manufactured in China.

Your audit firm has set overall acceptable audit risk at a level of 5%.

Inherent risk in the case of Importers Limited is assessed as being high: 90%.

The client appears to have strong internal controls and control risk has been assessed as being low: 40%.

required

What level of detection risk is acceptable in this case?

solution

Audit risk	=	Inherent risk	x	Control risk	x	Detection risk
5%	=	90%	x	40%	x	?

By calculation it can be found that detection risk is 14%*. This means that a 14% chance that audit procedures will not pick up errors or omissions is acceptable.

*Calculation: Detection risk = 0.05 ÷ (0.90 x 0.40) = 0.14 = 14%

Lastly, it is very important to remember that risk must be constantly reviewed during the course of the audit. Factors may come to light during audit testing that will change the level of risk, and this will have an immediate impact on the amount and focus of audit work.

dealing with fraud

ISA 240 'The auditor's responsibility to consider fraud in an audit of financial statements' states:

'The auditor should maintain an attitude of professional scepticism throughout the audit, recognising the possibility that a material misstatement due to fraud could exist, notwithstanding the auditor's past experience with the entity about the honesty and integrity of management and those charged with governance (ie the directors)'.

We have seen in Chapter 2 that the auditor is not responsible for setting out to detect fraud. ISA 240 does not change the position. What it does is to increase the emphasis on the auditors' approach to fraud during the risk assessment and planning stages of the audit.

Auditors need to separate deliberate fraud from accidental error. The simple fact that something has been misstated in, or omitted from, the financial records isn't necessarily fraud. What the good auditor does is consider the possibility that it might be.

There are two types of fraud identified in ISA 240: **theft** and **misstatement**.

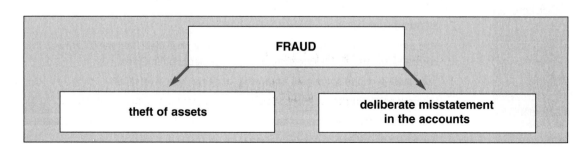

Theft is the straightforward misappropriation of assets. Examples include:

- theft of cash or company property
- diverting company funds into a personal account

Misstatement = Deliberate.

Misstatement is a deliberate misrepresentation in the accounts – in other words, disguising the true nature of a transaction in order to present the accounts in a more favourable light. Examples of this might include:

- suppressing details of claims against the business
- falsifying the valuation of contracts in progress
- accounting for sales revenues in periods earlier than the ones they really relate to
- suppressing costs or deliberately not matching costs with revenues

Auditors should be alert to the possibility of fraud when carrying out the audit. The possibility of a serious fraud occurring should form part of the assessments of risk discussed above. In addition, during the course of the audit the audit team should discuss these possibilities among themselves and evaluate the likelihood of serious fraud occurring.

It must be remembered that many of the most spectacular business failures caused by fraud have involved collusion by senior management. Audit teams must be alert to the possibility that systematic and widespread fraud, of sufficient size to distort the reported results, could be carried out by the directors and management conspiring together.

THE AUDITORS' PERMANENT FILE

Before the auditors can decide on the nature and volume of audit work they have to carry out, they need to gain a clear understanding of the way in which the client operates. This will include an understanding of the client's business, its management and its financial systems. Much of this information will remain unchanged from one year to the next, and once recorded by the auditor, will require only minimal updating each year.

PERMANENT AUDIT FILE

Information that remains 'permanent' for the business is recorded in the **Permanent Audit File**. We referred to this earlier in the section on the engagement letter and will look at it in more detail now.

the permanent file

As its name suggests, the permanent file is used to document those aspects of the client's business which are expected to remain more or less unchanged from year to year.

Permanent
File

The permanent file should contain sufficient information so that any member of the audit team who has no previous knowledge of the client can pick it up and gain a clear picture of the client company, its ownership, management, activities, and very importantly, its financial systems.

The information included in the permanent file will be obtained largely from the client's management and staff. Before recording any information in the permanent file, the auditors must satisfy themselves that all information to be included is accurate. Consequently, at the planning stage of each annual audit visit, the permanent file must be reviewed to ensure that it continues to be relevant, up-to-date and accurate.

gathering information for the permanent file

Auditors can obtain information about their client by:

- touring the client's premises and asking questions about what is going on
- talking to the employees
- interviewing directors, managers and other key personnel
- reviewing original documentation such as minutes of meetings, internal reports and management accounts
- approaching banks and other lenders for details of finance arrangements – always with permission from the client

It is important that, wherever possible, the auditors obtain information from as wide a range of sources as possible and obtain independent evidence to support the information included on the permanent file. Any copies of documents to be included in the file should be taken directly **by the auditors** from the original documents. These copies should then be initialled and dated to evidence that the original of the document has been inspected.

contents of the permanent file

The permanent file should include:

- a description of the client's business activities
- details of ownership, including lists of shareholders, if relevant
- details of group structure, divisions or branches where appropriate
- management structure including relationships between the client's owners/directors and other senior executives
- financial structure, including details of loan and overdraft arrangements
- significant stakeholders other than owners and lenders who might influence business activities, eg a major customer or supplier
- the auditors' view of the business approach adopted, eg risk-taking and unplanned, or conservative and planned

- relationships with other auditors or specialists involved in the audit
- an overall risk assessment
- an assessment of the control environment
- the signed engagement letter
- detailed descriptions of the financial systems

A typical index to a permanent file is shown in the Appendix on page 302.

DOCUMENTING THE CLIENT'S FINANCIAL SYSTEMS

The final point on the list of items included in the permanent file is probably the most important. In order for the auditors to plan their audit work they must have a thorough understanding of the client's financial systems. To that end the auditors must prepare detailed descriptions of these systems.

The main client systems that need to be documented are:

- sales
- purchases
- wages and salaries
- fixed assets
- stock
- investments

Documentation of the systems should include as much information as possible relating to:

- all documents involved including where they are kept
- the way in which transactions are verified
- the personnel involved in the various systems and their roles
- levels of responsibility of staff
- reporting schedules
- the books of accounts maintained and where they are located

There are two main methods of documenting the client's systems:

- narrative notes
- flowcharts

narrative notes

Compiling a series of narrative notes is the simplest way of recording the client's systems. It is best to record the final version on computer file, as it makes them easier to update. A set of handwritten notes prepared on previous audit visits can be time-consuming to revise and is not recommended.

Auditors must ensure that the notes that they produce describing the client systems contain sufficient detail for the user to gain a good understanding of how the system operates.

flowcharting

The danger of using complex narrative notes to document a financial system is that they can become extremely detailed and ultimately may become confusing to the reader, who gets 'lost in the detail'.

It is much easier for the reader to have a diagram showing how the financial system operates. With this in mind, auditors will often use flowcharts, together with brief narrative notes, where necessary, to describe and explain the system.

Flowcharts show the systems in picture form with common symbols used to represent particular documents, and their physical movement. Flowcharts can be used to show the flow of information as well as documents.

As with narrative notes, the auditors will review these charts each year and update for changes and developments in the systems.

The basic flowcharting symbols commonly used are shown below.

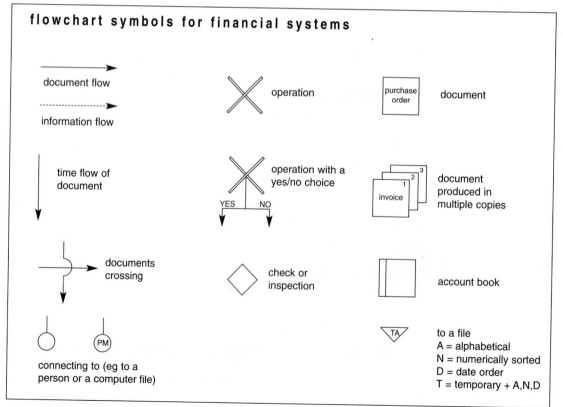

flowcharting rules

There are some key rules for flowcharting:

■ use standard flowcharting symbols wherever possible

■ keep the charts simple – unless the system is very simple do not try to get it all on one sheet; break the chart up into a series of sub-systems and link them together

■ document flows should start at the top left of the sheet and finish at the bottom right

■ chart all documents from 'cradle to grave' – ie from their origination to their final filing, and do not leave any loose ends

■ connecting lines should not cross unless this is unavoidable

A simple flowchart of a goods received and invoice processing system is shown on the next page.

You should notice three things when you look at this flowchart:

■ each operation within the flowchart is separately numbered with a brief narrative where required

■ the chart is divided by functional departments, making it easier to see which department is responsible for which function, and where responsibility for checking transactions lies.

■ the chart does not attempt to describe the whole system at once, for example it does not deal with payments which would be included in a different chart; this simplifies reporting and makes identification of internal controls easier

advantages and disadvantages of flow charts

The **advantages** of flowcharts are:

■ they can be prepared relatively quickly

■ by linking flowcharts even quite complex systems can be described relatively clearly

■ as standard symbols are used they can be easily followed by anyone familiar with flowcharting procedures

■ flowcharts make any weaknesses or gaps in the system or sub-system being described relatively easy to spot

■ there are a number of computerised flowcharting software packages available

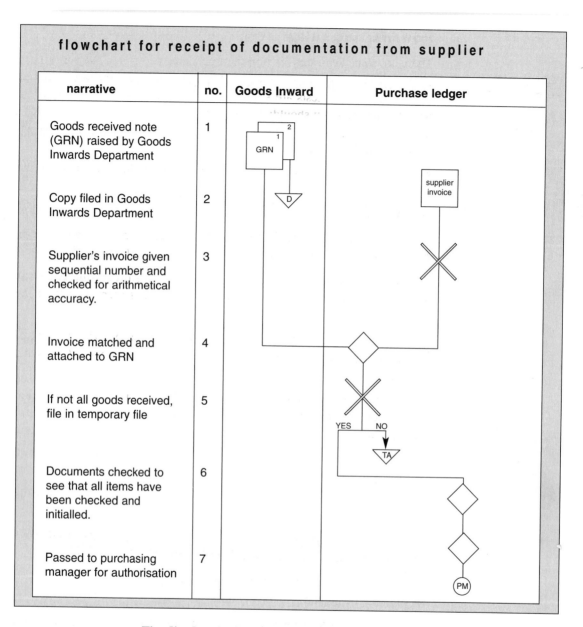

flowchart for receipt of documentation from supplier

narrative	no.	Goods Inward	Purchase ledger
Goods received note (GRN) raised by Goods Inwards Department	1		
Copy filed in Goods Inwards Department	2		
Supplier's invoice given sequential number and checked for arithmetical accuracy.	3		
Invoice matched and attached to GRN	4		
If not all goods received, file in temporary file	5		
Documents checked to see that all items have been checked and initialled.	6		
Passed to purchasing manager for authorisation	7		

The **disadvantages** of flowcharts are:

■ they have to be redrawn if systems change, even to a limited extent

■ they are fine for standard systems but for non-standard transactions they may become unwieldy and require too many narrative notes

■ they are fine for describing accounting processes where documents are moving through the system, but once the documents stop moving they cannot describe controls – for example, flowcharts can describe procedures for controlling goods inward and goods outward but not the controls over stock in the stores

walk through tests

When the flowcharts and accompanying narrative descriptions have been drafted, the auditors should test out the systems to ensure that they work as documented. These tests are known as **walk through tests**. To carry out a walk through test you should:

- choose a small sample of transactions, two or three, from the part of the system being verified
- follow them through the system, using the flowcharts as a guide
- ensure that the flowchart and any notes accurately record the system as it operates in practice

A walk through test should be performed each year before any audit testing begins to ensure that there have been no changes since the preceding audit.

Auditors must document their walk through tests, recording details of the transactions they have chosen to follow through the system, and keep the details on their permanent file.

As soon as the auditors consider that they have a sufficient understanding of the client's systems they can create a programme of audit work to test the internal controls within the system.

The way in which the auditors produce the audit programme will be covered in detail in Chapter 4 but at this point we must ensure that you have clear understanding of what is meant by internal control.

INTERNAL CONTROL

ISA 315 'Obtaining an understanding of the entity and its environment and assessing the risks of material misstatement' states:

'internal control consists of the following components

(a) the control environment

(b) the entity's risk assessment process

(c) the information system, including the related business processes relevant to financial reporting and communication

(d) control activities; and

(e) monitoring of controls

As you will appreciate, at some time or another, everybody makes mistakes. A good financial system has within it a series of checks and procedures designed to prevent, detect and correct mistakes or errors that could occur during the processing of transactions. The prime aim of these checks is to ensure that as many errors as possible are picked up so that there are no material errors in the financial statements.

In all but the very smallest companies there will be a number of layers of management, each with their own role in supervising and directing areas of the business and its workforce. The managers will therefore be the key to the effective operation of these controls within the company's systems. They will be the individuals responsible for the checks, authorisations and approvals that will make up the internal controls of the business.

It is important for you to understand that internal controls are not there primarily to detect fraud.

The purpose of internal control is to provide assurance to managers that:

- the risk of serious error or misstatement in the financial records is minimised

- the assets of the business are safeguarded
- all liabilities are identified and properly recorded
- financial records are kept up to date and as accurately as possible

Internal control is made up of two elements:

- the control environment
- control activities and procedures

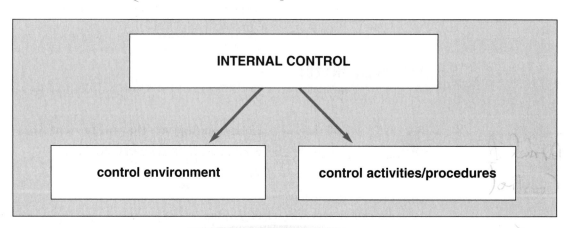

the control environment

ISA 315 'Obtaining an understanding of the entity and its environment and assessing the risks of material misstatement' states:

'The control environment includes the attitudes, awareness and actions of management and those charged with governance (ie the directors) concerning the entity's internal control and its importance in the entity. The control environment also includes the governance and management

functions and sets the tone of an organisation, influencing the control consciousness of its people. It is the foundation of internal control, providing discipline and structure.'

The **control environment** is, fundamentally, the philosophy and operating style of the organisation as set by its directors and senior management, ie the managerial attitude to, and awareness of, internal controls.

In order to assess the internal controls, auditors must to able to understand the culture of an organisation and the way it is reflected in:

- the attitude of its management and staff, and
- the effect this attitude has on the organisation's procedures

What makes a good internal control environment?

It should have the following characteristics:

- competent, reliable staff who demonstrate a high level of integrity and commitment in their attitude to work
- a clear, well-understood management structure with defined authority limits
- involvement by the management in the day-to-day activities of the business
- operating procedures which are understood and accepted by the employees who have to implement them

It is important that you are familiar with key aspects of evaluating a control environment, as this often forms the basis for tasks set in the Simulation for Unit 17.

The following Case Study will illustrate these main points.

Case Study

COUNTIT & CO: THE CONTROL ENVIRONMENT

situation

You are an audit manager for Countit & Co, a firm that has recently gained two new audit clients of a similar size.

Your audit staff have completed their preliminary investigations of the two clients. You are reviewing their notes which can be summarised as follows:

Client 1 - Floggers Ltd

Floggers Ltd is an old-fashioned family company which has been in business for over a hundred years and trades as wholesalers of fruit and vegetables.

Its management structure is divided into five layers ranging from supervisor, deputy manager, manager, senior manager and director. The senior managers and directors have been with the company for many years.

Each level of management has clear authority limits set down in the company manual, which also sets out detailed written procedures for every job.

Management at all levels generally has an unforgiving attitude to errors and inefficiencies.

Most of the systems are paper-based, although the accounting ledgers are maintained on a computer and there are rigid systems of authorisation before transactions can be processed.

Staff turnover in clerical posts and at supervisor and deputy manager level is high.

Client 2 - Creatit Ltd

Creatit Ltd is a new company set up six months ago. It trades as a website design business and as an advertising agency.

Creatit Ltd is run by two brothers who manage the business jointly.

Creatit Ltd mostly employs creative people but it does have a small clerical staff to deal with billing and time recording.

The approach to work is casual, spontaneous and rather uncontrolled.

Error detection is not seen as a priority. The management's view is that they will deal with errors and problems when they arise.

Staff are happy and so staff turnover is low.

required

In your review of the control environment for each of these clients, what conclusions would you draw about the risk of error arising in the accounts?

solution

Floggers Ltd

The key points are as follows:

- Floggers has very rigid systems with a high level of internal control where error detection is seen as a priority and mistakes are not tolerated

- the senior management of Floggers is separated from the day-to-day activities of the business by several layers of administrative hierarchy

- Floggers has a high level of staff turnover which may indicate that staff have a low level of commitment to the company

- following on from the point above – there is a higher risk that frequent mistakes could be made by new, untrained staff

- there may be a temptation for staff to hide mistakes because of the attitude of the management

- Floggers management may take a negative approach to the audit and see it as an intrusion into their business

Creatit Ltd

The key points are as follows:

- Creatit has a much more 'hands on' approach to management and a more forgiving attitude to errors; their priority is the product rather than the accounts

- Creatit's financial systems will contain little in the way of formal internal control checks, but managers are much more aware of what is happening on a day-to-day basis as they are actively involved in the company

- the low level of staff turnover indicates that the employees are loyal to the business and have a strong commitment to the company

Your conclusions from an audit point of view are:

1   Providing the systems at Floggers are working correctly there would be very little likelihood of mistakes being made when recording transactions in the financial systems. The risk is more likely to be transactions which are not being recorded at all. Consequently the audit approach would focus on omissions rather than errors.

2   The business that Floggers operates involves processing large numbers of transactions of easily identifiable goods. Their systems have been in existence for years which means that the risk of posting errors can be assessed as low.

3   As far as Creatit is concerned, the financial statements may well contain errors or omissions and the lack of formal procedures might give cause for concern. However, the close involvement of the management and the commitment of the staff to the organisation would indicate that they will take a positive approach to the audit rather than see it as an intrusion.

4   The trade of Creatit is project work which carries a higher level of audit risk.

Your estimate is that the control environment in both companies is generally good, although the focus of your audit work in each business will differ.

control activities and procedures

ISA 315 'Obtaining an understanding of the entity and its environment and assessing the risks of a material misstatement' states:

> 'Control activities are the policies and procedures that help to ensure management directives are carried out ... Control activities, whether within IT or manual systems, have various objectives and are applied at various organisational and functional levels'.

These are the detailed policies and procedures which are designed to:

- minimise the possibility of mistakes or fraud
- detect errors within the accounting system

When documenting the systems of internal control, the auditors will need to highlight these control activities as they become apparent. It is important to remember that, in order for these control activities to operate effectively, there must also be a good internal control environment.

In practice, if the management and staff of the client company do not have a positive attitude towards the control environment, they will not be carrying out the relevant internal checks effectively, even if good control procedures are in place. This will lead to an increased risk of error or fraud.

forms of internal control

The internal controls that are present in the client's systems will take a number of different forms.

Examples are shown in the table below:

FORMS OF INTERNAL CONTROL	what they involve
Organisational controls	Defined management structure Clear responsibilities for supervision Authority limits for expenditure Written procedures
Segregation of duties	The involvement of a number of different people or departments in recording a transaction to minimise the risk of error or fraud
Physical controls	Restricting access to information or assets
Authorisation and approval of documents	Fixed levels of authority to authorise specific transactions or sign cheques to specified levels Documented procedures Evidence of authorisation
Competency and reliability of staff	Staff training based on identified training need Clear Human Resources policies about recruitment and retention of staff
Arithmetical and accounting checks	Month-end routines to balance and reconcile accounts Checks of calculations on documents generated and received

examples of control activities and procedures

Examples of specific control activities and procedures that relate to the forms of internal control listed on the previous page are set out in the table below.

INTERNAL CONTROL	CONTROL ACTIVITIES AND PROCEDURES
Organisational controls	Company Procedures Manual Company registered under a quality standard eg ISO 9001 with documented procedures Internal auditors operating as part of the internal control environment
Segregation of duties	Staff responsible for sales invoices are not responsible for recording cash received Staff responsible for purchase ordering are not responsible for checking delivery notes or purchase invoice processing
Physical controls	Limiting access to computer applications and processes Menus on computers limiting areas to which operators have access Password controls Regular physical verification of fixed assets by managers Restricted access to ownership documents eg title deeds, vehicle log books
Authorisation & approval of documents	Authorisation of orders Approval of invoices for payment Matching invoices to delivery notes and original orders Two signatures on cheques
Competency and reliability of staff	Regular staff training Encouraging staff to achieve professional qualifications Clear guidelines for recruitment of staff Staff appraisal and review systems
Arithmetical and accounting checks	Checking calculations on invoices Bank reconciliations Reconciliation of suppliers' statements with purchase ledger Maintaining control accounts Monthly trial balance Comparison of financial records with actual counts of stocks and cash

INTERNAL CONTROL QUESTIONNAIRES

As we have seen, auditors have to identify the internal checks operating within the financial system and test them to ensure that they are operating effectively. One technique is to use an **Internal Control Questionnaire (ICQ)**. This consists of a series of questions drawn up by the auditors and designed to identify all internal checks present in each department's systems. The example below assesses the purchasing system of a client company.

INTERNAL CONTROL QUESTIONNAIRE

Client name Bobupandown Ltd   prepared by   JT   date 28/09/05

period to   31 March 2005   reviewed by   DB   date 12/10/05

Purchases System Purchase Ordering

Process	Yes	No	Comments
1 Are all purchases made as a result of written orders?	✔		
2 Are all orders sequentially numbered?	✔		
3 Are all numbers accounted for?		✔	Spoiled orders destroyed
4 Do all orders have to be authorised by a senior manager?	✔		MD, Purchasing Manager
5 Are orders only sent to approved suppliers?	✔		
6 If there is no approved supplier, is the procedure for approving a new supplier carried out before the order is placed?	✔		Only recognised suppliers used

7 Do all purchase orders show:
        quantities
        prices
        terms
        initials of authoriser
        date
	
	✔
	✔
	✔
	✔
	✔		

8 Is there a limit to individual order values?	✔		MD- no limit, Purchasing Manager £50,000

9 Are copies of the purchase order sent to
        Purchase ledger
        Stores
	
	✔
	✔		

10 Are purchase orders matched to invoices?	✔		
11 Are all orders retained in the Purchasing Department?	✔		

■ Before accepting an assignment, auditors must consider any legal, ethical or practical problems, including the size and resources of the audit firm.

■ The arrangement between the auditors and the client should be agreed and formalised in an engagement letter, which sets out the responsibilities of each party and sets out the precise scope of the auditors' duties.

■ Auditors must obtain sufficient knowledge of the client to be able to understand the nature of the business and its transactions and should make themselves aware of the general environment in which the client operates.

■ The auditors are required to assess and document significant areas of audit risk, both at the level of the financial statements and also at the individual item disclosure level.

■ Auditors have to evaluate the risks involved in undertaking the audit. These are based on three types of risk:
- the inherent risk, which is based on the client's activities, operations, and management
- the control risk, based on the ability of the internal controls of the financial system to detect and correct errors or misstatements
- the detection risk, which is the risk that an error or misstatement will not be detected by the audit procedures carried out

■ The audit risk model is an assessment of combined risks using the formula: *inherent risk x control risk x detection risk*

■ The overall audit risk is the probability of auditors giving an incorrect opinion; if the level of audit risk is high, the amount of detailed testing the auditors will carry out will be greater than it would be if the risk were low

■ The auditors document the client's system using a combination of methods including narrative notes, flowcharts and internal control questionnaires. Auditors can confirm their system documentation using walk through tests.

■ General client documentation will be retained on the permanent file and reviewed annually.

■ Auditors have to evaluate their clients' internal control by examining the control environment and control procedures.

■ The control environment is the overall attitude of the organisation towards control procedures and activities including the audit.

■ Control procedures are designed to minimise the possibility of errors or misstatements and to safeguard the assets of the business.

■ Control procedures and activities should include the segregation of duties, limiting access to information, authorisation of transactions, checking and reconciliations.

Key Terms		
	engagement letter	a formal letter signed by the company directors and the auditors, setting out the basis of the agreement between the client and the auditors, establishing their respective responsibilities
	permanent file	ongoing information about the client which will be used for successive audits; it includes a copy of the engagement letter and provides a clear picture of the client company, its ownership, management, activities, and its financial systems
	audit risk	the risk that an auditor might give an inappropriate opinion on the financial statements – the higher the risk the greater the investigative work that will have to be carried out
	risk assessment	a documented process by which auditors assess the likelihood of a material misstatement in the accounts going undetected
	inherent risk	the risk that the accounts will contain a material error or misstatement because of the nature of the client's business, activities, operations and management
	control risk	the risk that the client's internal controls will fail to detect errors or mis-statements
	detection risk	the risk that audit procedures will fail to detect errors or misstatements
	audit risk model	the formula that links the types of risk: *Audit risk = inherent risk x control risk x detection risk*
	flowcharts	a system of documenting financial procedures using standardised symbols to create a diagram of the system
	walk through test	a test involving a small number of transactions which an auditor follows through the system to confirm that the systems notes and flowcharts are a true representation of what actually happens
	internal controls	the policies, procedures, attitudes and internal checks which together combine to ensure that the likelihood of significant error or material misstatement is minimised
	control environment	the overall context within which internal controls and internal checks operate, founded on management attitude and awareness of internal controls
	control procedures	detailed procedures operating within the control environment which minimise the risk of an error or misstatement going undetected
	internal control questionnaire (ICQ)	a series of questions which auditors use to identify the internal checks operating in various parts of the client's financial system

answers to the asterisked (*) questions are to be found in the Student Resources Section of www.osbornebooks.co.uk

Student Activities

3.1* A trainee auditor has been asked to prepare a briefing for clients as to how an audit assignment is planned. Among other things the briefing contained the following statements:

(a) Engagement letters exist so that both the client and the auditors understand who is responsible for what.

(b) The engagement letter is the basis for agreeing how much work the auditor has to do.

(c) Control procedures are what the auditor relies on. If these exist the auditor can sign the report without worrying about the financial statements being wrong.

(d) Walk through tests are there to support flowcharts. If these tests are satisfactory, the auditor can feel confident that the control procedures are working satisfactorily.

(e) Audit risk is the risk of being sued.

(f) Auditors need to find out all about their clients so they can make a decision about the level of inherent risk.

(g) Segregation of duties is an important part of the control environment.

Which of these statements are incorrect, and why?

3.2* You are working on the audit of your client Sweetie Ltd for the year ended 31 March 200X. The company employs one hundred workers in a doughnut manufacturing plant. Wages are paid weekly. The following procedures are carried out:

Wages are paid weekly on a Friday afternoon.

Staff are paid a consistent weekly wage for the standard hours that they work. Overtime is paid for on the Friday following the week in which it is worked.

Employees' clock cards are signed by supervisors and brought to the wages office every Monday morning.

Hours worked in the week are taken from the cards. Overtime hours are calculated and entered on an overtime sheet which is then used to calculate overtime payments.

The overtime sheet is authorised by the production manager.

Wages are prepared using a standard computerised Sage payroll software package.

Standard hours and overtime hours are entered into the payroll by the wages clerk using the input screen.

Any amendments to employees' details, eg changes of personal details, tax code or deductions, are entered on each employees computer file by a member of the personnel department and approved by the personnel manager.

Details of any new starters are notified to the wages department by personnel. Once they have been entered on to the system they are reviewed by the personnel manager to ensure that they are accurate.

Leavers are removed from the system once their final week's wages have been calculated.

When all the information has been entered into the payroll system, it is then processed and authorised by the production manager.

The data is then passed to the accounts department who prepare BACs payments for each employee.

Wages are paid on Friday, so the payroll has to be prepared in time to ensure employees are paid promptly.

An ICQ was prepared for last year's audit and used again for this year's audit.

You are to:

Assess the payroll system details set out above and complete the ICQ on the next page.

INTERNAL CONTROL QUESTIONNAIRE

Client name..

Period to .... Reviewed by .... Date ....

WAGES SYSTEM CONTROL PROCEDURES

Process	Yes	No	N/A	Comments
Is there an individual file recording each employees details?				
Are rates of pay authorised by a responsible official?				
Are there procedures to remove leavers from the payroll as soon as they have been paid their final wages?				
Are there procedures to ensure new starters are included on the payroll correctly?				
Are there procedures to ensure that changes in employees' details are properly recorded?				
Is the payroll software a standard package? (Record details of the package used)				
Is there a timetable for preparing and calculating wages?				
Do employees have to record start and finish times?				
Are overtime rates approved by a responsible official?				
Are hours worked authorised by a responsible official of the company? (Record details)				
Is the payroll approved by a responsible official before wages are paid?				
Is the payroll reconciled on a monthly basis to net pay and deductions?				
Are employees paid by bank transfer?				
Are the people involved in making the payments different to those who prepare the payroll?				

3.3 * Your audit firm has recently merged with another firm and you are reviewing the audit files of some of their clients.

(a)   Castles in the Air Ltd is a recently formed IT consultancy controlled by two brothers who are the only directors. Neither has any financial experience.

(b)   Wheels Ltd is a long established motor dealership which has been the client of your audit firm for ten years. During that time there have been no changes to their financial and management systems and no significant audit problems.

(c)   Tightly Ltd is a large manufacturing business owned and managed by Vera Tightly. Within the factory are six production lines which use state of the art equipment to manufacture high precision drilling equipment. The company has three main clients and the contracts they have with these companies sometimes take over a year to complete.

(d)   Swizzles is a small chain of café bars selling wines and food from sites in three towns in the region. The chain is owned and managed by Antonio Swizzler who has an office in the central site in Newtown. The majority of the company's transactions are for cash as they do not accept credit or debit cards.

Based on the information set out above what would be your assessment of the level of inherent risk for each business? Give reasons for your answers.

3.4   You have been approached to take over the audit of a manufacturer of high quality, high specification components for nuclear reactors.

The components are made from specialised metals and are made to very fine tolerances. There is only one other such manufacturer in the world which is based in the USA. Contracts for component manufacture can sometimes last for two to three years.

In order to finance these contracts the company has a series of complex financial arrangements with banks and investors.

You wish to take on the assignment but are worried about what risks taking on such a client might pose.

Using the information set out above state three audit areas which appear to have high inherent risk. For each area state the factors that have led you to this assessment.

3.5   You have just taken over the audit of a new client and are in the process of assessing audit risk. You have identified the following factors:

The client runs a chain of twenty public houses and restaurants spread throughout England.

The businesses have been acquired piecemeal and each business operates their own stand alone financial system.

Your client's senior management consists of a managing director, sales director and operations director.

During the last two years four managers have been caught defrauding the business and were sacked but not prosecuted.

The previous auditor was a smaller firm than yours which meant that they had to rely on local firms to audit several of the restaurant and pubs. None of these small firms have expressed any doubt as to the truth and fairness of the accounts.

Your firm is big enough to audit all of the businesses without using the small local firms mentioned earlier.

The head office has a team of internal accountants and stock checkers who from time to time turn up unannounced at one of the businesses and perform stock checks and audits. It is they who caught the four managers who were defrauding the businesses.

You have a great deal of experience in the industry as you have three other similar clients.

Using the background information set out above,

(a) Set out two factors you would take into account when evaluating each of the following components of audit risk: inherent risk, control risk and detection risk.

(b) Set out the main areas of the audit where errors are likely to arise and where audit work should be concentrated.

3.6 You are the audit manager on the audit of Piccolo Ltd, a firm of house builders whose business consists of:

■ the construction of small housing developments in association with a local architect's firm and a property developer

■ small building contracts and household repairs

You are reviewing the audit file, before sending it to the audit partner, and you notice a number of items which have been recorded by staff during the audit. They immediately raise concerns in your mind and you consider the partner should be made aware of them. They are as follows:

■ As part of the audit work on sales, the numbering of invoices was checked to ensure they were complete. During the period selected six invoices for small building work and repair jobs could not be traced. These types of invoices are raised by the building contracts manager who often receives payment directly from the customer when the job is completed.

■ A review of the complaints file revealed letters from two customers who complained about being sent an invoice when they had already paid the contracts manager. In each case he claimed a mistake had been made and issued credit notes to cancel the invoices.

■ Analytical review (ratio analysis) revealed that the gross margin on small building and repair work had dropped by nearly 5% from 14.8% last year to 9.9% for the current year. The company prices all these jobs on a cost plus basis and never gives discount. There is a standard mark up of 20% on materials and labour cost.

■ There were three building contracts in progress at the year end. One was a conversion of an old cinema into offices. The contract, which was for a fixed price, had been subject to major problems and costs had been escalating. Examination of the cost accounts revealed two journal entries transferring costs to another, newer contract. The journals simply said 'Transfer'. The production director, who was responsible for these types of contract, could not give a satisfactory explanation for these journal entries.

■ Examination of the cost ledger indicated that cash payments have been made to building workers employed by the company. The production director stated that these were a bonus for working over weekends to finish off a contract.

(a) Draft a memo to the audit partner setting out any concerns raised by these situations.

(b) Describe what course of action should be taken by the auditors in relation to the potential problems you have identified.

This chapter explains how auditors plan and carry out detailed testing of the client's financial systems. It describes how auditors record their work in their working papers and how they deal with the client staff on a day-to-day basis.

This chapter covers:

■ creating the audit plan

■ drawing up the audit programme

■ materiality – deciding on whether an issue is important to the financial statements

■ testing internal controls

■ sampling – selecting transactions to test

■ substantive testing, including analytical procedures such as ratio analysis

■ audit working papers – documenting the evidence gathered

■ working with client staff – maintaining a good relationship

PERFORMANCE CRITERIA COVERED

unit 17 IMPLEMENTING AUDITING PROCEDURES

element 17.1: contribute to the planning of an audit assignment

D   Record significant weaknesses in control correctly.

E   Identify account balances to be verified and the associated risks.

F   Select an appropriate sample.

G   Select or devise appropriate tests in accordance with the organisation's procedures.

H   Follow confidentiality and security procedures.

I   Formulate the proposed audit plan clearly and in consultation with appropriate personnel.

J   Submit the proposed audit plan to the appropriate person for approval.

element 17.2: contribute to the conduct of an audit assignment

D   Identify and record material and significant errors, deficiencies or other variations from standard and report them to the audit supervisor.

F   Conduct discussions with staff operating the system to be audited in a manner which promotes professional relationships between auditing and operational staff.

G   Follow confidentiality and security procedures.

AUDIT TESTING AS PART OF THE AUDIT PROCESS

We saw, in Chapter 3, how the auditors:

- document the client's systems
- identify the internal controls
- perform walk through tests to ensure those controls really do exist and are working in the way in which they have been documented by the auditors

In this chapter we will examine how this information is used by the auditors to design tests to determine how effectively the client's internal controls are operating.

The identification of controls in the client's systems and the testing of them is a key area of your studies. It is often used in the Simulation to examine your knowledge of planning procedures, sampling theory and materiality which we are now going to cover in more detail.

We will first explain what is known as 'substance over form'.

SUBSTANCE OVER FORM

Before we examine the processes of how auditors plan an audit and carry out tests on the client's financial systems you need to understand one of the fundamental principles of auditors' work.

Auditors are not employed merely to check that the financial statements agree with the books and that everything adds up and is neatly reconciled.

A key part of the auditors' role is to gather enough evidence to satisfy themselves that a transaction or a balance in the client's accounts really is what the financial statements say it is.

This is what is known by auditors as **substance over form**.

For example, the auditors need to gather sufficient evidence to prove that:

■ the assets shown on the balance sheet exist, are described correctly and are worth what the directors state they are worth

■ all liabilities have been fully quantified, are correctly described and are included in the financial statements

■ any estimates are based on reasonable assumptions and are properly disclosed

■ sales and costs relate to genuine transactions for the accounting period and relate only to that period

In short, auditors are expected to do more than simply accept what they are told by the client. They must gather sufficient evidence so that they can be confident that in their professional opinion what they have been told is a true reflection of what has actually occurred.

The next step in the process of deciding what audit evidence must be gathered is the formulation of the audit plan.

CREATING THE AUDIT PLAN

It is worth reminding ourselves that the purpose of carrying out audit work is so that the auditors can gather **sufficient** and **appropriate** evidence to support their opinion on the truth and fairness of their client's financial statements.

ISA 500 'Audit Evidence' states:

'Sufficiency is the measure of the quantity of audit evidence. Appropriateness is the measure of quality of audit evidence; that is its relevance and its reliability in providing support for, or detecting misstatements in, the classes of transactions, account balances and disclosures and related assertions.

The quantity of audit evidence needed is affected by the risk of misstatement (the greater the risk the more evidence is likely to be required) and also by the quality of such audit evidence (the higher the quality the less may be required).

Accordingly the sufficiency and appropriateness of audit evidence are interrelated. However merely obtaining more audit evidence may not compensate for its poor quality.'

The two key points that are made by ISA 500 about audit evidence are therefore that it should be:

■ sufficient

■ appropriate

Put simply:

Sufficient relates to the quantity of evidence – is there enough?

Appropriate relates to the quality of the audit evidence – is it the right type of evidence?

It is important to understand that whilst quality and quantity of evidence are important factors, auditors cannot make up for a lack of good quality evidence by simply gathering large amounts of poor quality evidence.

We will discuss what constitutes good quality evidence later in the chapter.

The production of the audit plan will allow the auditor to decide what constitutes sufficient and appropriate evidence for the particular audit they are doing. They will use the information that they have gained from evaluating the client and the client's systems using the process summarised below.

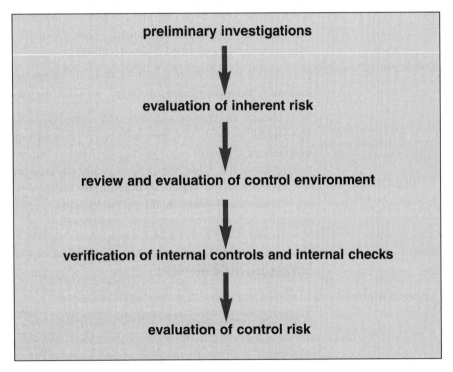

preliminary investigations

evaluation of inherent risk

review and evaluation of control environment

verification of internal controls and internal checks

evaluation of control risk

Auditors must take the information they have gathered and use it to prepare a formal written plan.

audit plan or audit programme?

Before we go on to describe the audit plan in more detail, you must be clear about the difference between the audit plan and the audit programme. Briefly, the audit plan is the general strategy and scope of the audit. The audit programme is the detailed audit work to be carried out, including details of specific individual tests to be performed. The audit programme is covered in the next section.

audit planning memorandum

Evidence of the detailed planning of the audit is recorded in a written document called the **Audit Planning Memorandum (APM)**.

When the planning has been completed, the Audit Planning Memorandum is usually drafted by the **audit manager**, who is responsible for the day-to-day running of the audit assignment.

The Audit Planning Memorandum is approved by the audit partner who carries overall responsibility for the audit and who will, eventually, sign the auditor's report (covered in Chapter 7).

The Audit Planning Memorandum sets out all the key matters relating to the audit for the year. This will include administrative matters such as staffing and timetable and, more importantly, how the audit will be carried out to ensure it meets its planned audit objectives.

The sample Audit Planning Memorandum shown on the next two pages illustrates the main sections included and what they cover.

In addition to the production and approval of the Audit Planning Memorandum, there will normally be an audit planning meeting where all members of the audit team get together before the audit commences to be briefed about the client, the audit plan and the areas of the audit which they will be working on. This is an opportunity for the audit manager to explain any complicated issues in the Audit Planning Memorandum to the audit team.

THE AUDIT PROGRAMME

When the Audit Planning Memorandum has been completed, the audit manager will review the audit programme or, in the case of a new client, prepare an audit programme containing all the audit tests to be performed.

The audit programme contains the detailed instructions for the audit staff regarding the tests which they must carry out.

It should be based on:

■ systems weaknesses identified in last year's audit

■ appropriate, relevant tests of internal controls

(continued on page 81)

AUDIT PLANNING MEMORANDUM

Prepared by

Date

Reviewed by

Date

1 Changes since previous audit   **Comments/ref**

- changes to client's business

- changes to management structure

- changes to accounting system /personnel

- external reporting requirements (IASS/legislation etc)

2 Audit planning focus

- changes to previous year audit programme

- changes to sample sizes

- key areas of internal control considered weak

- key areas of internal control considered strong

- indicate areas where material errors have been detected in previous periods

- systems to be flowcharted

- update permanent file

- specialist assistance required

- schedules to be provided by client

- other services to be provided to client

3 Evaluation of audit risk

Inherent risk   %

Control risk   %

Audit risk (at 95% confidence level)   %

4 Observations

Attendance at client's premises for:

- stock taking

- wages payout

5 Visit rota

- branch visits to be undertaken this year

6 Audit focus

- areas for particular attention this year

7 Systems documentation

- confirmation that the systems documentation is up-to-date
- arrangements for documenting the system

8 Internal audit

- reliance to be placed on internal audit
- liaison arrangements

9 Specific briefing notes

- particular matters to be dealt with by the audit team

10 Staffing

- Partner
- Reviewing partner (if required)
- Manager
- Senior
- Junior

11 Timetable and budget

12 Analytical review

- Ratios over three years, to include gross and net profit %, ROCE, stock turnover, debtor days, creditor days, current ratio and gearing.

13 Conclusion

- derived from analysis and audit points arising
- leading on to audit planning focus (item 2)

an example of an audit planning memorandum (blank)

- key areas identified in the planning process that require close attention
- tests to confirm the figures included in the balance sheet and profit and loss account

The audit programme sets the following for each audit area:

- the objectives which the tests are designed to achieve
- details of actual tests to be performed – including the sample sizes

To show you how this is set out in practice, a sample section from an audit programme for Sales & Debtors is shown below.

As you will see in this example of an audit programme, the person who carries out the test will initial and date the audit programme as evidence that every test included in the audit programme has been completed.

AUDIT PROGRAMME

Audit area Sales & debtors	**Prepared by**
Client	**Date**
Period	**Reviewed by**
	Date

Tests of control

Control objectives

- Sales are made to approved, creditworthy customers in accordance with company objectives.
- Customer orders are authorised, controlled and recorded.
- Uncompleted orders are controlled and recorded so as to be fulfilled at the earliest opportunity.
- Goods delivered are controlled and recorded to ensure that invoices are issued for all sales.
- Goods returned and claims by customers are controlled to ensure that claims are valid and credit notes are approved and issued as appropriate.
- Invoices and credit notes are authorised and checked before being entered in the debtors ledger.
- Procedures are in place to ensure that overdue debts are pursued and appropriate provisions made in respect of debts where recovery is doubtful.

Tests of control	**Initial & date**
Test new customer procedure to ensure credit checks and references completed	
Test allocation of credit limits	
Check sample of customer orders to ensure they are approved by sales department	
Check sample of delivery notes to ensure goods signed for by customer on receipt	

	Initial & date
Check sample of sales invoices for authorisation by sales department	
Check sample of sales invoices for matching against sales order and delivery note	
Check sample of sales invoices for evidence of arithmetic checks	
Check batching procedure for posting sales invoices to sales ledger	
Confirm all order forms, sales invoices and credit notes are numerically sequenced	
Review selection of customer claims and check authorisation of credit note or refund	
Check selection of credit notes with copy goods returned note	
Check credit notes authorised by sales manager or equivalent	
Check statements are sent to customers monthly	
Confirm aged debtors printout produced monthly and confirm evidence of review by sales manager	
Substantive procedures	
Check sample of sales invoices for:	
- arithmetical check	
- match to sales order	
- match to delivery note	
Vouch sample of sales invoices to customer account in sales ledger	
Check numerical sequence of:	
- customer order forms	
- sales invoices	
- credit notes	
Ensure all sequence numbers accounted for and cancelled documents retained on file	
Test batch processing procedures and ensure batch totals agree	
Check sample of authorised credit notes against customer claims	
Review period-end aged debtor analysis for possible doubtful debts	
Review subsequent payment or clearance	
Check client's provision for doubtful debts	

Note

Each of the tests of control and the substantive tests will be evidenced by working papers in the current audit file.

You will see from the sample audit programme on the previous two pages that there are a number of individual sections covering classes of items included in the financial statements. In this chapter we will be concentrating on the types of testing that are carried out on the client's financial systems, covering control (or compliance) testing and substantive testing. In Chapter 5 we will focus on the way in which the auditors test the three main areas of sales, purchases and payroll transactions. Finally, in Chapter 6, we describe how the auditors test specific items on the balance sheet.

In the next section we will examine how materiality affects the development of the audit programme.

MATERIALITY

ISA 320 'Audit Materiality' states:

> *Information is material if its omission or misstatement could influence the economic decisions of users taken on the basis of the financial statements …*
>
> *The assessment of what is material is a matter of professional judgement.'*

Materiality is effectively a measurement of how important something is within the financial statements. As the above quote from ISA 320 states, something will be considered to be material if leaving it out of the financial statements or getting it wrong would give the reader/user a misleading view of the state of the company's affairs.

There are three points to understand about materiality:

■ the auditors will use their professional judgement to decide what is material

■ it cannot be defined as one specific value

■ the auditors' decision as to whether an error is material depends on the context of the financial statements as a whole

Something can be material to the financial statements for **qualitative** or **quantitative** reasons.

qualitative aspects

Qualitative means that an error or omission that the auditors have discovered is material because of the **nature** of the item, regardless of its financial value. In this case the error or omission is unacceptable and the auditor must highlight this to the client management for adjustment.

Examples of qualitative aspects include:

■ a disclosure required by the Companies Act or Accounting Standards which has been omitted completely or partially from the accounts, eg director's emoluments

■ an item which is misstated, eg a short-term loan shown as a long-term loan

■ an item which might affect the accounts but which has not been included because it cannot be quantified with a reasonable degree of certainty, eg the outcome of a significant court case

It is the responsibility of the auditors to remind the directors of their duty to comply with legislation and with relevant Accounting Standards and to rectify errors and omissions.

quantitative aspects

Whereas 'qualitative' refers to the nature of errors and omissions, **quantitative** refers to quantity, ie to the size (value in £s) of any errors found during the audit.

The auditors must take a view as to whether the value of errors found, individually, or taken all together, is sufficiently significant (material) for the auditors to request the management to adjust the financial statements.

For each audit assignment, the auditors will set a level of materiality.

In order to determine a numerical value for materiality, the auditors will often use percentages of some of the key numbers in the draft financial statements. For example:

■ 5% - 10% of pre-tax profits

■ 1% of turnover

■ 5% of net asset value

Alternatively, they may decide to calculate these figures and then to use a combination of all three. The figures on which the auditors will base their calculation of materiality will depend on the nature of the client being audited.

It is important to understand that these figures are given as examples only and that you should not see them as a definitive guide to setting materiality. It is also important for materiality levels to be constantly reviewed during the course of the audit where the level of inherent or control risk changes or where errors are found in audit testing.

When, during the audit, the auditors find errors in the accounts, these should be noted on a schedule of errors and misstatements. At the end of the audit all errors and misstatements that have been found should be aggregated and considered together. The auditors must then assess whether they have a material impact on the financial statements and also whether they affect the truth and fairness of the financial statements.

In most cases the directors will be happy to adjust the financial statements for errors found by the auditors because they are keen for the accounts to be as accurate as possible. However, if the directors refuse to amend the accounts, the auditors will have to consider whether the error or mistake is serious enough that they should highlight it in their final audit report. This issue will be covered in detail in Chapter 7.

Case Study

MATERIALITY: LEMON LTD

situation

You are the audit manager covering the year-end audit of Lemon Ltd. You are reviewing the audit files before sending them to the audit partner for final review. Two specific points have been drawn to your attention by the audit staff.

(a) The draft accounts currently do not include any reference to the fact that the client's Sales Director owns 15% of Tonic Ltd, a major supplier to Lemon Ltd.

(b) One of the company's major customers has gone into liquidation, owing them £40,000 which is unlikely to be recovered. Profits for the year are £200,000 and debtors are shown in the balance sheet at £650,000.

Materiality on the audit has been set at 10% of the pre-tax profit. However, the client's management say they have not provided for this, as it is not material and if necessary they will write it off next year.

required

What recommendations will you make to the audit partner regarding these two issues?

solution

(a) This is automatically material (for qualitative reasons) and must be disclosed. The director has an interest in a major supplier to the business and the Companies Act requires that this type of information is disclosed in the Financial Statements.

(b) This is not automatically material as there is no requirement on the company to disclose this item simply due to its nature. The auditor must look at the issue in the context of the accounts as a whole. Would failure to amend the accounts for this item mean that the financial statements were misleading to the reader?

In this case the profits would be reduced by 20% to £160,000 and debtors by about 6% to £610,000. Whilst the effect on the balance sheet may not be considered material the reduction in profit is large. The materiality here is clearly quantitative. The audit partner should therefore encourage the directors of Lemon Ltd to provide for this debt in the financial statements for the current year.

AUDIT TESTING

In this chapter so far we have covered the planning of the audit and the formalising of the audit plan. We will now examine in detail the various types of testing that are included in the audit programme, starting with the testing of internal controls.

internal controls

In Chapter 3 we examined the function of internal controls within the client's financial systems and established that their role is to ensure that the risk of a material error or omission in the financial statements is minimised.

The auditors will take the effectiveness of these controls into account when assessing the risk of a serious misstatement in the accounts not being picked up by the client.

Part of the audit process is to test and evaluate these controls in order to ensure that:

- they have been **designed** to pick up material misstatements
- they **operate** effectively for the whole accounting period

The type of testing carried out on the controls will depend on how effective the auditors consider the controls in the system to be.

Chapter 3 explained that the auditors use walk through tests and internal control questionnaires (ICQs) to find out how strong the internal controls are. The auditors' assessment of the strength of the internal controls will determine the type of audit approach that they take.

There are two main approaches that the auditor can take when testing internal controls:

- a **risk based approach** where they rely heavily on the fact that internal controls function effectively
- a **systems based** approach where controls are tested but are generally not found to be effective, so the auditors consider that they need to carry out a substantial amount of detailed testing

The diagram on the next page shows the process the auditors will go through to decide which of the two approaches to adopt.

The table that follows the diagram summarises this decision making process. Note that where **compliance testing** is referred to, it means testing of the effectiveness of the client's own internal controls. **Substantive testing** is additional testing carried out by the auditors, eg by examining transactions, balances and ratios, to ensure that the accounts are free from errors or misstatements. These types of testing are explained in more detail on the pages that follow.

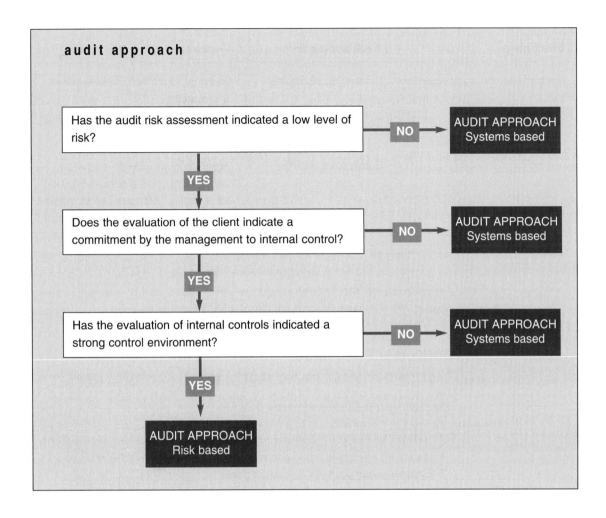

audit approach

a comparison of the risk based and systems based approaches

Description	Audit approach	Features
Risk based audit approach	Evidencing of controls	Audit tests show that strong controls exist
	Compliance testing	Compliance testing indicates controls functioning effectively
	Substantive testing	Low levels required – substantive testing should be confined to areas where audit risk is considered to be high

table continued on next page

Description	Audit approach	Features
Systems-based audit approach	Evidencing of controls	Tests show control weaknesses in the systems
	Compliance testing	Tests indicate a strong possibility of material error or misstatement
	Substantive testing	Medium/High levels required – substantive testing should be used to quantify the size of possible errors and also for areas where audit risk is considered to be high

We referred on the last two pages to compliance testing and substantive testing. We will now describe in detail what we mean by these two terms.

COMPLIANCE TESTING

ISA 500 'Audit Evidence' states:

'When the auditor's risk assessment includes an expectation of the operating effectiveness of controls the auditor is required to test those controls to support the risk assessment.'

Compliance testing, or testing of controls, will test to assess whether the internal controls have been operating effectively throughout the period. The way in which the auditors do this is through:

- **inspection** – eg looking at sales invoices to ensure that they are authorised for payment

- **re-performance** – 'doing something again', eg preparing a bank reconciliation to ensure that the client has done it properly

- **observation** – eg watching the client operate the system

- **sample tests** – eg select a sample of transactions covering the whole accounting period and check whether the controls on this sample have been applied effectively.

The Case Study that follows gives an example of how compliance testing operates in practice.

SIMPLE SALES LTD:
COMPLIANCE TESTING – SALES SYSTEM

situation

Simple Sales Ltd is a wholesaler of imported Russian dolls and wooden toys.

The sales system is as follows:

Sales orders are received from customers by telephone, email or fax. When an order is received the sales department transfer it to a multi-part, pre-numbered order form, which is signed by the member of staff taking the order.

One copy of the order goes to the customer as confirmation, one copy goes to the warehouse for packing/despatch, one copy goes to the accounts office and one copy is retained in the sales office.

Goods are despatched from the warehouse which raises a despatch note; these are also multi-part and pre-numbered. One copy of the despatch note goes with the goods when they are sent to the customer, one copy goes to the sales office, one copy to the accounts office and one copy is retained in the stores.

The sales office invoices the client and sends a copy of the invoice to the accounts office.

Staff in the accounts office:

- check the calculations on the invoice
- match the invoice to the order and the despatch note
- enter the details into the sales day book and from there to the sales ledger
- annotate each invoice to ensure that these checks have been carried out

If the order is only partly completed due to goods being out of stock, the stores department pin the original order onto a board in the stores with the missing items highlighted. When these are received into stock they raise a despatch note in the usual way.

required

What compliance tests would the auditors need to carry out in order to establish that internal controls were effective?

solution

The auditors will check the client's internal control systems by performing the following compliance tests:

■ Select a sample of sales invoices from throughout the year and agree with the sales order and despatch notes to ensure:

- quantities and details of goods on the sales invoice agree to what was originally ordered and to what was despatched
- the sales order has been authorised by a member of the sales staff

- prices on the order and on the invoice match and agree to the client's official price lists
- the invoices are arithmetically correct
- VAT has been calculated and applied correctly

■ In addition the auditors should:

- match the sample of sales invoices to the Sales Day Book and to the customer accounts in the Sales Ledger
- review the sales invoices either side of each of the sample selected to ensure that there are no gaps in the sequence of numbers

Provided that all these controls are found to be functioning satisfactorily, the auditors will conclude that the sales system for Simply Sales has operated effectively for the accounting period.

SAMPLING

In the section on compliance testing (see page 88) we referred to the auditors selecting a **sample** of transactions to test. The question is how do the auditors select which items to include in this sample?

ISA 530 'Audit sampling and other means of testing' states:

'When designing audit procedures, the auditor should determine appropriate means for selecting items for testing so as to gather sufficient appropriate audit evidence to meet the objectives of the audit procedures.'

It is impossible for auditors to test all the transactions a company makes and they are clearly not required to do so. What they have to do is test a sample of transactions and, from the results that they find, draw a conclusion about all transactions. The statistical term used to describe all the items that could be sampled is the **population**.

The decision facing the auditors is how many items from the 'population' to include in the sample. If a client issues 3,000 sales invoices in the year does the auditor test a sample of ten, 25, 50 or even 100?

Before they can make this decision a number of factors need to be taken into account:

■ the number of items in the population from which the sample is selected

■ sampling risk – the risk of choosing a misleading sample and reaching the wrong conclusion

■ tolerable error – the maximum acceptable error in the sample (in £s)

■ expected error – the level of error expected from previous audits of the client

Another factor is the expected level of risk. We have covered risk in some detail already (see page 45). However, it is worth pointing out that if inherent risk and control risk are considered to be high, the auditors will increase their sample sizes in order to reduce detection risk as much as possible.

You are unlikely to be asked in the skills test to determine an actual sample size, but you may well be asked to identify the factors that the auditors will take into account when deciding on the number of items to include in a sample.

We will now look at the factors other than risk that affect sample sizes.

population

As noted earlier, the **population** in relation to audit is the total number of transactions of a particular type which the client has carried out. For example:

- the total number of purchase invoices processed
- the total number of stock issues made
- the total number of sales credit notes issued

The sample to be tested should be selected from the population and should be a representative sample of the population as a whole. There are two important points to remember here:

- all the transactions in the population must be of the same type to ensure that the sample chosen has the same characteristics as the rest of the items in the population
- if there has been a major change in the nature of the population during the period – for example, a change during the year from manual invoicing to computerised invoicing – the auditors might be dealing with different populations

This point is illustrated in the Case Study that follows.

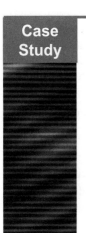

Case Study

HILO LTD: SAMPLING METHOD

situation

The auditors of HiLo Ltd are planning the audit testing that they will perform on the sales system. As part of their testing they need to select a sample of sales invoices.

The year end is 31 December.

HiLo Ltd has always processed the sales invoices manually rather than using a computer accounting package. Each invoice is allocated a sequential number.

However, in August this year, the company installed a new computer system with an integrated accounting package. This has meant that from the end of August all sales

invoices have been printed by the computer from information entered on to the sales ledger by sales staff, and invoice numbers have been allocated automatically.

required

What factors will the auditors need to consider when defining the population from which they will select the sample of sales invoices to be tested?

solution

Step 1

The auditors should obtain the first and last invoice numbers for the sales invoices issued during the financial year. This will show the range of the total population of sales invoices. They should also confirm that the number of the first computer generated invoice followed on sequentially from the number of the last manual invoice to be issued.

Step 2

The auditors should ensure that the population consists solely of sales invoices and does not include credit notes, as these should be tested separately.

Step 3

There are two separate populations of sales invoices with different characteristics which will need to be tested differently:

- The first population consists of sales invoices prepared manually by sales staff on a word processor. For these invoices there may be typing and calculation errors as the preparation of the invoices is a separate process from entering the sales information into the customers' accounts in the sales ledger.

- The second population consists of sales invoices produced automatically from information entered into the computerised sales ledger. In this case, entering the sales information onto the system and updating the customers' accounts are automatically linked, so the risk of error is reduced.

Step 4

Separate samples should be taken from each population. The size of the sample to be selected from each population is likely to be different because the risk of errors being found in each sample will vary.

sampling risk

The reason for testing a sample is so that the auditor can draw a conclusion about the population as a whole. **Sampling risk** is the risk that the auditors' conclusion about the whole population, based on the sample, is different from the conclusion they would have reached if they had performed the same test on the whole population.

One possible reason for this happening is if the auditors select a sample which is not truly representative of the population as a whole, even though it has been selected from transactions which are all of the same type.

For example, suppose the auditors decide that they wish to test sales invoices issued in the year by selecting a sample of ten invoices. They then choose five invoices issued in June and five in July because the files containing these invoices are the most convenient to find. Clearly, this will not be a representative sample of sales invoices issued during the year as it does not include any invoices from the other ten months of the year.

The auditors must be sure that a representative sample is selected which reflects, as closely as possible, the entire population from which it has been chosen.

There are a number of methods which auditors use to select a representative sample and so minimise sampling risk. The main methods are shown in the table below.

basis of selection	methodology
random selection	the auditors select the sample to be tested on a random but organised basis, for example by using random number tables or by computer generated random numbers; if the auditors use this method, each item has an equal chance of being selected
systematic selection	using this method, the auditors select items with a constant interval between each one, for example if there are 200 items in the population and the sample size is to be ten then the auditors would select every twentieth invoice (note also that the first item to be included in the series should be randomly generated)
haphazard selection	this is similar to random selection but may not be based on tables or any other mathematical tool used for selecting the items to test – care has to be taken that the sample is truly haphazard and that the sample is not biased towards the items most easily located

tolerable error

When testing a sample of transactions the auditors will often find errors which need to be recorded because they are material or significant. The

tolerable error, as the name suggests, is the maximum error (in £) in the population as a whole that the auditors are willing to 'tolerate' and still be able to conclude that the objective of the audit test has been met. Because the auditors are testing a sample and not the whole population, they must consider the errors that they have found as being representative for the population as a whole. This process is known as extrapolation. Provided that this error level is below the tolerable error limit that has been set (see above), the auditors can conclude that the test has successfully achieved its objectives.

There are some errors which should not be included in a calculation of tolerable error which might result in an alteration to the accounts.

For example, if the auditors discover that in a test of twenty invoices one invoice has been posted to the wrong purchase ledger account, this will not affect the overall creditors figure on the balance sheet and so does not affect the accuracy of the financial statements.

In this situation, the auditors should still find out why this error has occurred to ensure that it is not a weakness in the system rather than human error.

If the extrapolated error level for the whole population, based on the sample, exceeds the level of tolerable error that has been set for the audit, the auditors will then have to consider how to deal with the situation.

Case Study

SAM PULL LTD: INVOICE SAMPLING

The auditors of Sam Pull Ltd are testing a sample of sales invoices.

They select and test a sample of 50 invoices out of a total population of 6,000 and discover calculation errors on those invoices amounting in total to £180.

The objectives of the audit test are to assess the reliability of the controls in the sales ledger processing system and also ensure the accuracy of the sales figure in the financial statements.

required
How should the auditors deal with their findings?

solution
Extrapolating the error from the sample for the population as a whole (ie all the invoices) would be calculated as follows:

      Total number of sales invoices
÷   the number of sales invoices in the sample
x   the errors found in the sample

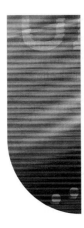

ie   6,000 ÷ 50 x £180 = £21,600

This means if the rate of errors occurring in the population is the same as that for the sample, the total errors would be £21,600.

The auditors must then decide whether this total error is within the tolerable error for the audit, given the level of turnover of the company. A significant error is one which would affect the auditors' opinion as to the truth and fairness of the accounts.

If the error is considered to be significant, the auditors will have to take a view as to whether to extend the sample and test further items to see if this level of error is maintained in the remainder of the population.

As with any error found by the auditors, they may still wish to comment to the client's management about weaknesses in their systems that have allowed these errors to go undetected.

expected error

Where auditors have been involved in the audit of a client for a number of years they will have experience of errors that have been found in the past in certain areas. Over time they will come to expect a certain level of error due to the nature of the client's business or the inadequacy of their records. This is known as **expected error**.

Clearly, in some circumstances, if the auditors have encountered a high level of error historically then, at some point, they will have to decide whether using sample testing is still an appropriate way of gathering audit evidence.

SUBSTANTIVE TESTING

ISA 500 'Audit Evidence' states:

> *'there are inherent limitations to internal control including the risk of management override, the possibility of human error and the effect of systems changes. Therefore substantive (testing) procedures for material classes of transactions, account balances and disclosures are always required to produce sufficient appropriate audit evidence'*

Substantive testing procedures are designed to support test of controls and to provide sufficient appropriate audit evidence to ensure the accounts are free from material misstatements.

There are two main types of substantive testing:

- **detailed testing** of transactions and balances
- **analytical procedures** to test the reasonableness of account balances

As far as substantive testing of financial systems is concerned, there are a number of similarities between the techniques used for compliance testing and those for substantive testing. The main difference is the amount of testing that is carried out.

Substantive testing techniques are also used to verify assets and liabilities on the balance sheet. We will deal with this in Chapter 6.

detailed testing

Detailed tests take several forms which are summarised in the table below.

TYPE OF TEST	DEFINITION	EXAMPLE
Inspection	Physically examining records, documents or assets	Examining fixed assets to verify existence (but not necessarily ownership or value) Inspecting documents relating to arrangements with providers of loan finance
Vouching	Checking an entry in the accounting records back to the original document	Vouching an entry in the sales day book with a copy sales invoice Vouching the hours worked recorded on the payroll system back to the original clock cards
Posting	Checking amounts entered in the books of prime entry with the ledger accounts or checking between ledger accounts, to ensure entries are made in the correct account	Sales Day Book entries to Sales Ledger Cash book payments to Nominal Ledger accounts
Enquiry	An independent verification of balances Requests for information from client staff	Independent circularisation of debtors Questions such as 'Why is invoice number 32187 not here?'
Computation	Checking the arithmetical accuracy of accounting records	Testing calculations on stock sheets Testing VAT calculations on invoices
Reconciliation	Reconciling balances in the accounting records with independent evidence	Bank reconciliation Reconciliations between suppliers statements and purchase ledger balances

The auditor will apply a combination of tests to different aspects of the system under review.

They will also ensure that, where necessary, they test transactions in both directions, ie:

- **forwards** – from the original document to the final entry in the accounting records, eg from the sales invoice to the sales ledger

- **backwards** – from the entries in the accounting records to the original documents, eg from the wages control account to the timesheet

Case Study

SIMPLE SALES LTD:
SUBSTANTIVE TESTING – PURCHASES

situation

You are a member of the audit team that is auditing Simply Sales Ltd. You have been allocated responsibility for testing the purchases system.

The objective of the audit testing is to ensure that the procedures for processing purchase invoices are being operated correctly.

required

Following compliance testing of the internal controls of the purchases system, your team has identified a need for substantive testing. What forms of substantive testing might the auditors carry out on the purchases system?

solution

The auditors' tests will take a variety of forms and will use various types of substantive testing in order to gather the evidence needed. These are summarised below.

PURCHASE LEDGER INVOICE PROCESSING	
Test	**Type of test**
For a sample of purchase orders: - Check that the supplier is on the approved supplier list	Inspection
For a sample of Goods Received Notes (GRN's): - Check that details agree with the original order	Inspection
For a sample of purchase invoices: - Check the details agree with the GRN - Check details agree with Purchase Order	Inspection Inspection

- Check all calculations - Check VAT computation	Arithmetical Arithmetical
For a sample of entries in the purchases day book: - Check with purchase invoice	Vouching
For a sample of entries in the purchases ledger: - Check back to the purchase day book entry	Posting

analytical procedures

The other type of substantive testing involves **analytical procedures**, which analyse and compare financial and other information over time periods in order to detect any inconsistencies in the accounts.

ISA 520 'Analytical Procedures' states:

'The auditor should apply analytical procedures as risk assessment procedures to obtain an understanding of the entity and its environment and in the overall review at the end of the audit. Analytical procedures may also be applied as substantive procedures.

Analytical procedures means evaluations of financial information made by a study of plausible relationships among both financial and non-financial data. Analytical procedures also encompass the investigation of identified fluctuations and relationships that are inconsistent with other relevant information or deviate significantly from predicted amounts.'

ISA 520 then goes on to describe the nature and purpose of analytical procedures as follows:

'Analytical procedures include the consideration of comparisons of the entity's financial information with, for example:

■ *Comparable information for prior periods.*

■ *Anticipated results of the entity, such as budgets or forecasts, or expectations of the auditor, such as an estimation of depreciation.*

■ *Similar industry information, such as a comparison of the entity's ratio of sales to accounts receivable with industry averages or with other entities of comparable size in the same industry.*

Analytical procedures also include consideration of the relationships:

■ *Among elements of financial information that would be expected to conform to a predictable pattern based on the entity's experience, such as gross margin percentages.*

■ *Between financial information and relevant non-financial information, such as payroll costs to number of employees.'*

comparison of financial information

The simplest method of performing analytical review is to compare the financial information for the current period to the same information for previous periods. Provided that the client's business has not changed significantly, the auditors would expect the financial information to be consistent from year to year.

In the case of the company below, for example, the financial period being audited is 2005 and the auditors have summarised the following information for further analysis:

Year	2002 £	2003 £	2004 £	2005 £
Sales	702,000	744,000	748,000	776,000
Cost of Sales	428,000	447,000	452,000	476,000
Gross Profit	274,000	297,000	296,000	340,000
Closing Stock	60,100	63,800	65,600	81,200
Debtors	86,500	88,100	88,700	93,600
Creditors	58,500	59,700	56,900	64,200

A study of this table suggests that there is a steady upward trend in the results of the client. However, in order to test the information fully the auditors will perform additional detailed analytical procedures.

You will have come across accounting ratios at various stages in your AAT studies to date. A number of the ratios that you are familiar with can be calculated as part of analytical procedures, including:

Gross profit %	(Gross Profit/Sales x 100)
Net profit %	(Net Profit/Sales x 100)
Debtor days	(Debtors/Sales x 365)
Creditor days	(Creditors/Cost of sales x 365)
Stock days	(Stock/Cost of sales x 365)

In this example the auditors would calculate the following:

	2002	2003	2004	2005
Gross Profit %	39%	39.9%	39.6%	43.8%
Stock days	51 days	52 days	53 days	62 days
Debtors	45 days	43 days	43 days	44 days
Creditors	50 days	49 days	46 days	49 days

Having performed these more detailed calculations it can be seen that both the gross profit % and the stock days have risen significantly in 2005 whilst all the other ratios have remained reasonably constant.

As part of their analytical procedures the auditors would now investigate the reasons for these increases in the current financial period. From the original data it can be seen that closing stock has also risen significantly. If for any reason the closing stock was incorrectly stated and should be lower, this could be the explanation for the increase in gross profit margin and stock days. An overstatement of closing stock would mean that cost of sales would be lower than it should be, and hence gross profit margin would be higher than it should be.

The same sort of analysis could also be used to compare the results of different branches of a business or to compare information to budgeted figures for the year. However, in all cases, the auditors must investigate any inconsistencies that are discovered.

Analytical procedures can also use other ratios where there are direct relationships – between figures, for example:

■ selling expenses as a percentage of sales

■ direct wages as a percentage of direct costs

The auditors can also calculate expected relationships such as applying the average pay rise for the year to the previous year's total wages and salaries and comparing the result to the current wages and salaries figure.

comparison of non-financial information

Non-financial data can also be used as part of analytical procedures. This analysis can often identify inconsistencies that simple financial calculations will not reveal.

An example of this (from ISA 520) is the comparison of payroll costs to the number of employees (the non-financial information). A significant increase or decrease in payroll costs over the year could indicate an error or misstatement of the payroll costs.

Other examples of the analysis on non-financial data include:

- monthly wastage as a percentage of raw materials quantities for a manufacturing company; a large increase could highlight problems in production or could be as a result of theft
- weekly bed nights in a hotel to establish levels of occupancy from period to period
- miles per gallon for individual vehicles in a transport fleet

analytical procedures – a summary

The analytical procedures that the auditors use will vary from client to client and not all the ratios are appropriate in all situations. However, in all cases the auditors will be looking to:

- investigate any unusual or inconsistent variations in ratios
- obtain explanations and substantiate the variations
- evaluate the results of analytical procedures in relation to other audit evidence

We will examine analytical procedures again in Chapter 7 'Audit completion and audit reporting' when the auditors will use them to assess the overall reasonableness of the financial statements.

AUDIT WORKING PAPERS

It is very important that the auditors are able to demonstrate that sufficient work has been carried out to justify their audit opinion; consequently every step of the audit, from planning to completion, must be thoroughly documented on appropriate **audit working papers**.

ISA 230 'Documentation' states:

> *'The auditor should document matters which are important in providing audit evidence to support the auditors opinion and evidence that the audit was carried out in accordance with ISAs.'*

audit files

There are two main types of audit files that the auditor will produce for each client audit:

- the permanent file
- the current year file

The permanent file was covered in detail in Chapter 3, so we will now focus on the current year files.

current year audit file

The current year audit file will contain the results of all the audit testing, including the tests of control, substantive tests and analytical procedures carried out as part of the audit. These will normally be filed in separate sections for each of the main audit areas, with a schedule at the front of each section summarising the figures that have been audited.

The current year audit file will also include:

■ copies of the draft financial statements

■ letters of representation from management (see Chapter 7)

■ management letters (see Chapter 7)

■ the audit planning memorandum

■ the audit programme

■ schedules and supporting documentation for each balance sheet item

■ checklists for accounts presentation and audit work completion

■ queries raised and explanations received

■ extracts from minutes

■ statistical and analytical review information

A sample current file index is included in the Appendix (page 304).

recording audit tests

Every procedure carried out by the auditors must be evidenced by working papers, whether the procedures are:

■ compliance tests of controls

■ substantive testing of transactions

■ specific tests to confirm balances

If the results of audit testing are not recorded, or details of work carried out on the client's systems are not documented, the auditors cannot prove that the work has been carried out.

By convention, audit working papers are prepared in a certain way. This can be illustrated by the example shown on the next page.

Firms of auditors generally have pre-printed paper for use on audits. You will notice from the example that the sheet is pre-printed with space for:

■ the name of the client

■ the financial period end

■ the initials of the person who carried out the test and the date on which it was carried out

continued on page 104

| Client: | Heather Walker plc | Prepared by: | JT |
| | | Date: | 22.1.06 |

| Period: | Year ended 31 December 2005 | Received by: | |
| | | Date: | |

Objective:

Test of control to confirm that sales invoices are matched against order and delivery note.

To ensure goods ordered and delivered have been invoiced.

Customer name	Delivery note no	Date	Sales order no	Date	Sales invoice no	Date	Agreed
Willco plc	D11021	27.1.05	1002	16.1.05	00684	30.1.05	✔
Harris Bros	D20413	22.9.05	1704	10.9.05	08482	23.9.05	✔
Morton	D19875	16.6.05	1506	10.6.05	06281	17.6.05	✔
PGW Ltd	D13743	2.2.05	1104	28.1.05	01723	4.2.05	✔
Simple Bys	D41026	11.12.05	1911	2.12.05	10416	13.12.05	✔
Ross Dryer	D16424	13.4.05	1251	9.4.05	04783	14.4.05	✔
Ample Charm	D15817	27.3.05	1207	20.3.05	02961	30.3.05	✔
Montaigne	D31041	31.10.05	1802	17.10.05	09281	2.11.05	✔

Conclusion:

All deliveries are matched to sales orders and sales invoices, so goods ordered are delivered and invoiced. The objective is achieved.

sample audit working paper

■ the initials of the person(s) who reviewed the work and the date that they did so

All of these details must be completed on each working paper that is prepared during the audit. The working paper should also include clear evidence of:

■ the test being performed

■ the objective of the test, for example:

  'To ensure that purchase invoices are matched with approved orders'

■ details of the test carried out in order to demonstrate that the objective has, or has not been achieved

■ a conclusion as to whether or not the objective has been achieved

Note that there is a pre-printed space on audit working papers for the reviewer to initial and date. This is because every piece of work prepared by any member of the audit team must be reviewed by a more senior member of the team. The audit senior, for example, may review work performed by the audit junior, the audit manager may review work performed by the audit senior and so on.

The reviewer will use his/her experience of the client and of auditing in general to assess the audit test that has been performed. In particular he/she will need to ensure that the conclusion that has been reached is supported by the work carried out. The reviewer will also produce a schedule of audit review points to pass back to the auditor who carried out the test indicating areas where the work performed is unsatisfactory, where further work is required or where the work performed does not support the conclusion that has been reached.

WORKING WITH THE CLIENT'S STAFF

The final section of this chapter discusses the way in which the auditors approach client staff to obtain information and audit evidence. Throughout the planning and testing stages, the auditors will come into contact with the client's staff at all levels in the organisation.

Audit staff need to maintain good working relationships with the staff operating the systems they are testing. It is important that the audit staff conduct themselves professionally at all times. Particular points that audit staff should remember are:

■ client members of staff may feel defensive and protective about their work as they may see the auditors as there 'to check up' on them

■ staff are usually busy and the auditors may place additional demands on their time

■ client staff may not have a precise idea of what the auditors are there to do – they may believe that the auditors are working for senior management and there to find out if they are doing their jobs properly

Audit staff should bear these points in mind in their general approach to the organisation's employees. Consequently, they should:

■ be polite, courteous and professional at all times

■ when asking for information, explain why it is needed

■ take account of the staff's workload when asking for information to be produced

■ keep a list of queries and arrange a meeting with the relevant member of the client staff to deal with in one go rather than continually interrupting them as each query arises

■ remember their duty of confidentiality regarding everything to do with the client's affairs – this means that confidential information should not be shared with other members of the client's staff

■ do not get involved in office politics or disputes – the auditors must remain independent

■ although the auditors have power under the Companies Act with regard to obtaining information, audit staff should be reminded that this is a last resort and denial of access should be dealt with at a senior level

If the auditors can build and maintain a good relationship with the client's staff, the audit can be conducted in a spirit of mutual co-operation. This should in no way compromise the auditors' independence, but it will help the audit to progress to a satisfactory conclusion.

Chapter Summary

■ Substance over form means that the auditors have to evaluate what a transaction actually is, not just what it appears to be.

■ All audits must be planned, and details of the planning is set out in an Audit Planning Memorandum (APM), which includes all key matters relevant to the current year's audit. All members of the audit team should read the Audit Planning Memorandum.

■ The auditors need to obtain evidence that is both sufficient and appropriate to support the audit opinion as to whether the financial statements give a true and fair view.

■ A detailed list of all the audit tests that are to be carried out is contained in the audit programme.

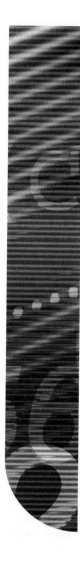

- Materiality is an important factor and the audit must consider the significance of errors found from the point of view of a user of the accounts.

- Auditors carry out compliance tests to see if internal controls are working effectively. Depending on the results, they will decide on the level of additional testing that is required.

- Where the audit test requires a sample to be selected, the auditors must ensure that the sample is representative of the population as a whole.

- Errors may be found when testing a sample of transactions, but if the level is below the tolerable error that has been set, the test may still achieve its objective.

- Substantive testing of transactions and balances will always be required in order to provide evidence to support the audit opinion.

- Analytical procedures are a form of substantive testing which analyse the relationships between financial (and non-financial information) to establish inconsistencies and unexpected patterns which must then be investigated by the auditors.

- All the audit work for the current year should be filed in a separate current year audit file.

- Every test undertaken during the audit must be documented on a working paper, and all working papers must be reviewed by a more senior member of the audit team.

- Auditors should always remember to be polite and professional when dealing with client staff.

Key Terms

substance over form	the principle that requires the auditors to confirm that a transaction is what it appears to be
audit plan	a document setting out the general strategy and scope of the audit
audit planning memorandum	a document detailing all key matters relevant to the current year's audit.
audit programme	a comprehensive list of all the audit tests to be completed, including a detailed set of instructions for the audit staff to follow

materiality — the level of significance or importance of a matter detected by the auditors in relation to the accounts as a whole

compliance testing — testing of internal controls to ensure that they are functioning correctly

sample testing — the testing of a sample of transactions to enable the auditors to come to a conclusion about all transactions of that type

population — the total number of transactions from which a sample is taken

sampling risk — the risk that the auditors will draw the wrong conclusion about the population as a whole based on the sample selected

tolerable error — the level of errors in a population which the auditors are prepared to accept and conclude that the objective of the test has been met

expected error — the level of error auditors expect to find based on previous experience of auditing the client

substantive testing — all tests other than compliance tests, including analytical review

inspection — the examination of assets, records or documents

vouching — matching an entry in the accounting records with an original source document

analytical procedures — analysis of the relationships between financial and non-financial information to establish inconsistencies and unexpected patterns which must then be investigated by the auditors

permanent audit file — ongoing information about the client which will be used for successive audits; it includes a copy of the engagement letter and provides a clear picture of the client's organisation, ownership, management, activities and its financial systems

current audit files — the audit files containing all the work relevant to the current year's audit

audit manager — person responsible for the day-to-day running of the audit

audit partner — person ultimately responsible for the audit and for signing the auditor's report

Student Activities

answers to the asterisked (*) questions are to be found in the Student Resources Section of www.osbornebooks.co.uk

4.1* One of your junior staff has prepared some slides for a presentation to a client on the practical procedures involved in auditing. The slides contain the following statements:

(a)   Materiality is generally defined as being about 5% of gross profit or 10% of net profit.

(b)   Audit sampling is always based on the level of materiality – the higher the level the less work you need to do.

(c)   Vouching is a test of transactions between books of original entry.

(d)   Analytical procedures are a form of substantive testing where you calculate all the financial ratios you can think of.

(e)   Auditors need to select samples which represent the population as a whole.

(f)   Providing the financial statements comply with the law, auditors have to accept them.

Which of these statements should you remove from the slides before the presentation is given and why?

4.2* The balance sheet of Huba Ltd has a net asset value of £5.6m. Its turnover is £15m and its net profit is £250,000.

During the course of the audit the following errors are discovered:

(a)   Out of a population of 25,000 sales invoices the auditors have taken a sample of 50. This revealed errors amounting to £120.

(b)   The financial statements do not refer to accounting policies on depreciation.

Are either of these two errors material, and if so, what action would you take as auditor?

4.3* You are carrying out audit work on the accounting records of Doggies Ltd, a company which manufactures pet food for pedigree dogs and rare breeds.

You will be carrying out some transaction testing for sales and purchases. As part of this testing you will be selecting a representative sample of transactions in each area.

(a)   What type of population should a sample be drawn from when carrying out this kind of audit testing? Illustrate your answer by describing the population that the sample should be drawn from when testing sales.

(b)   State three factors you would take into account when deciding on any sample size.

4.4* You work as an audit senior for Additup & Co, a firm of registered auditors.

The senior audit partner has asked you to carry out a training session with new trainees who are about to go out on audit.

In particular he has asked you to explain the difference between:

(a) tests of control

(b) substantive testing

(c) analytical procedures

Prepare a handout to give to the trainees describing the three different types of tests and giving an example of the use of each one when auditing purchases and creditors.

4.5 You are carrying out the audit of McColl & Co, a manufacturer of souvenirs for the Scottish tourist industry for the year ended 31 December 2005.

You have been asked to carry out an analytical review of the results for the previous four years in order to identify any areas of the audit which might require particular attention this year.

As far as you are aware, there have been no exceptional circumstances which have made this year different from any other.

You have worked out the following ratios:

McColl Ltd	2005	2004	2003	2002
	£000's	£000's	£000's	£000's
Sales	10,450	9,420	8,350	7,980
Gross profit margin %	52%	45%	46%	45%
Closing stock	502	341	309	317
Stock days	37	24	25	26
Debtor days	49	41	40	42
Creditor days	52	51	50	52

From the analysis above identify two areas where you think the audit team should concentrate their work. Explain your reasons for this.

4.6   You are an audit senior involved in the audit of Dunbar & Co for the year ended 30 June 200X. Your audit junior has prepared the working paper below analysing legal and accountancy fees which comprise nominal ledger account 7500 'Professional fees'. This has now been passed to you for review.

(a)   Review the working paper she has produced and list at least four review points.

(b)   Apart from verifying the correct charge to the profit and loss account, what other aspect of legal and professional fees might the auditors have to consider?

Client   Dunbar &Co

Prepared by

Date

Period end   31 June 200X

Reviewed by

Date

Object of test

To confirm that professional fees are fairly stated in the Profit & Loss Account

Professional expenses – Nominal account 7500

	£	
Debt collection expenses	267.45	
Advice re employment contract	564.87	
Taxation advice	1,298.00	
Advice re preparation of VAT return	763.00	
Legal fees - purchase of freehold land	7,349.00	✔
Land registry fees re purchase of land	539.00	
Employment advice re dismissal claim	2,654.00	✔
Drafting new terms of trade wording	432.00	
Advice on new budget system	4,300.00	✔
Legal advice re ongoing product liability claims	5,000.00	✔
Advice re new computer system	2,300.00	
Donation to political party	500.00	
Fees re purchase of house – Mr Dunbar	453.00	
Provision for audit fee – 200X	10,500.00	✔
	36,920.32	

Work done

Based on the materiality limit of £2500 I've checked all the items above that value, marked √, back to an invoice and they're all OK.

Conclusion

No errors found.

4.7   You are the audit manager planning the audit of W.H. Inger & Co Ltd, a company which manufactures lenses for telescopes and binoculars.

The audit partner tells you that after last year's audit he had received a complaint from the client.

The client made several points:

(a)   The staff had been harassed by a constant stream of questions from audit staff.

(b)   Audit staff did not seem to understand what the business actually did.

(c)   One of the accounts staff had been reduced to tears because a member of the audit team had described a schedule she had produced as 'rubbish'.

(d)   A member of the audit team had revealed that two accounts clerks doing more or less the same work were paid different salaries.

The audit partner has asked you to draw up some guidelines for a briefing to be given to this year's audit team prior to the commencement of the audit.

Set out four guidance points to pass on to this year's audit team.

5

Auditing accounting systems

In this chapter we will explain what constitutes 'good' audit evidence and describe the detailed audit testing that is carried out on the three main accounting systems operated by an organisation – purchases, sales and payroll. We will also examine the issues involved when auditing in a computerised environment.

This chapter explains:

■ audit evidence

■ testing system components – the stages in the accounting process

■ auditing purchases

■ auditing sales

■ auditing payroll

■ auditing in a computerised environment

PERFORMANCE CRITERIA COVERED

unit 17 IMPLEMENTING AUDITING PROCEDURES

element 17.2: contribute to the conduct of an audit assignment

A   Conduct tests correctly and as specified in the audit plan, record test results properly and draw valid conclusions from them.

C   Identify all matters of an unusual nature and refer them promptly to the audit supervisor.

D   Identify and record material and significant errors, deficiencies or other variations from standard and report them to the audit supervisor.

E   Examine the IT environment and assess it for security.

F   Conduct discussions with staff operating the system to be audited in a manner which promotes professional relationships between auditing and operational staff.

G   Follow confidentiality and security procedures.

AUDIT EVIDENCE

the background

In Chapter 4 we examined the various approaches that auditors can take, and showed how they evaluate the client's **internal control systems** to establish the level of audit work they need to carry out.

Remember the basic requirement is that auditors need to gather sufficient and appropriate evidence to support their audit opinion as to whether the financial statements give a true and fair view.

This chapter will focus on the three main accounting systems – purchases, sales and payroll – and describe the audit evidence that must be gathered to ensure that these systems operate effectively and produce accurate figures for the profit and loss account.

Although debtors and creditors form part of these systems, the testing of these balance sheet items will be covered separately in Chapter 6.

what is audit evidence?

First we must consider what we mean by **audit evidence** and how we decide what is considered good evidence and what is not good evidence.

ISA 500 'Audit Evidence' states:

> *'The auditor should obtain sufficient appropriate audit evidence to be able to draw reasonable conclusions on which to base the audit opinion.*

> *'Audit evidence' is all the information used by the auditor in arriving at the conclusions on which the audit opinion is based, and includes the information contained in the accounting records underlying the financial statements and other information. Auditors are not expected to address all the information that may exist.'*

This extract from the international standard tells us two things:

- evidence has to be 'sufficient' and 'appropriate' – a point that we examined in Chapter 4 when creating the audit plan
- auditors do not have to investigate everything

So, what do auditors have to do in order to ensure that the evidence they investigate is both sufficient and appropriate?

assertions

The audit procedures that are planned and carried out should be designed to validate the financial statement **assertions**. These are basically a set of statements about what the financial statements say about the assets and liabilities and the transactions of the company. Set out below is the full list of assertions included in ISA 500, Section 17. It is split into three sections:

(a)   **transactions and events** – which will be covered in this chapter

(b)   **account balances** – which will be covered in Chapter 6 (which deals with auditing the balance sheet)

(c)   **presentation and disclosure** – which will be covered in Chapter 7

The list of assertions in ISA 500, Section 17 is shown in the table below (note that the text in italics has been inserted here to explain the assertions):

(a) Assertions about classes of transactions and events for the period under audit	
Occurrence	transactions and events that have been recorded have occurred and pertain to the entity (*ie they relate to the organisation being audited*)
Completeness	all transactions and events that should have been recorded have been recorded
Accuracy	amounts and all other data relating to recorded transactions and events have been recorded appropriately
Cut–off	transactions and events have been recorded in the correct accounting period
Classification	transactions and events have been recorded in the proper accounts
(b) Assertions about account balances at the period end	
Existence	assets, liabilities and equity interests (*shares held*) exist
Rights and obligations	the entity holds or controls the rights to assets, and liabilities are the obligation of the entity (*the organisation being audited*)
Completeness	all assets, liabilities and equity interests that should have been recorded have been recorded
Valuation and allocation	assets, liabilities and equity interests are included in the financial statements at appropriate amounts and any resulting valuation or allocation adjustments are appropriately recorded
(c) Assertions about presentation and disclosure	
Occurrence and rights and obligations	disclosed events, transactions, and other matters have occurred and pertain to the entity (*the organisation being audited*)
Completeness	all disclosures that should have been included in the financial statements have been included
Classification and understandability	financial information is appropriately presented and described, and disclosures are clearly expressed
Accuracy and valuation	financial and other information are disclosed fairly and at appropriate amounts

You will probably have noticed from the table on the previous page that there is some repetition between categories of assertions. If the auditors wish to do so, they can perform tests that cover the same assertion for both transactions (a) and balances (b). For example, one test can be used to cover completeness of transactions and completeness of balances. Similarly, testing can cover more than one assertion about a class of transactions or account balance.

When the auditors have gathered sufficient and appropriate evidence to validate these assertions they can then form a valid audit opinion on the financial statements.

One factor that the auditors must remember is that the audit evidence which is used to validate one assertion may not be sufficient to validate another. Performing a detailed test on a class of transactions may not cover all the assertions in (a) above.

This point is illustrated in the Case Study below.

Case Study

BANJO LTD:
SUFFICIENT AND APPROPRIATE EVIDENCE

situation

You are a member of an audit team testing the controls on the sales system of an audit client, Banjo Ltd.

One of the audit tests to be performed is as follows:

'Select a sample of invoices and vouch them to the sales ledger. Ensure that all details for each item have been entered in the correct customer account and have been recorded at the right amount.'

required

Which of the assertions for classes of transactions (in this case, sales) will be covered by this test?

solution

If this test is carried out with few errors found, it should support the conclusion that:

■ Sales invoices are posted to the sales ledger in the correct period and at the correct amounts.

■ With regard to the assertions about transactions, this should provide the following evidence:

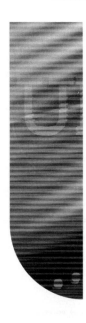

Occurrence	the auditor will check the invoice to ensure that the transaction has occurred and relates to the client
Accuracy	the amounts on the invoice have been checked and have been vouched to the sales ledger
Cut–off	the test includes checking the details on the invoice to the customer account which should include the date
Classification	part of the test is to ensure that the invoice has been posted to the correct customer account

The assertion that has been omitted from this list is Completeness. This test would not be good evidence of completeness because the sample has been selected from all sales invoices issued by the client, and so would not detect transactions which had not been invoiced.

quality of audit evidence

When gathering audit evidence the auditors must always consider the quality of the information that they are gathering. The source of the evidence is one of the key factors that will affect the quality of the audit evidence collected.

The following table will give you a general indication of what constitutes good quality and reliable audit evidence and what does not.

Type of audit evidence	Which is the more reliable?
Evidence from external sources, eg the client's bank _or_ from internal sources, eg client staff?	External sources
Evidence gained directly (eg a letter sent to the bank to confirm the balance at the year end) _or_ gained from the client (eg the balance on the cash book)?	Evidence gained directly from an external source
Documentary evidence (eg a supplier statement) _or_ oral evidence (eg discussions with client staff)?	Documentary evidence
Original documents (eg a letter from a debtor confirming their balance with the client) _or_ photocopies?	Original documents

Therefore examples of the **most reliable** evidence gathered by auditors would be:

■ a letter from the client's bank, sent directly to the auditors' office, confirming the balance on the client's bank account at the year end

■ replies from a sample of the client's debtors sent directly to the auditors' office stating the outstanding balance they believe they have with the client at the year end

Examples of **less reliable** evidence would be:

■ an emailed confirmation of the bank balance at the year end from a member of the client's staff

■ a photocopy of a supplier statement taken by the client rather than by the auditors

The decision as to what is good audit evidence will also be a matter of common sense on the part of the auditors. Professional judgement is as much a factor here as the general rules described above.

TESTING SYSTEMS

important note!

The next section of this chapter will provide you with the practical information and instructions you will need to perform detailed audit testing on the three main financial systems that operate in most commercial organisations – purchases, sales and payroll.

There is necessarily a large amount of detail covering a very wide range of possible tests that can be carried out. This section should be used as a reference point for possible tests. You will be relieved to hear that you will not have to learn it all off by heart!

system components

In order to test a system that operates in an organisation, you must be able to analyse the system into its component parts and understand how they link together.

For example, in the case of purchases, the system can be sub-divided into:

■ placing the order

■ receiving the goods

■ receiving the invoice from the supplier

■ recording the transaction in the accounts

■ paying the invoice

Auditors will need to identify each of the following:

■ the assertions that the audit work must cover

■ the objectives that the controls in the system aim to achieve at each stage of the process – for example at the ordering stage, the objective may be to ensure that all orders are properly authorised

■ the type of controls that the auditors would expect to be in place at each stage of the system – for example, all orders should be made on standard order forms and should be authorised before being sent to the supplier

■ finally – the best way of testing these controls

In their audit work the auditors will need to:

■ test every component part of the system

■ provide evidence that the assertions which are relevant to the system being tested have been properly covered

■ satisfy themselves that there is sufficient and appropriate evidence to justify the audit conclusions

In this section therefore we will cover each of the three main systems – purchases, sales and payroll – by focusing on four areas:

1   audit objectives

2   the internal control objectives of the system

3   system controls

4   audit testing

THE PURCHASES SYSTEM

audit objectives – purchases system

The audit objective is to carry out audit work to gather sufficient appropriate evidence to validate the assertions about the purchases system. These can be summarised as:

■ purchases of goods and services relate only to the company being audited (occurrence)

■ all purchases that should have been recorded have been recorded (completeness)

■ purchases of goods and services have been recorded at the correct amounts (accuracy)

■ all the relevant purchase transactions have been recorded in the correct accounting period (cut–off)

■ purchases have been recorded in the correct accounts in the nominal and purchase ledgers and any other related records, eg stock records (classification)

internal control objectives – purchases system

To re-cap – there are five main sections of the purchase system:

■ placing the order

■ receiving the goods

■ receiving the invoice from the supplier

■ recording the transaction in the accounts

■ paying the invoice

The control objectives for the system can be identified for each stage of the system as follows:

ordering

- all orders for goods and services are properly authorised

- orders are made only from approved suppliers

receipt of goods

- all goods and services received are for the purposes of the business and not for private use

- only goods and services that have been ordered are accepted

- goods ordered are received in a satisfactory condition

- unsatisfactory goods are returned to suppliers

- all receipts of goods and services are accurately recorded

- receipt of goods or services is evidenced

receipt of invoice

- liabilities are recognised for all goods and services received

- all invoices received are authorised

- any credits due to the business for faulty goods and services have been claimed

- liabilities can not be recorded for goods or services which have not been received

accounting for purchases

- all expenditure is correctly recorded in the books and records of the business

- all credit notes are properly recorded in the books and records of the business

- all entries in the purchase ledger are to the correct suppliers' accounts

- all entries in the nominal ledger are to the correct account

- all purchases are recorded in the correct accounting period (cut-off)

payment

- all payments have been properly authorised

- all payments are for goods and services which have been received (completeness)

system controls – purchases system

Now that we have identified the internal control objectives of the purchases system, we can examine the controls and procedures that the system should have in place to ensure that these objectives are achieved and also to minimise the risk of fraud and error.

Throughout the whole purchase process there should be formal written procedures for ordering, receiving and paying for goods and services.

Another key control within the system is segregation of duties – there should ideally be separate staff responsible for raising orders, receiving goods, and approving and paying invoices.

ordering

organisational controls	- ordering is only allowed from approved suppliers
physical controls	- blank order forms are kept secure
authorisation	- there are recognised authority levels for orders above defined limits
arithmetic and accounting checks	- standard pre-numbered order forms are always used
	- regular review of orders placed but not received

receipt of goods

physical controls	- quantity and condition of goods received are properly checked

- pre-numbered goods received notes (GRNs) are always used

authorisation — GRNs are signed off for all goods received

receipt of invoice and accounting

organisational controls — stated authority levels should exist for approving invoices

authorisation — all invoices are approved for payment

arithmetic and accounting checks

- invoices are matched with orders and GRNs

- prices on invoices are agreed to standard supplier price lists

- arithmetic accuracy of invoices is checked and evidenced

- regular reconciliations of suppliers' statements with purchase ledger balances

- controls exist for processing purchase invoices (eg batch totals)

- regular reconciliations of purchase ledger control account with purchase ledger balances

- cut-off checks are performed to ensure goods received but not invoiced are accounted for in the correct period

payment

physical controls — cheque books are securely located

- cancelled cheques are retained

authorisation — recognised list of authorised cheque signatories

- a minimum of two cheque signatories for all payments

arithmetic and accounting checks — regular bank reconciliation performed

audit testing – purchases system

The auditors' objective is to test whether the controls listed above are functioning properly within the system being tested.

In Chapter 4 we described the two types of testing that auditors carry out :

■ **compliance testing** of the system of internal controls

■ **substantive testing** of transactions and balances

ISA 500 'Audit Evidence' states:

'When substantive procedures alone do not provide sufficient appropriate audit evidence the auditor is required to perform tests of controls to obtain audit evidence about their operating effectiveness

... substantive procedures for material classes of transactions, account balances and disclosures are always required to obtain sufficient appropriate audit evidence.'

Auditors must therefore use both types of tests in order to provide the evidence they need.

Remember – the amount of testing carried out and the emphasis of the tests will be decided by the risk assessment. If the assessment of risk is high, the audit will focus on testing a larger number of transactions and balances and so samples will be large. If the risk assessment is low, the audit approach will be based on testing controls in the system to ensure that they operate effectively.

audit tests – purchases system

Set out below is a detailed list of the audit testing that would be performed to cover each part of the purchases system. Most of these tests would normally be performed on a selected sample of transactions.

ordering

- check that approval has been obtained and is evidenced for purchases

- check sequence of purchase orders to ensure none is missing

receipt of goods

- observe client staff receiving goods into stores to ensure documented procedures are followed

- ensure goods received are checked to the purchase order before they are accepted

- check sequence of GRNs and investigate any missing numbers

- ensure all returns to suppliers are suitably documented and regularly followed up

- ensure correct entry of goods received in the client's stock records

receipt of invoice and accounting entries

- check all invoices are matched to GRNs and orders

- check details on invoices and ensure invoices are arithmetically correct

- ensure prices agree to the approved supplier price list

- check authorisation of invoices for payment

- check posting of invoice to purchase day book

- check postings to the nominal ledger and the purchase ledger control account

- ensure invoices are posted to the correct supplier account

- check purchase ledger control account reconciliations

- check evidence of reconciliation of purchase ledger balances with suppliers' statements and re-perform a sample of reconciliations

- obtain explanations for items long outstanding, eg unmatched orders or GRNs or unprocessed invoices

- check GRNS issued are matched to credit notes from the supplier

payment

- for a sample of payments in the cash books:
  - check to approved supplier invoice
  - check details and amounts on the invoice to supplier statements

- check payments to suppliers are debited to correct supplier accounts in the purchase ledger

- review bank reconciliations to ensure they are accurately carried out on a regular basis

cut-off

- for the few days immediately before and after the financial year end, review GRNs to check for:

  - goods received for which no invoice has been received

  - goods received for which invoices have been received but which have not been posted in the purchase ledger

  - goods received that relate to the financial year being audited but which have been accounted for in the following year

- for goods returned immediately prior to the year end, ensure that relevant credit notes have been posted correctly

- review credit notes posted immediately after the year end to ensure that they do not relate to the financial year being audited

analytical procedures for purchases

As part of their testing, the auditors may carry out some analytical procedures as follows:

- compare monthly purchases for the year with monthly purchases for previous years and obtain explanations for any unusual variances

- compare sales with purchases on a monthly basis using the gross profit margin and investigate any unusual results

- compare ratios such as gross profit margin, stock turnover and creditor days with ratios derived from budgeted figures and prior year figures

- consider the effect of price changes on the value of purchases

a note on the testing process

This comprehensive list of testing for the purchases system may on a first reading appear very long and complicated. However, if you take the information step-by-step, the process is quite logical. The auditors in each case are testing to see whether the control procedures within the client's purchases system are operating satisfactorily.

THE SALES SYSTEM

The objectives for auditing the sales system are again based on the assertions relating to transactions and events.

We will again – as with the purchases system – describe in turn the audit objectives, the internal control objectives, the system controls and the audit testing.

audit objectives – sales system

The audit objective is to carry out audit work to gather sufficient appropriate evidence to validate the assertions about the sales system. The objectives can be summarised as:

- sales of goods and services relate only to the company being audited (occurrence)
- all sales that should have been recorded have been recorded (completeness)
- sales of goods and services have been recorded at the correct amounts (accuracy)
- all the relevant sales transactions have been recorded in the correct accounting period (cut-off)
- sales of goods and services have been recorded in the correct accounts in the nominal and sales ledgers and any other related records, eg stock records (classification)

internal control objectives – sales system

As with purchases there are five main sections of the system:

- receiving the order (and granting credit)
- despatching the goods
- raising the invoice
- recording the transactions in the accounts
- receiving payment

The control objectives can be identified for each stage of the sales system as follows:

receiving the order (and granting credit)

- goods and services are only supplied to customers on credit if their credit rating is good

- orders are recorded correctly when they are received

despatching the goods

- goods are only despatched on the basis of approved orders

- all despatches of goods and services are accurately recorded

- all returns from customers are recorded and the reasons for rejection are investigated

invoicing

- all invoices raised relate to goods and services supplied by the business

- all despatches of goods or provision of services are invoiced at the correct price and on authorised terms

- credit notes are authorised and only issued for a valid reason

accounting for sales

- all sales are properly recorded in the books and records of the organisation

- all credit notes issued are properly recorded in the books and records of the organisation

- all entries in the sales ledger are to the correct customer accounts

- all entries in the nominal ledger are to the correct account

- all sales have been recorded in the correct accounting period (cut-off)

- procedures exist for identifying bad debts

receiving payment

- all receipts from customers have been properly recorded

- all payments received are for goods and services which have been supplied

system controls – sales system

Now that we have identified the internal control objectives of the sales system, we can examine the controls and procedures that the system should have in place to ensure that these objectives are achieved and also to minimise the risk of fraud and error.

In businesses where sales income involves a significant number of cash transactions, there is an increased risk of fraud and auditors have to be very aware of this when they are designing their procedures. For this reason, cash sales will be dealt with separately at the end of this section.

Throughout the sales process there should be formal written procedures for receiving orders, granting credit, despatching goods and collecting payment for goods and services supplied.

There should also be segregation of duties within the system with different staff responsible for taking orders, granting credit, despatching goods and receiving payment.

receiving orders and granting credit

organisational controls - there are recognised authority levels for accepting new customers

- procedures are in place to credit check all new customers

physical controls	- blank sales order forms are kept secure
authorisation	- there are recognised authority levels for changes in customer data (eg increasing discount allowed)
	- all increases to customer credit limits are authorised
arithmetic and accounting checks	- pre-numbered sales order forms are always used
	- prices quoted to customers are checked to standard price list and appropriate discounts applied

despatching goods

organisational controls	- delivery notes are matched with orders and invoices
physical controls	- the quantity and condition of goods supplied are properly checked
	- pre-numbered delivery notes should always be used
	- proof of delivery is obtained for all goods despatched (signed delivery notes)
	- returns from customers are recorded (pre-numbered goods returned notes)

invoicing and accounting for sales

organisational controls	- invoices and credit notes are pre-numbered and sequentially issued, and spoilt invoices are not destroyed
authorisation	- all credit notes are authorised
	- all non-standard discounts are approved
arithmetic and accounting checks	- invoices are matched with orders and delivery notes
	- credit notes are matched with goods returned notes

- controls are in place for processing invoices (eg batch totals)

- invoices and credit notes entered into the accounting records promptly

- invoices are posted to the correct customer account

- regular up-to-date statements are sent to customers

- regular reconciliation of sales ledger control account with sales ledger balances

- cut-off checks are performed to ensure goods that have been despatched but not invoiced are accounted for in the correct period

receiving payment

physical controls

- all money received from customers is recorded by two people

- all money received is banked intact on the same day

arithmetic and accounting checks

- regular bank reconciliations are performed

- all cash received is posted to the correct customer account

audit testing – sales system

As when they are dealing with purchases, auditors must use a mixture of compliance tests and substantive procedures in order to obtain the evidence they need. For most of the tests, unless otherwise stated, they would normally be performed on predetermined samples.

receiving orders

- check new accounts to ensure that credit checking has been performed and credit limits properly authorised

- check that orders are only processed for customers who are within their credit limit

- check the sequence of internal sales orders to ensure none is missing

- ensure that unfulfilled orders are regularly reviewed and that either the goods are despatched or the order is cancelled

despatching goods

- observe client staff to ensure documented procedures are followed

- ensure goods being sent out are checked to the order before they are despatched

- check sequence of despatch notes and investigate any missing numbers

- check that proof of delivery is obtained on the despatch note or the GRN from the customer

- ensure all returned goods received from customers are supported by appropriate documentation

- check correct entries are made in client stock records for goods despatched

invoicing and accounting for sales

- check sequence of sales invoices and investigate any missing numbers or cancelled invoices

- check all invoices are matched to despatch notes and orders ensuring all details agree

- ensure prices and discounts agree to standard price list and have been approved for the customer

- check arithmetic accuracy of sales invoices, including calculation of discounts and VAT

- check posting of invoice to sales day book

- check posting to nominal ledger and to sales ledger control account

- ensure invoice has been posted to the correct customer account in the sales ledger

- ensure sales ledger control account reconciliations are performed regularly

- obtain explanations for long outstanding items, eg unfulfilled orders or unmatched goods returned notes

- check goods returned notes are matched to authorised credit notes issued to the customers

- review non-routine sales, eg scrap items, sales of fixed assets to ensure:

- • appropriate authorisation
- • the asset is removed from the fixed asset register
- • profit/loss on sale is acceptable
- ensure list of aged debtor balances is maintained for credit control purposes and long outstanding amounts are regularly followed up

payments received

- observe client staff to ensure procedures for receiving cash are properly followed
- investigate any payments on account or round sum amounts received from customers
- check amounts received from customers are credited in full to the correct account in sales ledger
- review bank reconciliations to ensure they are accurately carried out on a regular basis

cut-off

- for the few days immediately before and after the financial year end, review despatch notes and customer returns to ensure:
  - • invoices have not been issued in the current financial year for goods despatched after the year end
  - • credit notes have been accounted for in the correct financial year
- review significant invoices raised in the period immediately after the year end to ensure that they are accounted for in the correct accounting period

analytical procedures for sales

As part of the testing process, the auditors may carry out some analytical procedures as follows:

- compare monthly purchases for the year with monthly purchases for previous years and obtain explanations for any unusual variances
- compare sales with purchases on a monthly basis using the gross profit margin and investigate any unusual results
- compare selling expenses to sales to ensure they are appropriately proportional to each other
- compare ratios such as gross profit margin, stock turnover and debtor days with budgeted figures and with figures from previous periods
- consider the effect of prices changes on the value of sales

audit of cash sales

There are certain types of business where a significant volume of sales is received in cash. Examples include supermarkets, bars, restaurants, taxi firms and hairdressers. You will be able to think of others.

When auditing these types of organisations, the auditors have to consider the increased likelihood of fraud. Inadequate controls in the client system over the collection and recording of cash receipts could lead to misappropriation of cash.

Consequently there are additional audit procedures that need to be carried out to ensure the completeness and accuracy of the recording of cash sales.

Audit procedures for cash sales include:

- review procedures for collecting cash sales and observe client staff collecting cash and entering it into the till

- ensure cash is banked intact (cash should not normally be taken from cash sales to pay wages, small bills or petty cash items)

- if the client does allow expenditure to be made out of takings, vouch a sample to supporting documentation (receipts, wages schedules)

- for a sample of cash sales:
    - check record of cash takings (eg daily summary sheet) to an independent record (eg a till roll total) and ensure any differences are investigated
    - check total from the daily takings sheet to the bank statement
    - ensure total on the daily takings sheet is correctly entered in the sales account

- observe client staff counting cash takings at the end of the day and ensure correct amount is entered on to the daily takings sheet and matched to the till roll total

- ensure that there is appropriate segregation of duties between staff carrying out the sales and staff counting and banking the cash

- ensure takings are banked daily to reduce risk to cash retained on the client's premises

- if cash is held overnight on client premises, ensure client has set up adequate physical controls to ensure its safekeeping

analytical procedures for cash sales

It is often difficult for the auditors to obtain conclusive proof that all cash sales have been recorded unless the client has very strong controls in place. The auditor will therefore rely on analytical procedures to test the accuracy of the sales figure by comparing with figures from previous periods. However, the auditor must take into account external factors such as seasonal variations, weather and public holidays, all of which may have a direct effect on the amount of cash takings.

Auditors will often be able to recommend straightforward and practical improvements to the client's systems where cash sales are involved.

THE PAYROLL SYSTEM

The payroll system contains details of the organisation's staff and their wages and salary payments. The organisation's objectives when operating the payroll system are to ensure that it pays the correct rate of pay for the actual amount of work done.

The principal differences between wages and salaries are:

- wages tend to be paid weekly and salaries monthly
- wages can vary from week to week, whereas salaries are generally a set payment, and only vary if commission or bonus payments are included

It is becoming increasingly rare for wages to be paid in cash; for security reasons most staff are paid directly into their bank account by BACS. If payments are still made in cash there are a number of issues that are raised which we will look at later in this section.

Key points that relate to both wages and salaries are:

- all employees must have a contract or written terms of employment
- rates of pay must be agreed
- all deductions from gross pay must be statutory (eg PAYE and NI) or authorised by the employee (eg pension contributions)
- there are defined rules for calculating tax and national insurance contributions, whatever method is used for paying staff
- staff must be paid regularly and on time

Businesses may have a mixture of staff paid a weekly wage and staff paid a monthly salary. In this case they may operate two payrolls. If this is the case, the auditors will need to carry out separate tests on each payroll to ensure that both are operated correctly.

confidentiality

In Chapter 1 we explained how auditors must treat all the information they obtain during the audit as confidential. This is particularly important when auditing payroll. Matters such as rates of pay and individual's salaries can be a very sensitive area and one that can be of particular interest to other employees!

The payroll system contains much personal information about employees including:

■ the hourly rate of pay or annual salary

■ additional benefits

■ home address

■ bank details

■ date of birth

■ national insurance number

It is the duty of the organisation under the Data Protection Act to ensure that all this information remains confidential.

This duty of confidentiality extends to the auditors which means that it is only the more senior members of the audit team who are allowed access to payroll details. Where possible, the auditors should try to identify client staff by payroll or clock card number rather than by name.

audit objectives – payroll system

The audit objectives are to carry out audit work to gather sufficient appropriate evidence to validate the assertions about the payroll system. They can be summarised as:

■ payment for wages and salaries relate only to work done for the company being audited (occurrence)

■ all payments for wages and salaries that should have been recorded have been recorded (completeness)

■ wages and salaries and any deductions have been calculated and recorded at the correct amounts (accuracy)

■ all the relevant payments and liabilities have been recorded in the correct accounting period (cut-off)

■ payments for wages and salaries have been recorded in the correct accounts in the nominal ledger and any other related records (classification)

In addition to the objectives above, the auditors must pay particular attention to businesses where staff are employed on a casual or seasonal basis. This can often mean that there are large numbers of staff coming and joining, often with little documentation of previous employment (P45s). This can then make it difficult for the organisation to comply with tax and NI requirements.

Casual and seasonal staff are often paid in cash, sometimes with little documentation. In situations such as this, there is a risk of fraud which means that the auditors must ensure they cover this risk when designing their procedures.

internal control objectives – payroll system

The main stages of the payroll system are as follows:

■ hours are input into the system as required and amendments to staff details are made when necessary

■ gross pay, deductions and net pay are calculated and payslips produced

■ transactions are recorded in the accounts

■ payments are made to staff and HM Revenue & Customs

The control objectives for the system can be identified for each stage of the system as follows:

inputting hours and amending staff details

- all amendments to staff details are properly authorised

- hours worked are approved at an appropriate level

- staff are only paid for hours worked

- only staff who work for the company are included on the payroll

- details of leavers and joiners are authorised and promptly entered onto the payroll system

- staff details remain confidential at all times

calculating payroll and deductions

- payroll is calculated based on approved rates and hours worked

- statutory deductions for PAYE and NI are correctly calculated

- voluntary deductions (eg pension contributions or share save schemes) are correctly calculated

accounting for payroll and payments to staff and HM Revenue & Customs

- net pay is accurately calculated and paid to the correct employee

- payroll figures are correctly recorded in the books and records of the business

- all payments for PAYE and NI are paid on the due date

- wages and salaries are paid on the right date

systems controls – payroll

Now that we have identified the internal control objectives of the payroll system, we can examine the controls and procedures that the system should have in place to ensure that these objectives are achieved and the risk of fraud and error minimised.

Throughout the whole payroll process there should be formal written procedures for recording and inputting hours worked, amending staff details, and paying wages and salaries.

There should also be segregation of duties between staff responsible for approving hours worked, making changes to staff details and inputting and calculating payments. Where wages are paid in cash, one person should be responsible for counting the cash and another more senior person should check the amounts paid.

inputting hours and amending staff details

organisational controls
- a written record is kept for each employee containing details of rates of pay and contracted hours; any changes should require appropriate authorisation

- formal procedures are followed for starters and leavers

- timesheets and clock cards are approved before hours are entered onto the system

physical controls
- access to the payroll office is restricted to authorised personnel only

- access to the payroll and staff records is restricted to authorised personnel only

authorisation
- all changes to rates of pay, bonus payments and commission earned should be authorised

- written approval from employees should be obtained for all voluntary deductions from wages or salaries

calculating payroll and deductions

organisational controls
- up-to-date versions of payroll software should be installed, using the latest tax and national insurance rates

- staff are fully trained on PAYE and NI issues

                                   - changes to staff tax codes are promptly and accurately entered on the payroll system

authorisation   - payroll schedules are approved before payment

arithmetic and
accounting checks   - wages and salaries control account is regularly reconciled

                                   - commission and bonuses are reconciled to source documentation (eg sales records)

                                   - piecework payments (ie payments based on the number of items produced) are regularly reviewed against levels of work completed

                                   - unusual changes in payments to individuals from month to month are identified

accounting for payroll and payments to staff and HM Revenue & Customs

organisational controls   - a timetable for payment of wages and salaries is maintained and adhered to

physical controls   - staff who count wages in cash are not the same as those who prepare the payroll

                                   - cash for payment of wages is stored securely at all times

                                   - payslips are handed to staff members personally or are sent to their home address in sealed envelopes

authorisation   - pay packets can only be signed for by individual staff member

                                   - BACs payment schedules are authorised by an appropriate person before processing

arithmetic and
accounting checks   - the wages control account is regularly reconciled

                                   - a comparison is made between wages paid and budgeted figures for wages

                                   - a regular check is made of deductions by accounts staff to ensure consistency with previous periods' deductions

- reconciliations are regularly performed between the total net pay figure and payment shown on the bank statement

- a regular review of national insurance and PAYE accounts to ensure no outstanding balances remain after payment to HM Revenue & Customs

audit testing – payroll

Relatively few organisations now pay their staff in cash. The introduction of reliable payroll software and the use of the inter-bank computer payment system (BACS) has significantly reduced the opportunity for defrauding a business through the payroll.

This does not, however, reduce the auditors' responsibility to ensure that the controls within the systems are operating effectively. As with purchases and sales the auditors will use a mixture of compliance tests and substantive procedures, including analytical procedures in order to obtain the evidence they need for payroll.

The key areas of audit testing are designed to ensure that:

- all employees exist
- all employees are paid at the correct rate
- all deductions from wages are properly calculated
- net pay and deductions are accounted for correctly in the accounts of the organisation

audit tests

- review a sample of joiners in the year to ensure that they have been correctly recorded in the appropriate month

- review staff files to check that changes in personnel details have been promptly updated on the payroll system

- for a sample of employees:

  - check individual wages or salaries figures from the payroll schedules against individual personnel records to verify rates of pay or salary figures

  - re-perform calculation of gross pay and deductions (eg PAYE, NI, pension) to ensure the calculations are correct

  - ensure voluntary deductions (eg pension contributions) have been authorised by the member of staff

- confirm existence of staff members by arranging to meet them

- check details of hours worked from payroll records to individual timesheets or clock cards

- ensure clock cards and timesheets have been approved

- ensure all overtime payments have been approved

- re-perform commission and bonus calculations to ensure they are consistent with supporting documentation (eg sales schedules or approved bonus schemes) and ensure that they have been approved for payment

- where staff have been paid piecework, check the production figures on which the payments are based to ensure that the payments have been correctly calculated

- check the calculation of benefits

- confirm payment of net pay to the BACS summary or the cash payments summary

■ review the wages control account and ensure that it is regularly reconciled and all outstanding items are investigated

■ check payroll software to ensure that up-to-date income tax and national insurance rates are being used to calculate payroll figures

■ check figures from the payroll summary to the nominal ledger

■ for a sample of payments to HM Revenue & Customs:

- ensure that the amount paid agrees to the liability shown on the payroll schedule

- ensure that the payment was made to HM Revenue & Customs within the permitted period to clear the income tax and NI liability account

■ for payment of cash wages, observe distribution of pay packets to employees to ensure that:

- each employee receives a pay packet and no more than one pay packet

- procedures are in place to ensure that cash payments are secure

- all wage packets are signed for by members of staff

- a record is kept of unclaimed wages

- explanations are obtained for unclaimed wages

analytical procedures for payroll

As part of their testing, the auditors may carry out some analytical procedures as follows:

■ comparing wages and salaries month-by-month with previous year figures

■ comparing average salary per employee with previous year figures

■ review increases in pay rates by comparison with previous year's payroll figures – eg if pay rises were generally 4% during the year, is the current wages and salaries figure approximately 4% greater than last year's figure?

Most payroll systems operate on broadly the same principles, although there are often particular arrangements for calculating items such as overtime, commission or bonuses. Auditors should apply the principles outlined above to their audit testing of both weekly and monthly payrolls, ensuring that they are adapted, where necessary, to suit the particular circumstances of each client.

AUDITING AND COMPUTERS

Nowadays even the smallest organisation is likely to use computers, and many use computerised accounting packages to maintain their accounts. Examples of well known computerised accounting packages include Sage, Pegasus, Quickbooks and MYOB.

Computerised systems have the following advantages:

■ information can be processed quickly, accurately and efficiently

■ up-to-date management information is available at the press of a button

■ they have built-in controls over input into the system, including:
  - mandatory fields to ensure that sufficient information is entered for each transaction
  - they do not permit single entry, ie for every debit input there must be a credit, and vice versa

But there are problems associated with automatic accounting systems if they are not properly controlled. In particular, the auditors will be concerned about the loss of a tangible audit trail. Because the system generates transactions electronically the auditor cannot follow the flow of documents which evidence a transaction because there are not any physical documents to follow.

At the planning stage, auditors will have to consider how the computerised aspect of the accounting system affects the tracking of information and the flow of documents, and consequently how this affects audit risk.

audit risk and computers

There are several specific aspects of audit risk which have to be considered in connection with computerised systems, as shown in the table below.

RISK	FEATURES
inherent risk	- computerised systems are more susceptible to fraud if access to information is not suitably restricted - management may have little understanding of the detailed operations of the computer system and may leave it in the hands of computer specialists - many of the operations within the system occur automatically and inaccurately input data will continue to generate inaccurate transactions until it is detected – for example a wage rate or a sales price that has been entered incorrectly
control risk	- it is often difficult to detect a case where software has been tampered with or illicit software introduced onto the computer - computerised systems require fewer staff, which can mean there is a lack of segregation of duties - authority for transactions can be difficult to trace where the transaction has been generated by the computer

One advantage of a computerised accounting system is that managers within an organisation are able to produce a large amount of information at the press of a button. This will allow them to analyse data and may lead to improved control procedures.

the control environment

The principles of good internal control described in Chapter 3 apply equally to computerised and manual accounting systems; therefore the auditor will be looking for many of the same features.

These can be summarised as:

- organisational controls
- physical controls, including restricted access to information

■ segregation of duties

■ authorisation

■ arithmetic and accounting checks

These principles are covered by the specific controls detailed below. The auditors should concentrate on these when testing in a computerised environment.

CONTROLS OBJECTIVE	CONTROL PROCEDURES
documented procedures	- all staff should be trained to use computer software and should be encouraged to follow documented procedures
systems documentation	- copies of the supplier's handbook should be available to all staff members, together with a telephone helpline number
control of access	- access to modify computer software should be restricted to authorised personnel only - logical access controls should be in place to ensure that staff are only allowed access to parts of the system that they require for their work, eg an accounts assistant would have access to the sales ledger but would not have access to personnel records or to payroll
password controls	- access to the system should be restricted by passwords and authorised log-ons; passwords should be changed regularly and should not be disclosed or shared
application controls	These include: - authorisation of input documentation - batch controls for processing batches of documents, for example agreeing manual batch totals with computer batch totals - sequential numbering systems for entries onto the system - rejection messages for incorrectly entered data (eg inputting four digits for an account number when all accounts have six digit numbers - automatic range checks to ensure data input is within acceptable limits, eg hours worked by a member of staff are not more than 50 per week - automatic records maintained of who has processed each document, and when

audit approach for computerised systems

There are two approaches that the auditors can take when auditing in a computer environment:

■ audit 'around' the computer – ie largely ignoring the computer

■ understand and interrogate the computer system

auditing around the computer

When the use of computers in the workplace was less common, the auditors would take the view that they could carry out their audit procedures by concentrating on the inputs and outputs from the computer system and ignoring 'the bit in the middle', ie procedures that occur within the computer system.

This approach is now limited to the audits of smaller organisations using standard 'off the shelf' accounting software packages. The auditors take the view that the computer simply replaces manual records and there are few, if any, automated routines.

Because it is standard software, it is likely to be well tested and error free and the audit is more likely to be familiar with its inputs and outputs. The audit approach in this situation is to:

■ check the controls for data input to ensure that appropriate authorisation, coding and use of batch totals are used for this data

■ examine standing data which is held on the computer programme to perform calculations – eg standard wage rates, sales price list, rates of VAT – and ensure this standing data is accurate and is currently used by the computer

■ check outputs from the system against relevant input documentation, for example a selection of sales invoices input on to the system could be traced to the customers' accounts in the sales ledger

■ check output from the system against external evidence, for example purchase ledger balances with statements from suppliers

understanding and interrogating the computer system

Where computerised systems are more complex, and the computer program contains predefined routines to generate information automatically, the auditor needs to adopt a different approach.

There are two problems faced by the auditor in this situation:

■ in complex bespoke ('one-off') systems, even the client's own IT staff may not be able to explain all the details of the programme; they may know what the system can do but they may not know how it does it

■ management may consider that because they do not understand the computer system, they have no wish to become involved in its day-to-day operations – this can result in a loss of control on their part, and may lead to a dependence on one or two experts within the company

In cases like this, auditors will adopt an approach where they use the computer's ability to process data to interrogate its operations using **computer assisted audit techniques (CAAT)**. Larger audit firms now have dedicated audit staff who are experts at using CAAT.

There are various types of CAAT, including:

■ **audit interrogation software** – a computer program which examines data in the client's computer files, for example reconstructing the aged debtors listing from invoices on the sales ledger and comparing it to the client's version

■ **test data** - this comprises 'dummy data' which is input into the system and for which the company has already predicted the results – the problem with this type of CAAT is that it may corrupt the client's live data or may be difficult to remove from the system after the test has been completed

■ **embedded audit files** – audit facilities are set up within the client's systems which can be used by the auditors to obtain information on demand or on a continuous basis

All of these audit techniques will allow the auditors to carry out equally effectively all the detailed testing that we have considered earlier in this chapter.

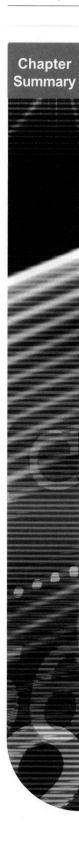

Chapter Summary

- Audit evidence must be sufficient and appropriate. Auditors do not have to examine every transaction, but what they do examine must be representative of all transactions of the same type.

- ISA 500 sets out assertions which are a set of statements regarding what the accounts state about the transactions of the business and its assets and liabilities.

- Audit evidence is gathered to validate a series of assertions which relate to occurrence, completeness, accuracy, cut-off and classification of transactions.

- Good audit evidence is evidence that auditors gather for themselves or which comes from a reliable independent source.

- Systems can be divided into component stages and internal controls identified for each component. Audit procedures can then be designed to test these internal controls.

- The three main financial systems operated by most organisations are purchases, sales and payroll.

- Audit testing takes the form of a combination of compliance and substantive testing.

- Some substantive testing is always required when validating transactions and balances.

- Auditors must take additional steps to ensure sales are complete and accurate if the sales are made for cash.

- Confidentiality is a key point to consider when auditing payroll.

- Auditing in a computerised system environment requires the auditor to specifically evaluate the internal controls which relate to the computer system.

- Auditors can use two approaches to auditing computerised systems: auditing around the computer or using computer assisted audit techniques (CAAT).

- CAAT systems may require specialists to operate them in order to obtain information from client files and to maintain the audit trail.

Key Terms		
	internal control environment	the client's system comprising internal controls and control procedures
	audit evidence	the information used by the auditors in arriving at the conclusions on which the audit opinion is based
	assertions	statements about the validity and recording of transactions, balances and disclosures which form the basis of audit testing work
	compliance tests	tests of internal controls and procedures
	substantive testing	tests to detect material misstatements or errors in the financial statements – this includes detailed tests of transactions and balance and analytical review
	piecework	wages paid based on the amount of work an employee has carried out rather than the time spent at work
	computerised information system	the computer, software and files which make up all or part of the client's financial records
	CAAT	computer assisted audit techniques – specialised audit software designed to assist the auditor in evaluating controls within a computerised information system
	audit trail	a series of entries in a set of financial records documenting a transaction through the system

Student Activities

answers to the asterisked (*) questions are to be found in the Student Resources Section of www.osbornebooks.co.uk

5.1 * You are marking some test papers given to a group of trainee auditors. Among the answers are the following statements:

(a) Substantive testing is always necessary to provide good audit evidence.

(b) Documentary evidence is better than oral evidence, but oral evidence is better than nothing at all.

(c) Assertions are the statements about the accounts which audit tests are designed to prove.

(d) Cut–off means that all the transactions are recorded in the correct accounting period.

(e) Completeness can be tested by checking a selection of sales ledger balances to make sure that there is one for every credit customer.

(f) You can audit a computer by ignoring it and just testing the output.

(g) Computer-assisted audit techniques include special software to tell the auditor what is going on inside the computer.

Which of these statements are incorrect, and why?

5.2* You are carrying out audit tests on the payroll for Sharkey Ltd, a small finance company.

The company employs ten staff. These are:

■ the office manager who is paid a fixed salary each month

■ the sales manager who is paid a small fixed basic salary plus a monthly commission based on the total value of new business generated by his sales team each month

■ three telephone sales staff who are also paid a fixed monthly salary plus a commission based on the amount of new loans they negotiate with customers in the month

■ three office and accounts staff on fixed salary each month

■ two casual staff who are brought in when required and as weekend cover – they are paid at an hourly rate based on the number of hours worked

(a) Identify any issues which increase the risks involved in paying commissioned staff as opposed to salaried staff.

(b) What controls would you expect in the system for hourly paid staff to ensure they are only paid for hours worked?

(c) Outline three audit tests that you would carry out to ensure that the controls over commissions and hourly paid staff are functioning correctly.

5.3* Happy Homes Ltd builds houses on sites across the North of England.

You are the audit senior currently engaged in the audit of the purchases system.

This is the first year your firm has done the audit.

You have discovered the following about the system for purchasing raw materials.

- Site managers send a list of materials required to the head office ordering department, based on the architect's drawings. The site managers are solely responsible for deciding materials quantities.

- The ordering department raises purchase orders direct to suppliers by telephoning a range of suppliers to find the cheapest quote. When they have identified a suitable supplier they raise a three-part purchase order which sets out a description of the goods required and the agreed price. The top copy goes to the supplier, the middle copy goes to accounts and the bottom copy stays in the ordering department.

- Materials are delivered direct to site and should be signed for by the site managers who are supposed to issue a goods received note and send a copy together with the suppliers' delivery note to the accounts department. Often they forget to raise a GRN. Sometimes they send the GRN and delivery note to the accounts department very late and covered in mud.

- When the supplier's invoice arrives it is checked by the accounts department to the original order and any proof of delivery. If there is no proof of delivery, the accounts department telephone the site manager and request oral confirmation the goods were delivered. They then note this on the invoice. Prices and calculations are checked and, if the accounts office are satisfied with their checks, the invoice is posted to the purchase ledger.

Using the information set out above:

(a) Identify three weaknesses in the current purchases system and suggest improvements to the company's system of accounting for purchases.

(b) Set out four audit tests you would use to test that the purchases system is functioning properly.

(c) State what analytical procedures could be used to verify the purchases figure in the accounts.

5.4   You are an audit senior working on the audit of Walters Woodworking Ltd. The company makes wooden toys and games for nurseries and schools and also for sale to the public.

Sales and debtors

Walters sells most of its goods through either a mail order catalogue or on-line though a website.

Mail order customers use pre-printed forms and can pay by instalments over six months. There are no credit checks but no customer can have a balance outstanding of more than £100.

On-line customers are required to pay by credit card or debit card at the time of order.

Invoices are raised based on orders received.

Goods are despatched to customers in a haphazard manner and there is no formal notification to the sales office that goods have been despatched.

Purchases and stocks

Goods are purchased exclusively from overseas suppliers. Prices are agreed before the start of the financial year as are total order quantities for the year. Walters places orders whenever it needs more stock. In total they must order the agreed quantity by the end of its financial year, irrespective of how much of any particular line has been sold.

Goods are stored in a warehouse and are packed by casual staff, many employed on a week by week basis depending upon demand. Goods are parcelled and sent by courier to the customer.

Wages and salaries

There are twenty full-time staff paid on a standard weekly rate plus overtime.

All weekly paid employees have to clock in and out of the premises.

There are four supervisors, four office staff, three sales order clerks and the manager all of whom are paid a fixed monthly salary.

For each of the three audit areas outlined above identify two audit tests using:

■ compliance testing

■ transactions testing

■ analytical procedures

5.5   Sailor Sam Ltd operates a ferry services between Hopetown and Oldport which lie either side of a bay. The ferries take cars and foot passengers and are very popular in the summer months because the alternative route, by road, is a long one down narrow country lanes.

There are two areas of the business which the audit manager has highlighted as containing a high level of audit risk.

Cash sales

All fares are collected on board the vessel by a member of the crew. Prices are fixed per foot passenger or per car, irrespective of the number of occupants. A car with one person in it pays the same as a car with four people in it. Only cash is accepted.

The crew gives each foot passenger or car owner a ticket from a pre-numbered pad. Foot passenger tickets are green and car tickets are yellow. When the tickets are torn from the pad they leave a stub behind.

The ticket stubs and the money collected are bagged after each voyage and sent through to the accounts office at the end of each day. The money in the bags should tally with the tickets of each type sold.

Payroll

The business is very seasonal. During the summer months the company takes on a large number of casual workers, some of whom sail as crew members and some of whom work as cleaners and shore staff.

All staff who work on the ferries are paid a fixed weekly amount in cash and are required to sign for their wages. The ferries sail at fixed times, so there is no overtime.

Throughout the season the company employs a large number of workers but often only for short periods of a week or two. All workers are entered on the payroll irrespective of the duration of their employment. Students usually bring some form of identification but many of the other workers have no documentation to show.

Many of the casual workers leave shortly after being paid without giving any notice.

There are separate payrolls for permanent and casual staff. Full-time permanent staff are paid monthly by bank transfer.

(a)   For each of the two areas of the business described above, list three issues which would affect the evaluation of control risk, particularly with regard to possible fraud. Suggest one improvement to each system which would help reduce the level of control risk.

(b)   For both cash takings and the casual staff payroll suggest three substantive audit procedures which might provide evidence of accuracy and completeness.

6

Verification of assets and liabilities

This chapter explains the procedures auditors should follow to verify the existence, valuation and ownership of fixed and current assets and liabilities recorded in the Balance Sheet.

This chapter covers the audit of:

■ opening balances

■ fixed assets

■ stock and work in progress

■ valuation of stock and work in progress

■ cut off procedures at the year end

■ debtors

■ bank balances

■ liabilities

■ share capital and reserves

PERFORMANCE CRITERIA COVERED

unit 17 IMPLEMENTING AUDITING PROCEDURES

element 17.1
contribute to the planning of an audit assignment

G   Select or devise appropriate tests in accordance with the organisation's procedures

H   Follow confidentiality and security procedures

element 17.2
contribute to the conduct of an audit assignment

A   Conduct tests correctly and as specified in the audit plan, record test results properly and draw valid conclusions from them

B   Establish the existence, completeness, ownership, valuation and description of assets and liabilities and gather appropriate evidence to support these findings

C   Identify all matters of an unusual nature and refer them promptly to the audit supervisor

D   *Identify and record material and significant errors, deficiencies or other variations from standard and report them to the audit supervisor*

F   *Conduct discussions with staff operating the system to be audited in a manner which promotes professional relationships between auditing and operational staff*

G   *Follow confidentiality and security procedures*

AUDIT ASSERTIONS

In Chapter 5 we examined the way in which testing the client's financial systems allows the auditors to assess the effectiveness of the internal controls within those systems. The auditors can then form an opinion as to whether all the transactions which have passed through the company's financial systems have been entered in the correct nominal accounts. This testing is carried out using a combination of compliance and transaction testing.

The audit of assets and liabilities focuses on ensuring that the items in the balance sheet are correctly stated.

In Chapter 5 we introduced the **assertions** which auditors now have to use as the basis for gathering their audit evidence. The assertions about account balances at the period end are:

- **existence**
  assets, liabilities and equity interests (shareholdings) do actually exist

- **rights and obligations**
  the company holds or controls the rights to assets – ie the company owns them – and all liabilities are those of the company

- **completeness**
  all assets, liabilities and equity interests (shareholdings) that should have been recorded, have been recorded

- **valuation and allocation**
  assets, liabilities and equity interests (shareholdings) are included in the financial statements at appropriate amounts and any resulting valuation or allocation adjustments are properly recorded

For simplicity we will refer to the main assertions throughout this chapter as **existence**, **ownership**, **completeness** and **value.**

This chapter will cover the main categories of assets and liabilities in turn, identifying the relevant financial statement assertions and detailing the auditing techniques that are normally used to provide the evidence the auditors need to validate each item.

Remember that the auditors are always considering their evaluation of audit risk when designing audit tests. If you are not sure about what evaluating audit risk involves, refer back to Chapter 3 (pages 45-46).

OPENING BALANCES

Before the auditors can test the final balances included in the balance sheet, they must ensure that the opening balances are correct. Audit testing must therefore be carried out to confirm that the balances at the end of the previous accounting period have been brought forward correctly into the current one.

Where the current auditors were also the auditors last year, this should be relatively straightforward because it will simply be a matter of checking the opening balances to the previous year's audited accounts and audit files.

Where this is the first year that the auditors have been involved, it may require a bit more work. In this instance an unqualified ('clean sheet') audit opinion in the previous year is a good starting point, provided that the auditors check that the balances brought forward agree with the previous year's audited accounts.

In both instances the auditors must pay particular attention to provisions, prepayments and accruals which were calculated at the year end to ensure that they have been correctly journalled at the beginning of the current financial period. For example, the auditors will have verified that an accrual for the audit fee has been included in Creditors at the end of the previous period. However, it may not have been included in the Audit Fee Account in the Nominal Ledger at the last period end. The auditors must ensure that the outstanding amount is correctly included as a brought forward credit balance on this account.

When the auditors have established that the opening position is correct, they can examine the transactions in the period.

FIXED ASSETS

Fixed assets, because of their size, are often a material balance in the financial statements, although the audit risk may be relatively low. Fixed assets in the balance sheet may be categorised in two principal ways:

- **tangible fixed assets** – land, buildings, plant and machinery, vehicles
- **intangible assets** – patents, trade marks, goodwill, research and development

We will first relate the key financial statement assertions of **existence**, **ownership**, **completeness** and **valuation** to tangible fixed assets.

tangible fixed assets

Tangible fixed assets usually consist of such items as land and buildings, plant and machinery, fixtures and fittings and motor vehicles. Most companies of any size will record their fixed assets in a **fixed asset register**. Typically this will include such information as:

- a description of the asset
- purchase price or valuation
- the rate of depreciation
- depreciation to date
- location
- any serial number (or registration number of vehicles)

The fixed asset register is a useful document for the auditors, providing a significant amount of information to allow them to verify the company's fixed assets. However, auditors should also maintain their own records of opening balances, acquisitions and disposals for each of the main categories of fixed assets.

existence of fixed assets

Common sense would suggest that the most obvious way of ensuring that a fixed asset exists is to go and have a look at it. This is exactly what the auditors will do: the auditors should select a sample of assets from the fixed asset register and perform the following tests:

- physically inspect the assets
- check the identification/serial numbers are correct and that the asset is located where it is stated to be in the fixed asset register
- check that the asset is in use and is in a good condition
- reconcile opening and closing vehicles by registration number and inspect vehicle registration documents

Samples of fixed assets may not necessarily be representative and should include high value items together with a selection of additions made during the financial year.

ownership – fixed assets

The assertion of rights and obligations in relation to fixed assets effectively means asking the simple question: 'Does the client **own** the asset?'

Just because the auditors have verified that an asset included in the company's accounts exists, it does not necessarily mean that the company actually owns it. In order to confirm this the auditors must carry out some further testing:

- ■ **confirm that the organisation owns land and property** by reference to
  - title deeds
  - Land Registry certificates
  - leases

Note that, as with all such tests, auditors should inspect original documents and not copies.

Should any of these documents not be in the company's possession (eg if title deeds are held at the bank), the auditors should obtain a letter or certificate from whoever holds them to confirm their existence. Normally the client's permission will be needed to do this.

The auditors should also find out why a third party is holding these documents. It may be for safekeeping or alternatively it may be because the assets are security for loans. In this case, the auditors must ensure that this is correctly reflected in the financial statements.

- ■ **verify ownership of plant, machinery and motor vehicles** by reference to independent evidence including:
  - vehicle registration documents (log books)
  - invoices for additions
  - maintenance agreements
  - insurance documents
  - last year's audit file

completeness – fixed assets

To ensure that **all fixed assets** are included in the accounts, the audit tests to be carried out should be:

- ■ select a sample of assets that physically exist on the client's premises and check them back to the fixed asset register
- ■ agree the fixed asset register to the nominal ledger and investigate any differences
- ■ if there is no fixed assets register, the auditors will have to work from their own audit files – last year's files should contain details of all fixed assets verified at the end of last year and this can then be linked with schedules of additions and disposals in the current year to provide an analysis of fixed assets at the year end – the totals can then be reconciled to the nominal ledger

valuation – fixed assets

The auditors must also be sure that the tangible fixed assets shown in the balance sheet are **valued** at the correct amount. One of the characteristics of a fixed asset is that its usefulness to the business extends beyond the financial period in which it was purchased. In most cases, this results in the asset being depreciated over its expected useful life. Hence, unless an asset is revalued, the two components of an asset's value are its original purchase price and the depreciation charged to date.

To test the valuation of fixed assets the following tests should be performed:

- for a sample of tangible fixed assets, agree the purchase price as shown in the fixed asset register to the original purchase invoice or lease agreement
- where assets have been revalued since they were purchased, obtain a valuation certificate from a suitably qualified valuer, and, in the case of property valuations, ensure that they are based on market value
- review depreciation rates for all categories of fixed asset and assess them for reasonableness – for example, substantial profit or loss on disposals would indicate that the rates had not been set correctly
- check that the rates of depreciation have been properly disclosed in the Accounting Policies statement in the accounts
- re-perform depreciation calculations for a sample of assets

fixed asset additions

The area of highest risk in auditing tangible fixed assets is probably in carrying out **additions** and **disposals**. We will examine each of these in detail.

Most companies will have a policy that requires that only assets over a certain value are capitalised in the accounts. The auditors must ensure that when the company acquires a new asset the capitalisation limit is adhered to and assets valued below that limit are treated as expense items. Similarly, they must ensure that no items that should have been treated as expenses have in fact been treated as fixed assets.

Other areas that the auditors should consider when auditing additions to fixed assets are:

- whether the acquisition has been correctly authorised – for example, whether the purchase invoice was signed off with the appropriate level of authority, or whether substantial purchases have been approved in the board minutes
- whether the assets that have been purchased in the year are valid business expenditure and are not for private use by directors or management – for

example, the auditors must ensure that the new office furniture purchased during the year is not actually in the managing director's study at home (a review of the delivery address on the invoice would spot this)

fixed asset disposals

During the year, the company will probably have disposed of some of its fixed assets. The auditors must make sure that their audit testing covers certain points regarding these disposals. They should, for example:

- review the sales invoice or other relevant documentation to establish that a valid sale was made and the correct sale price has been recorded in the accounts

- ensure that the sale of the fixed asset was appropriately authorised

- check the calculation of the profit or loss on disposal and ensure that the sales proceeds have been correctly accounted for

- ensure that a reasonable recovery of any scrap value has been achieved – there is a risk that assets may be sold cheaply to employees or friends!

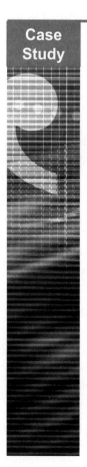

Case Study

BASHIT LIMITED: FIXED ASSETS VERIFICATION

situation

Bashit Ltd is a company which manufactures hospital beds and chairs from tubular steel. It is an old established company.

The major fixed assets of the company include:

- a freehold factory
- plant and equipment
- two delivery lorries
- three company cars

required

As the auditor of Bashit, how would you verify the existence, completeness, ownership and valuation of the motor vehicles, the property and the plant and equipment.

solution

Existence, completeness, ownership and valuation of motor vehicles

The auditors can test the existence and completeness of the motor vehicles by physically inspecting the five vehicles.

The registration numbers should be noted to ensure that they match with the records in the fixed asset register.

Ownership of the motor vehicles can be tested by inspecting original purchase invoices and also checking details to the vehicle registration documents (log books) and insurance documents.

Invoices will need to be inspected for all additions and sales invoices or other relevant documentation for all disposals. Details of the cost and descriptions of items should be checked to ensure that they agree with the fixed asset register.

If the vehicles were held at the beginning of the year, the auditors will be able to check the opening balances to the details of the vehicles in the previous year's audit file.

To confirm the valuation of motor vehicles is reasonable, the auditors should re-perform the depreciation calculation and check that the rates used are in accordance with the client's accounting policies.

Existence, completeness, ownership and valuation of freehold premises

In order to confirm existence, completeness and ownership of the freehold premises the auditors should inspect the title deeds and also physically inspect the premises.

If, as is often the case, the title deeds are not held on the client's premises, the auditors should obtain written confirmation from the organisation that holds them. This will normally be the client's solicitors or, if the premises are mortgaged as security for borrowing, the client's bank.

Valuation of the premises may require an independent valuation by a specialist valuer such as a chartered surveyor. This may not be necessary every year and will depend on whether the client wishes to disclose a revaluation of the premises in the financial statements.

Existence, completeness, ownership and valuation of plant and equipment

Physically verifying a sample of assets in the fixed assets register and also selecting a sample of physical assets located on the client's premises and checking that they are included in the fixed asset register will ensure that plant and equipment are complete and that they exist.

Ownership of the plant and equipment should be confirmed by reviewing the original purchase invoices. As with the motor vehicles, if the assets were held at the beginning of the year the previous year's audit file should also provide information on the ownership of these assets.

The valuation of the plant and equipment can be checked by agreeing opening balances to the previous year's file, checking any additions to purchase invoices and any disposals to sales invoices, re-performing depreciation calculations to ensure reasonableness, and checking that they are in accordance with the client's accounting policies.

Finally, depreciation policies should be re-assessed to ensure that they continue to be appropriate.

intangible fixed assets

Intangible assets include things such as patents, trade marks, licences, goodwill, and development costs. The main problem auditors have is that these assets cannot be physically inspected, so the auditors are reliant on documentation as the basis for audit evidence. This is an audit area which is rarely encountered in your assessment, but the principles which we applied to the audit of tangible assets also apply to intangible assets.

The auditors will seek as much independent evidence as they can find that these assets exist and are owned by the company. This will mean inspecting legal documents or obtaining written confirmation from people such as solicitors or patent agents.

Valuation is often the main issue with intangible assets. You should be familiar with the principles of IAS 38 (previously covered by SSAP 13), as part of your studies of Drafting Financial Statements. Valuation of intangible assets is a very specialised area and frequently auditors will refer to an independent, suitably qualified third party expert to assist them in the valuation.

INVESTMENTS

Investments are another form of asset encountered in the audit, for example:

- properties (held as an investment and not for a trade)
- listed or unlisted stocks and shares
- investments in subsidiary or associated companies

In principle, there is no difference between the audit approach to verify the existence, ownership and value of these types of assets, and that taken to audit tangible and intangible fixed assets, as described above.

In the case of investment properties, the auditors can verify the title deeds and a suitably qualified valuer should be asked to value them.

For investments in stocks and shares and subsidiary companies it will be the share certificates (or electronic equivalents) that the auditor will need to check. Investments in listed companies are relatively easy to value using the Stock Exchange Daily lists or the Financial Times.

Valuing unlisted shares can be complex and expert advice might have to be sought if auditors have any serious doubt as to their value.

As with tangible fixed assets, if title documents are not available the auditors should obtain a letter or certificate from whomever holds them to confirm their existence, and establish on what basis they are holding these documents.

The auditors must ensure that any title deeds and share certificates are held in the client's name.

STOCK AND WORK IN PROGRESS

One of the most significant figures in the financial statements is the stock and work in progress.

The closing stock figure forms part of the calculation of gross profit and is also shown as a current asset in the balance sheet. Material errors or mis-statements in the stock figures can have a significant effect on the truth and fairness of the accounts.

Over-valuation of closing stock will result in an overstatement of net assets and gross profit and potentially a higher tax liability.

Conversely, under-valuation of closing stock will result in an understatement of profits and potentially a lower tax liability.

Because of this, auditors will spend a considerable amount of time testing the organisation's stock.

categories of stock

Within the overall stock figure for the organisation, the auditors might be faced with several categories of stock for which they must assess the existence, ownership, completeness and valuation.

These include:

- goods for resale
- raw materials
- finished goods
- work in progress

Not every client will have every category of stock. For example, a shop will only have goods for resale, but a manufacturing company is likely to hold all categories except goods for resale.

The audit procedures described below relate to all categories of stock except for work in progress, which we will examine as a separate category.

If you ask any auditors what the best way of testing stock is, they will tell you that you must attend the client's year-end stock take. This will give the most reliable evidence of the existence of the stock at the year end.

stock taking procedures

ISA 501 'Audit evidence – additional consideration for specific items' states:

> 'When inventory (stock) is material to the financial statements, the auditors should obtain sufficient appropriate audit evidence regarding its existence and condition by attendance at physical inventory counting unless impracticable. Such attendance will enable the auditor to inspect the inventory, to observe compliance with the operation of management's procedures for recording and controlling the results of the count and to provide evidence for the reliability of management's procedures ...

> To obtain assurance that management's procedures are adequately implemented the auditor would observe employees procedures and perform test counts.'

Auditors must, therefore, include, as part of their audit procedures, a physical inspection of stocks. The reason for this is that, however good the company's financial systems and internal control procedures, and however frequently the company carries out its own stock taking, the auditors must always satisfy themselves as to the existence, ownership, valuation and completeness of all stocks held by the company at the year end.

There are two types of stock taking that the company can adopt:

- a year-end stock take, where all items of stock are counted once at the end of the year
- a continuous inventory system, where the management ensures that all stock is counted at some point during the year on a rotational basis

Even if stocks are maintained on a continuous inventory system there should be a full count at the year end.

Whatever system the client uses, the auditors should attend the year-end count and observe the organisation's staff counting the various categories of stock.

Client's stock takes are often performed outside normal working hours. This, coupled with the fact that the client may hold stock at a number of locations, will probably require a considerable level of staffing on the part of the auditing firm. This should have been taken into account during the planning stage of the audit (See Chapter 3).

If the client has a large number of locations where stock is held, the auditors may decide to attend the stock take at a sample of locations. This could be based on size, value of stock on site, results of previous stock takes, or the results of analytical procedures carried out at the planning stage.

organising the stock take

During an organisation's stock take there will be a high level of activity. It is therefore important that the organisation issues detailed written stocktaking instructions to all staff involved in the count. These instructions should include information covering the following areas:

■ **staff involved in the count**

Ideally, these should be staff who are not normally involved in the process of recording stock.

This helps enforce the principle of segregation of duties to the stock take, with staff normally involved in stock recording being involved in an advisory role.

■ **locations**

The instructions should identify all locations where stock is held and list the staff nominated to attend and the time at which stock taking will start.

■ **timing**

All stock counts should begin more or less simultaneously to minimise the risk of stock being moved between locations and consequently being counted more than once.

Counts should take place at a quiet time, eg a weekend, so that movement is kept to a minimum.

In addition **detailed instructions** should be given covering:

■ division of the count area into manageable sizes

■ individual responsibility for the count in each area

■ specific instructions for counting, weighing and measuring, where appropriate

■ cut-off arrangements –

These should include ensuring that the staff involved in the stock take are aware of the final goods received notes to be included in the stock figure. It should also be made clear to the staff that, where possible, no movements of stock should be made while the stock take is taking place.

■ procedures for identifying defective, obsolete and slow moving stock

■ identification of stock on the premises owned by third parties, eg goods which are being held on behalf of someone else should not be included

■ identification of the client's stock held at other company's premises

■ issue and return of pre-numbered stock sheets –

Pre-numbered stock sheets are used so that the count can be properly controlled and no 'unofficial' sheets included.

Auditors should note the numbers of the sheets issued and the areas of the stock take to which they relate.

- control of stock movements during the count
- any special problems such as dangerous areas or items, sealed containers or toxic substances (protective clothing might have to be supplied to staff and observers)

auditing the stock take

The main point that you should be aware of is that the auditors are there to observe the stock take. They are not responsible for counting the stock or for arriving at a valuation – that is the responsibility of the client's management.

The testing performed at the stock count will be partly **control testing** and partly **substantive testing**:

- the auditors must test that the **controls** that the client has put in place covering the stock count are effective and are carried out correctly during the count
- the auditors will also perform **substantive** testing to ensure that the year-end value of stock is accurate; this will involve the auditors re-performing some of the counting as part of their testing together with other audit work detailed later in this section

Before they attend the client's stock take the auditors should:

- review the details in the audit files of what happened in previous years and note any particular problems encountered
- review the client's stock taking instructions (see above) and highlight any specific areas for concern
- plan specific audit procedures to be carried out
- devise procedures to deal with any potential problem areas
- include any special arrangements, for example measuring equipment to be available where necessary or transport of staff between locations

It is important that specific areas of difficulty are discussed with the client's management before the stock take takes place.

The audit manager should also brief the audit staff who will be attending about the nature and extent of the stocks to be counted, and ensure that they are fully aware of any potential difficulties that they may encounter. For example, if they have to enter a special area such as a cold store, or carry out a physical procedure such as climbing storage tanks to observe the client staff checking the levels, this should be discussed with the staff concerned to ensure that there will not be any problems and to reassure them they will be safe and protected.

During the stock count the auditors should carry out all the procedures that have been planned. These will include:

- observe the client's staff carrying out the count in accordance with their instructions

- note any deviation from stock taking instructions for later discussion with the client's management

- select a sample of items and count them independently for comparison with the client's count

- ensure that all items checked are detailed on audit working papers, together with any observed problems with the count

- if any tests prove unsatisfactory, request a recount be performed by the auditors and client staff

- where boxed goods are stored in stacks, ensure the stacks are complete and not hollow

- ask the client's staff to open a sample number of boxes to ensure the contents are as stated on the label – this may disconcert the client's staff, but is an important part of the audit testing

- note any damaged, obsolete or slow-moving stock to ensure that these are separately identified and can be appropriately valued

- make a note of the count sheet numbers to ensure that all sheets are accounted for

- select a sample of the client's completed stock count sheets and take a copy for comparison with the final versions used for stock valuation

- note details of the last delivery of items into stock and the last issue from stock – details of the last delivery note or goods received note number should be recorded as this is to assist with cut off procedures which we will look at in more detail below

after the stock take

Attending the stock take is the first element of the auditors' work relating to stock. However, they must then check that a comparison is made between the result of the actual stock count and the numbers recorded in the client's stock records. The auditors must ensure that the client's management have appropriate procedures in place to carry out this important check and to ensure that all differences are investigated and the necessary adjustments made to the records.

The auditors will also need to follow up on the audit work that they themselves carried out during the stock take. Specifically they should:

- check the final stock sheets with copies they have taken of the actual sheets used in the count

- check details of any counts performed by audit staff to the final stock sheets

- check the final stock sheets for arithmetical accuracy
- ensure that certificates have been received for any stock held by a third party

When the auditors have satisfied themselves that the quantities of stock are materially correct, they will then have to consider the stock's value.

Now read the Case Study which follows; it recaps on the stock take process.

FRUITYCO LTD: ATTENDING THE STOCK TAKE

situation

Fruityco Ltd is a wholesaler of fruit and vegetables. The company buys in bulk directly from fruit and vegetable growers in the UK and also imports from overseas. Its main customers are fruit and vegetable retailers, small supermarkets and market traders.

Fruityco's year end is 30 June and you are the audit manager planning the audit of stock. As part of the audit procedures, members of your team will be attending the year-end stock take.

You have discovered the following key issues from last year's audit file:

- During the previous year's stock take there were still deliveries being made and goods being collected by customers. It was noted on last year's file that the client's attitude was that a few boxes of fruit was not material to the overall stock figure.

- There were no written stock taking instructions because stock was counted by the warehouse staff who knew exactly where the stock was, what it was, and how it should be counted.

- During the audit it was discovered that the company had included in stock a delivery which was still in a ship moored in the docks and hadn't been unloaded.

  The stock take was carried out very quickly and the audit staff attending were only able to independently count a few items themselves. The results of these counts were in accordance with the client's count.

- There did not appear to be any consideration by the client as to the age and condition of some of the stock or to its saleability.

required

What key points will you raise with the client's management following on from last year's stock take?

solution

Last year's stock take was unsatisfactory from an audit point of view because:

- There were continuous stock movements during the count; this meant that cut-off procedures could not be applied properly.

- There was no proper management control of the count – no instructions were issued and no independent staff appear to have been used. Management seem to have treated the stock take as a nuisance rather than as a key procedure.
- The stock take was carried out by people who were normally involved in maintaining stock records and handling the movement of goods in and out.
- The audit staff did not appear to have had time to carry out sufficient independent testing.
- Consideration had not been given to the true valuation of damaged stock, particularly with highly perishable items like fruit and vegetables.
- After the count had taken place, it was found that stock held at another location was included in the stock figures – and the auditors knew nothing about this.

As audit manager for this year's audit, you should make the following suggestions to improve the year-end stock take:

- Audit staff should be informed of all locations where stock might be located – including any in transit.
- Formal stocktaking instructions should be issued to staff involved in the stock take. Ideally these should be members of staff who are not normally involved in warehouse activities.
- The count should be recorded on pre-numbered count sheets and carried out in a systematic manner, with test counts and checks being made of the contents of individual sacks and boxes.
- All stock movement should be suspended while the count is carried out. Details of the last goods inwards note and goods outwards note should be recorded so that the cut-off can be properly carried out.
- A note should be made by company staff giving details of stock in poor condition.
- When opening boxes and sacks to confirm the quantities, audit staff should examine the condition of the contents. They should make a note of any stock which does not appear to be fit for resale.

VALUATION OF STOCK AND WORK IN PROGRESS

From your studies in Unit 11 'Drafting financial statements' you will know that stock and work in progress should be valued at the lower of cost and net realisable value.

You should also be aware that the principles of valuing stock are set out in International Accounting Standard 2 (IAS 2) – and previously in SSAP 9.

We will now examine briefly the key aspects of stock valuation.

cost

The cost of stock is taken as being:

■ purchase price where items have been bought in either as raw materials or goods for resale, or

■ production cost, including an allocation of overheads as appropriate

You will need to refer to your study of Unit 8 or Unit 33 which set out all the aspects of overhead allocation.

The individual items of stock should normally be valued on a First In First Out (FIFO) basis, which broadly means that the oldest stock is used up first.

Case Study

MAKEIT LTD: STOCK VALUATION

Makeit Limited has bought the following quantities of blottit, an ingredient of one of their products which has recently increased substantially in price.

11 August	200 kg @ £4.00 per kg	
4 September	200 kg @ £4.10 per kg	
12 September	150 kg @ £5.50 per kg	
Total	550 kg	

There was no opening stock of blottit.

At the year end (30 September) there were 235 kg of blottit in stock with the other 315 kg having been used in production.

The management have valued the stock at latest invoice price of £5.50 per kg and have arrived at a value of £1,292.50.

The total value of all stock held by Makeit at the year end is £54,000.

required

You are required as auditor to confirm the valuation of closing stock.

solution

Stock should be valued on a FIFO basis. This means that the earliest stock is issued to production first. What remains in stock are the latest purchases made.

The stock of 200 kg purchased on 11 August is used first so does not form part of the closing stock.

115 kg of the stock purchased on 4 September has been used for production leaving 85 kg of this purchase in stock.

None of the stock purchased on 12 September has been used.

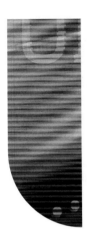

The correct closing stock valuation is therefore:

85 kg @ £4.10	=	£348.50	
150 kg @ £ 5.50	=	£ 825.00	
		£1,173.50	

The original valuation of closing stock of blottit is £1,292.50 and therefore overstates stock by £119. This is not material in the context of the total stock value of £54,000, but it does represent over 10% of the stock value for blottit.

If this policy of valuing stock at the latest invoice price has been used to value all individual stock categories, this could result in a material overstatement of stock in the financial statements.

analytical review

In addition to arithmetical tests such as those detailed above, auditors should also use analytical review to test the valuation of stock.

Analytical review used by auditors compares financial information from different periods to establish trends and to highlight consistencies and inconsistencies in the financial data of individual clients.

You will be familiar with ratios and performance indicators from your other studies. Several of these ratios and percentages relate to stock and can be calculated to substantiate the stock value at the year end.

Key ratios that can be calculated in relation to stock include:

$$\textbf{Gross profit \%} \quad = \quad \frac{\text{Gross profit} \times 100}{\text{Sales}}$$

If the gross profit percentage varies significantly from previous years, this could indicate that cost of sales is higher or lower than expected. An incorrect valuation of closing stock could be the cause of this.

$$\textbf{Stock turn} \quad = \quad \frac{\text{Cost of sales}}{\text{Average stock* or closing stock}}$$

$$\textbf{Stock days} \qquad \frac{\text{Average stock* or closing stock} \times 365}{\text{Purchases}}$$

* Average stock calculated as (opening stock plus closing stock) ÷ 2

An increase in stock turn or stock days could indicate slower moving stock. If all other factors in the business remain unchanged it could also indicate that the year-end stock has been overstated, as in the Case Study above.

Analytical procedures on their own will not satisfy the auditors of the accuracy of the stock valuation. However, they will indicate areas of inconsistency which should prompt further investigation.

net realisable value basis of valuation

Net realisable value means the price that the client would be able to sell the stock for in its present condition – which could be a lower price than cost price. Stock might have to be valued on this basis because:

■ it is damaged, or its condition has deteriorated, or it is obsolete

■ a decision has been made by the company to discontinue the product and sell off remaining stocks at a loss

■ the business is in difficulties and needs to raise cash urgently

In these cases the auditors have to base the stock valuation on what the stock would realise if sold. This may be simply scrap value or it may have no value at all. If it has been valued by the management at a nil value, auditors should still inspect the items to ensure that this value is appropriate.

The main way of checking the scrap value of unsaleable stock is to review the price obtained by previous sales of scrap or damaged stock, either during the year or after the year end.

If there is no available evidence to verify the valuation of stock at net realisable value, the auditors will have to use their professional judgement together with their knowledge of the client in order to judge whether or not the stock valuation is reasonable.

WORK IN PROGRESS

The audit approach to work in progress (WIP) will differ slightly from the approach to auditing stock. Physical inspection is a good way to establish that the work in progress exists, but inspecting something which is only part finished will not allow the auditor to assess the valuation with any accuracy.

The approach that the auditors take will be based on:

■ performing compliance testing on the accounting system to confirm that costs, particularly for materials and labour, are being correctly coded in the costing system

■ the use of analytical review techniques to look at the proportions of materials and labour used in production

- the use of analytical procedures to compare this years's value of work in progress for different stock lines with last year's figure
- checking the labour costs included in work in progress to wages records, material costs to stock records, and overhead costs to invoices

CUT-OFF PROCEDURES

The auditors must satisfy themselves that the client company has sufficient controls within its systems to ensure that stock movements are accounted for in the correct accounting period, ie

- if goods are included in stock, the costs relevant to those items have also been included in purchases and, if appropriate, in the year-end creditor figure
- if goods are included in sales and debtors they have been taken out of stock

This is known as **cut-off.**

The activities of the business continue from day to day and do not stop just because it is a period end. Therefore, cut-off must be considered at four separate points in the manufacturing process for the purpose of stock valuation:

- receipt of raw materials from suppliers
- issue of raw material into production
- transfer of work in progress to finished goods
- delivery of goods to customers

The key point is that stock should not be counted more than once and that creditors must be recorded for all stock received.

Specific points to consider here are:

- goods might have been received and included in stock, but the invoice may not have been posted to the purchase ledger
- goods might be received and included in stock, but the invoice may not have been received from the supplier
- goods could have been returned to a supplier before the year end and correctly excluded from stock, but the suppliers invoice could still be included in the purchase ledger awaiting a credit note
- stock could have been delivered to a customer close to the year end but not recorded as taken out of stock

Auditors must carry out procedures to make sure that creditors have been included for all the items included in stock, unless of course the goods have been paid for before the year end. Similarly they must carry out procedures to ensure that goods despatched to customers are invoiced and included in sales and debtors.

Looking back to the procedures that the auditors carried out during the stock take, they should have noted the number of the last goods received note (GRN) issued and the final despatch note raised before the stock take. This will enable them to audit the cut-off for stock, creditors and debtors.

The key procedures that the auditors will carry out are:

- review purchase invoices entered in to the company records shortly before and after the year and match them to the GRN to ensure that they are recorded in the correct accounting period

- review GRNs after the year end and ensure that none of these have been included in stock or creditors for the current financial period

- check records of goods returned to suppliers before the year end to ensure that any credit notes due have either been received or accrued

- check sales invoices before and after the year end to ensure that goods despatched to customers have been invoiced in the correct accounting period

Cut-off is often included in your assessment for this Unit. The following Case Study is a good illustration of how this could be tested.

Case Study

BRIGHTLY PLC: CUT-OFF

situation

Brightly plc is a manufacturer of lighting equipment. Its year end is 31 March and a stock count has taken place on this date.

The auditors have recorded the last Goods Received Note as no. 3487.

Inspection of invoices received shortly after the year end and posted to the purchase ledger includes the following:

Invoice	Supplier	Invoice date	GRN number	Amount
98984	Kings Ltd	30 March	3485	1200.50
12180	Bulbs & Co.	31 March	3486	750.00
38742	Lights Ltd	1 April	3487	150.00
23726	Phil Amment Ltd	31 March	3488	598.70
52832	Gleam Supplies	30 March	3489	740.00

required

Which invoices have been incorrectly recorded in purchases for the year and should be excluded from the list of creditors at the year end?

solution

The auditors recorded the last GRN number as 3487, so goods which were recorded on GRN numbers 3488 and 3489 were not delivered in time to be included in the stock take.

This means that the invoice from Phil Amment Ltd for £598.70 and the invoice from Gleam Supplies for £740 should not be in the list of creditors at the year end, despite the fact that the invoices are dated prior to the year end.

DEBTORS

The balance sheet heading of 'Debtors' generally includes two categories:

■ trade debtors

■ prepayments

We will examine each of these in turn from the point of view of verifying existence, ownership and value.

In the case of debtors, the auditors will rely much more heavily on compliance tests of the company's sales system for evidence of completeness than might be the case with fixed assets and stocks. The reason for this is that the sales ledger where the year-end debtors figure is taken from is the final part of the sales system.

trade debtors

These consist of sales ledger balances. The main objective of the auditors is to gather evidence to prove that these balances are either:

■ fully recoverable, or

■ a provision has been made against any doubtful debts

The compliance testing work that has been carried out on the internal controls in the sales system should provide sufficient evidence as to whether:

■ sales have been made to approved customers

■ all sales have been recorded

■ all amounts received from customers have been posted to the correct sales ledger accounts

In doing this, the auditors confirm that the sales ledger balances exist and that they belong to the client. The next step is to perform substantive tests to confirm the value of trade debtors.

The client will want its balance sheet to look as healthy as possible and so is more likely to overstate an asset than to understate it. Consequently, the audit objective when testing debtors is to ensure that they are not materially overstated.

The specific audit work that will be carried out on the list of sales ledger balances comprises:

- check that the balance on the sales ledger control account equals the total of the list of balances on the sales ledger
- test a sample of sales ledger balances to the sales ledger and vice versa
- review the cash book for receipts from customers after the year end to test if sales ledger balances have subsequently been paid – this is good evidence that the individual debtor's balance is correctly stated and recoverable at the year end
- review all credit balances and ascertain the reason for them: they may have been caused by an invoice being paid twice, or a credit note having being issued to the customer; it could also be that an invoice has been sent to the customer and payment received but the invoice has not been entered in the sales ledger

debtors' circularisation

One of the best ways for the auditors to establish the existence, ownership and value of debtors is to ask the debtor what they owe the company. This is usually done by selecting a sample of the year-end debtors and performing a **debtors' circularisation**. This involves sending each of the debtors a standard letter asking them to confirm their balance with the client.

In addition to confirming existence, ownership and value of the debtor balance a circularisation will also:

- provide evidence of the effectiveness of the system of internal control
- assist in the auditors' review of cut-off procedures
- identify items in dispute

The audit can take two possible approaches to the debtors' circularisation:

- a **positive circularisation**
  in this case the letter asks the debtor to confirm whether they agree with the balance or not; if they do not agree they are asked to supply the balance they believe that they owe to the client
- a **negative circularisation**
  in this case the letter asks the debtor to reply only if they do not agree with the balance

The problem with a negative circularisation is that the auditor has no idea whether the debtor actually agrees with the balance or has simply failed to bother replying. Consequently the auditors should always use a positive circularisation letter.

The process for performing a debtors' circularisation is as follows:

- select a **sample of balances** from the list of debtors in the sales ledger

  There are no rules as to what constitutes an appropriate number of accounts to be sampled, but the auditors have to be able to justify the size of the sample in the context of the total value of debtors and the total number of accounts.

  If you are not sure about this then look again at the section on sampling in Chapter 4 (pages 90-95).

- the sample should include not only active accounts but also:
  - nil balances
  - credit balances
  - accounts in dispute or where amounts have been written off in the period

- send letters to the sample of customers (see example on the next page)
  The letter must be signed and sent from the client as the client's permission is needed before debtors can be approached.

- the reply is requested to be sent to the auditors and a prepaid envelope is provided

- all the letters should be posted by the auditors to ensure that they have been sent

- replies are received and evaluated by the auditors and any queries fully investigated

- if replies are not received, these debtors should be followed up with a second reminder letter – this is often a problem in practice as there may be insufficient time to do this before the completion of the audit

The objective of the debtors circularisation is to ensure that debtors are correctly stated. Consequently the auditors are keen to achieve as high a response rate as possible to make the test as valid as possible. If the auditors feel that they have not received sufficient response to the debtors circularisation letters they will have to test the balances in other ways including a review of after date cash received, as detailed above.

When the replies have been received, the auditors should compare the value certified by the debtor with the balance on the sales ledger. Any differences should be reconciled and the reasons for these differences investigated.

These may be simply timing differences but may also be as a result of errors or mistakes which should be followed up.

To: Debtor Ltd
Address

Dear Sirs

Our auditors, Tickett & Wrunne, have requested that as part of their audit you kindly confirm whether you agree or disagree with our records of the balance you owe to us at close of business on 31 March 200X.

According to our records this amounted to £2,466.50 as shown on the enclosed statement.

If this amount agrees with your records, please complete and sign the slip below and return it to our auditors in the enclosed prepaid envelope.

If this amount does not agree with your records, please notify our auditors directly either by amending the enclosed statement or by providing a reconciliation of the difference.

This request is for audit purposes only and has no other significance.

Thank you for your co-operation.

Yours faithfully

John Brown

John Brown
Financial Controller

- -

Customer ..Debtor Ltd.................

The amount shown ~~does~~/does not* agree with our records as at 31 March 200X

Account number .DE1098....................... Signed ....I M Cross.............

Date..10 April 2006............ Position..........Accounts Manager...............

* The balance shown in our records is £..2,266.50.. A reconciliation is attached.

a debtors circularisation letter, completed by the debtor

provision for bad and doubtful debts

Clients that are concerned about being able to recover debts should make a provision in the accounts for bad debts. Ideally all provisions made by the management should be in respect of specific amounts due. However, companies sometimes make a general provision based on the value of total debtors – this general type of provision should be reviewed carefully as it may undervalue total debtors (the provision is deducted from debtors).

In assessing the reasonableness of the provision for bad debts the auditors should review the following:

- the adequacy of the credit control system – how effectively does the client chase debts?

- any disputes that are currently ongoing between the client and the debtor
- a comparison of the period of credit allowed and length of time the debt has been outstanding
- reports obtained from credit reference agencies regarding the solvency of the debtor
- the way the debt is made up – for example, is the debtor paying off specific invoices or are they simply making small payments on account which could indicate cash flow problems
- whether there have been any payments received since the balance sheet date
- the calculation of any general provision for bad debts – to ensure that it has been accurately calculated and that it is consistent with previous years' provisions

prepayments

Prepayments are amounts that the client has paid before the year end but which relate to the following financial period. Often they will be items such as rent where the amount is paid quarterly but the quarter ends after the client's year end. These can be audited relatively easily using the following audit procedures:

- check the calculation of the prepayments has been correctly done
- check the payment to the cash book and the invoice
- compare the calculations with previous financial periods to ensure that they are consistent with previous years and are prepared on a similar basis

BANK BALANCES

The auditors will rely on compliance testing of the client's financial systems to provide evidence of completeness of the bank figure in the financial statements – this should confirm that the cash book is being properly maintained. In addition to this they must confirm the balance at the period end.

year-end bank reconciliation

In a system with strong internal controls the auditors would expect to see the client performing regular (usually monthly) reconciliations between the balance of the bank account in the cash book and the balance on the bank statement received. The auditors will check the year-end reconciliation in detail by:

- agreeing the balance to the cash book

- agreeing the balance to the bank statement

- checking the arithmetic accuracy of the reconciliation

- tracing unpresented cheques and uncredited lodgements to the client's bank statement after the year end

- investigating any items in the reconciliation at the year end that have not appeared on the bank statement by the time of the audit

The auditors will normally take a copy of the client's bank reconciliation and mark it with appropriate audit ticks to demonstrate that they have checked each item.

bank confirmation letter

The strongest evidence of the accuracy of the year-end bank balance is independent confirmation from the bank itself. This is done by sending a standard request, known as a **bank confirmation letter**, to the bank.

The bank letter should always be in the standard form that has been agreed with the banking authorities and should be sent to all banks and branches where the auditor believes or knows the client has accounts.

The letter is sent directly to the bank by the auditors requesting confirmation of balances on all the client's bank accounts at the period end. It will also include permission from the client for the bank to disclose the information requested. Additional information can be requested by attaching a supplementary request.

Note that some of the terminology applies to specialist areas of bank services which are unlikely to be used by the client, for example 'derivative and commodity trading'.

An example of the standard bank confirmation letter is illustrated on the page opposite.

The bank will reply with details relevant to the client, providing details, for example, of:

- account balances

- loans

- overdraft facilities

- charges and mortgages held over the client's assets

- items held in safe custody, eg title deeds of client property (referred to in the letter as 'custodian arrangements')

The bank is likely to have instructions on its own files of what information needs to be provided to the auditors.

Date

The Manager
NE Bank PLC
High Street
Newtown
NE1 6HH

Dear Sirs

In accordance with the agreed practice for provision of information to auditors, please forward information on our mutual client(s) as detailed below on behalf of the bank, its branches and subsidiaries. This request and your response will not create any contractual or other duty with us.

Companies or other business entities

....Limited

.... Limited

Audit Confirmation Date : ....

Information required	Tick
Standard	
Trade finance	
Derivative and commodity trading	
Custodian arrangements	
Other information (see attached)	

The Authority to disclose information signed by your customer is already held by you. Please advise us if this Authority is insufficient for you to provide full disclosure of the information requested.

The contact name is : ....   Telephone: ....

Yours faithfully

Tickett & Wrunne, Registered Auditors

bank confirmation letter

When the auditors have received a reply from the bank they must ensure that all the information in the letter agrees to the financial statements and has been appropriately disclosed. The bank balance(s) shown on the bank letter should be agreed by the auditors to the balance(s) on the bank statement. Any discrepancies between the financial records and the bank letter must be followed up and the letter should be filed on the audit file in the bank and cash section.

CASH BALANCES

Clients do not normally hold significant amounts of cash, with most only holding small petty cash balances for day-to-day expenses. As the balance is unlikely to be material, the auditors will normally carry out only limited audit testing in this area to ensure that the amount shown in the financial statements agrees to the amount held in the petty cash tin.

For clients where cash plays a major part in the operation of the business – for example cafés, bars, shops and taxi firms – auditors may have to make arrangements to count it at the period end.

If a year-end count is not possible, auditors should make 'surprise' visits to the client's premises to count cash balances and reconcile them with the accounting records.

In all cases when the auditors are handling the client's cash, they must ensure that a member of the client's staff is present as the last thing they want is to be accused of misappropriating cash, particularly if testing shows that the balance of cash counted is less than the records show should be there!

In businesses where large amounts of cash are involved there is a higher level of inherent risk. The auditors will rely on their testing of the controls within the accounting systems to ensure that cash recording is being carried out properly. With the increased risk that comes with large amounts of cash the auditors must be alert to the possibility of fraud and must ensure that their audit procedures take account of this.

In order to gain assurance that cash takings are properly recorded and that cash is not being stolen or lost, the auditors must perform the following testing:

- review reconciliations between cash takings and till rolls or cash sheets
- carry out surprise cash counts
- perform analytical procedures, such as comparing gross profit margin to previous periods, to see whether the level of cash sales appears to be consistent

■ review the client's procedures for the safe custody of cash, eg that cash is locked away in a safe or lockable cabinets

■ review banking procedures – ideally cash should be banked daily and 'intact' (ie cash takings should not be used to pay for cash purchases)

■ check the adequacy of insurance arrangements for cash retained on the premises

LIABILITIES

In this section we will look at the methods that the auditors use to confirm the existence, ownership, valuation and completeness of liabilities.

The balance sheet heading of liabilities includes the following items:

■ purchase ledger balances (trade creditors)

■ accruals

■ provisions

■ long-term liabilities

When auditing liabilities, the auditors must consider the possibility of understatement. The client will be keen for the balance sheet to look as good as possible and understating liabilities will help to do this. This factor should be taken into account when the auditors are testing liabilities, particularly creditors, for completeness.

In the following pages we will look at particular aspects of each type of liability and the way in which the auditor should test them.

purchase ledger balances (trade creditors)

In the same way that the audit of debtors can be linked to the audit of the sales system, auditing creditor balances is linked with the work performed on the purchases system.

The audit work that has been carried out to assess the strength of the controls in the client's purchases system should test whether controls are in place to ensure that:

■ all purchases are authorised and made from approved suppliers

■ all liabilities owed to suppliers are correctly recorded in the purchase ledger

■ liabilities to suppliers are regularly settled

■ payments are made within the suppliers' terms of trade

To audit the year-end creditors, the auditor will carry out the following substantive tests:

- check the purchase ledger control account reconciliation with the list of individual purchase ledger account balances
- select a sample from the list of purchase ledger balances and reconcile them with statements from suppliers (we examine how this is done in more detail below)
- where supplier statements are not available for a number of suppliers the balance should be checked to the total of individual invoices and credit notes outstanding – this will verify that the balance exists but it does not provide evidence of completeness, ie that all invoices due to the supplier have been included in the balance
- review payments to suppliers after the year end – payment of the balance by the client is good evidence that the amount due to the supplier at the year end is correctly stated
- investigate all debit balances on the purchase ledger – the debit balance may have arisen because an invoice has not been posted to the account (in which case purchases and creditors may be understated) or an invoice may have been paid twice which could indicate a systems weakness
- perform cut-off procedures to ensure liabilities are included in the correct accounting period

In certain circumstances, the auditors may decide to perform a creditors' circularisation by sending out letters. As with debtors, this should be a positive circularisation (ie 'please reply anyway') and may sometimes be used when the auditors have assessed the controls in the client's systems as being weak. It may also be used as a method of confirming the creditors' balances if the client does not receive statements from many of its suppliers.

supplier statement reconciliations

The most conclusive way of testing creditors for existence, ownership, valuation and completeness is by performing supplier statement reconciliations on a sample, as this provides confirmation of the balance by a third party.

There are no rules as to what constitutes an appropriate number of creditors to be sampled, but the auditors must be able to justify the size of the sample in the context of the total value of the purchase ledger and the total number of accounts.

One point that must be remembered is that the auditors are seeking to ensure that creditors are not understated. Therefore the sample should be selected on the basis of the accounts with the greatest activity in the year rather than those with the highest balance at the year end.

If you need reminding about sampling, look at Chapter 4 (pages 90-95).

When the auditors have obtained copies of the supplier statements, they should reconcile the balance shown by the statement with the balance shown in the client's purchase ledger.

Differences are likely to relate to:

- invoices or credit notes in transit between the supplier and the client which will appear on the supplier statement but may not have been posted to the client's ledgers
- payments in transit which have been sent by the client but have not been received by the supplier in time to be included on the statement

Case Study

FANCY DANCER LTD: SUPPLIERS STATEMENT RECONCILIATION

situation

You are a member of the audit team currently auditing Fancy Dancer Ltd, a manufacturer of theatrical makeup and clothing which has a year end of 30 June 2005. As part of the process of verifying liabilities you have been asked to carry out a reconciliation of a sample of purchase ledger balances with statements from suppliers.

The following accounts have been extracted from the purchases ledger:

BADGERS PLC				
Date	Invoice no.	Dr	Cr	Balance
B/Fwd			1,872.89	
2.6.05	2389		9,653.09	
5.6.05	2345		6,785.02	
23.6.05	2453		5,457.98	
				23,768.98

SoSo Ltd				
Date	Invoice no.	Dr	Cr	Balance
B/Fwd			5,439.67	
1.6.05	2563		1,028.00	
6.6.05	2564		4,398.08	
7.6.05 Cash	52	5,439.67		
12.6.05	2578		7,449.90	12,875.98

BLUEBEARD LTD

Date		Invoice no.	Dr	Cr	Balance
B/Fwd				2,341.65	
2.6.05	CB	54	2,341.65		
19.6.05		2589		8,759.00	
22.6.05		2634		1,265.98	
					10,024.98

TRADERS

Date		Invoice no.	Dr	Cr	Balance
B/Fwd				2,341.65	
1.6.05		2689		1,564.65	
5.6.05	CB	61	3,906.30		
12.6.05		2703		6,784.09	
18.6.05		2734		2,567.78	
22.3.05		2745		7,649.67	
26.6.05		2786		9,864.45	
30.6.05	CB	62	6,784.09		20,081.90

SECONDSOUT

Date		Invoice no.	Dr	Cr	Balance
B/Fwd				3,576.98	
12.6.05		2854		12,765.89	
12.6.05	CB	63	3,576.98		
16.6.05		2874		19,564.34	
18.6.05		2984		12,675.42	
					45,005.65

SIMPLES

Date		Invoice no.	Dr	Cr	Balance
B/Fwd				543.98	
3.6.05	CB	63	543.98		
12.6.05	Credit	398	543.98		
15.6.98	Journal 2			543.98	
22.6.05	CB	65	543.98		-543.98

You have obtained the relevant statements for these suppliers:

BADGERS PLC
43 DOWNEER INDUSTRIAL ESTATE
FARTOWN
FX2 3ES

FANCY DANCER LTD

STATEMENT

DATE	INVOICE	DR (£)	CR (£)
Forward		1,872.89	
2.6.05	77456	9,653.09	
5.6.05	77891	6,785.02	
12.6.05	Credit 247		1,872.89
23.6.05	78012	5,457.98	

Amount due   **21,896.09**

SoSo Limited
Unit 2
Narrowly Street
Neartown
NE1 3RL

STATEMENT TO:
Fancy Dancer Ltd
Twinkle Street
Bigtown
BG2 4AU

Date	Invoice no.	Dr	Cr
May		5,439.67	
1.6.05	796	1,028.00	
6.6.05	801	4,398.08	
7.6.05	Cash paid		5,439.67
12.6.05	823	7,449.90	

Balance due   **£12,875.98**

---

bluebeard
downside works
Newtown
NE2 5LE

Fancy Dancer Ltd
Twinkle Street
Bigtown
BG2 4AU

STATEMENT

1.6.05	Fwd	2,341.65
2.6.05	CB56	-2,341.65
19.6.05	34567	7,859.00
22.6.05	34786	1,265.98

Total   **9,124.98**

TRADERS LTD
Roper Street
Bigtown
BG3 4LT

Fancy Dancer Ltd
Twinkle Street
Bigtown
BG2 4AU

	Ref	Dr	Cr
B/fwd		2,341.65	
1.6.05	984	1,564.65	
5.6.05	35		3,906.30
12.6.05	991	6,784.09	
18.6.05	1045	2,567.78	
22.3.05	1056	7,649.67	
26.6.05	1083	9,864.45	

Due   **£26,865.99**

SECONDS OUT LIMITED
Second House
Biggar Lane
Neartown
NE3 2TL

STATEMENT TO:
Fancy Dancer Ltd
Twinkle Street
Bigtown
BG2 4AU

		Dr	Cr
Fwd		3,576.98	
12.6.05	878	12,765.89	
16.6.05	891	19,564.34	
18.6.05	901	12,675.42	
19.6.05	2		3,576.98
23.6.05	942	14,202.83	
Balance		**£59,208.48**	

SIMPLES LTD
14 New Road
Neartown
NE1 4TH

Fancy Dancer Ltd
Twinkle Street
Bigtown
BG2 4AU

STATEMENT

1.6.05 B/FWD	543.98
8.6.05 Received	-543.98
BALANCE	0.00

required

(a) Using the information given to you on the last three pages, complete the table below.

Creditor	Balance as per client	Balance as per statement	Agrees to statement	Reconciled
Badgers plc	23,768.98	21,896.09		
SoSo Ltd	12,875.98	12,875.98		
Bluebeard ltd	10,024.98	9,124.98		
Traders	20,081.90	26,865.99		
Seconds out	455,005.65	59,208.48		
Simples	-543.98	0		

(b) State what the objective of this test is.

(c) Write notes about the tasks undertaken by the auditing team, mentioning any reconciliations performed and any further work needed in order to reach a conclusion.

solution

(a)

Creditor	Balance as per client	Balance as per statement	Agrees to statement	Reconciled
Badgers plc	23,768.98	21,896.09		✔
SoSo Ltd	12,875.98	12,875.98	✔	
Bluebeard ltd	10,024.98	9,124.98		✔
Traders	20,081.90	26,865.99		✔
Seconds out	455,005.65	59,208.48		✔
Simples	-543.98	0		✔

(b) The objective of the test is to ensure that creditors are correctly stated.

(c) It will be necessary for the auditors to follow up all the reconciling items on each of the reconciliations to ensure that they are valid. The invoices and credit note should be agreed to the original document and the cash in transit should be agreed to the bank statement.

The client has not picked up the transposition error in posting to the Bluebeard account and consequently this should be followed up.

The account with Simples Limited seems to have had several adjustments made to it, culminating in an invoice being paid twice. This has created a debit balance on the account which should be investigated to discover whether it is a simple mistake or if it results from a weakness in the systems, or even if it could be a possible fraud.

The workings are as shown below. Note that the comments column on the right sets out the client's explanation for the discrepancies.

Client: Fancy Dancers Ltd   **Prepared by:** JSO

Year end: 30-Jun-05   **Date:** 03-Aug-05

                                       Reviewed by:

                                       Date:

Purchase Ledger Balance Reconciliation with suppliers statements

Objective of test: To ensure that creditors are correctly stated.

Badgers plc   **Client's explanation**

Balance per purchase ledger   23,768.98

Credit note not included   -1,872.89   Account posted in July

Balance per Badgers Ltd   21,896.09

continued on next page

Client's explanation

SoSo Ltd

Balance per purchase ledger	12,875.98
Balance per SoSo Ltd	12,875.98

Bluebeard Ltd

Balance per purchase ledger	10,024.98	
Transposition error in posting: Invoice 2589 s/be £7,859.00 not £8,759.00	-900.00	Not amended by client
Balance per Bluebeard	9,124.98	

Traders Ltd

Balance per purchase ledger	20,081.90
Payment not received by supplier	6,784.09
	26,865.99

Secondsout

Balance per purchase ledger	45,005.65	
Invoice not posted	14,202.83	Included in accrued invoice list
Balance per Secondsout	59,208.48	

Simples Ltd

Balance per purchase ledger	-543.98	
Invoice paid twice CB 63 & CB 65	543.98	Duplicate invoice paid in error. Client will deduct from next payment.
Balance per Simples Ltd	0.00	

accruals

You will know from your accounting studies that accruals are amounts which are quantified and included in the accounts for the current year being audited, but for which payment is not yet due.

Examples include:

■ VAT liability

■ PAYE and NI

■ interest on borrowings

■ purchase invoices received but not entered in the ledger

In most cases, accruals can be checked by a combination of analytical procedures and professional judgement to assess reasonableness, ie the schedule of accruals for the current year end can be compared to the previous year for consistency. The auditors can also use their experience of the client to assess what accruals would be likely in such a business.

In addition to this, the auditors can specifically check the amounts accrued to supporting documentation. For example:

■ the VAT accrual can be agreed to the VAT control account

■ PAYE & NI deducted from wages but not yet paid to HM Revenue & Customs can be checked against payroll schedules

■ interest calculations can be re-calculated using the loan amount and interest rate verified by the bank letter

■ invoices received but not posted can be checked by examining the actual document

As the audit visit is made after the year end, in most cases accruals can be verified with payments made after the year end, or in the case of VAT to the VAT return submitted after the year end.

provisions

The client will make provision in the accounts for costs which may be incurred but which cannot be precisely quantified. One example of this might be a provision to cover the outcome of a legal claim that has been made against the client which has not yet been settled, or another could be a provision for a possible loss on a contract which has yet to be completed.

In other words, provisions are estimates based on the directors' judgement. This then presents a problem for the auditors, as there is often little reliable evidence to support the estimate. Consequently, the auditors may find it very difficult to find independent evidence to support the existence, ownership and value of these provisions.

You need to be familiar with the accounting rules set out in IAS 37 'Provisions, Contingent Liabilities and Contingent Assets' (and previously in FRS 12). This basically requires that a provision be made if it is likely that the client will have an obligation to pay something, as the result of a past event, even if the amount cannot be precisely calculated

When the auditors are testing the provisions in the accounts they need to ask themselves:

■ is the provision in respect of a liability which is likely to be incurred?

■ what is the probability of it being incurred?

■ on what basis has the provision been calculated and is there evidence to support it?

If the provision is to cover a legal claim made against the client, the auditors must contact the company's legal representatives to obtain sufficient independent evidence to support the provision.

If the auditors cannot find sufficient evidence to support the provision calculation, they may request formal written confirmation from the management of the business and will obtain representations from the management to support this. This will be covered in detail in Chapter 7.

long-term liabilities

Long-term liabilities are amounts that are due for payment in more than one year's time and are, generally, bank loans. Confirmation of loan balances will be included in the bank confirmation letter.

The auditor will also ensure that:

■ bank loans and overdrafts have been disclosed correctly in the financial statements in accordance with the provisions of the Companies Act

■ that the company has not breached the terms and conditions of the loans

■ that the loan facilities will continue for the foreseeable future

If the auditors believe that the client's long-term finance might be withdrawn they must consider whether this will have an impact on the client's ability to continue to operate as a going concern. If the auditors decide that this is an issue, it will have to be disclosed to the shareholders in the audit report. This situation will be discussed again when we examine reporting in Chapter 7.

SHARE CAPITAL AND RESERVES

The verification of the client's share capital and reserves should be relatively straightforward. Most matters relating to this area are recorded in the company's statutory books which are maintained by the Company Secretary.

The statutory books comprise several registers, including the register of shareholders and the register of directors. They also set out the details of share capital issued and contain the minutes of the board of directors and of the annual general meetings.

The procedures that the auditors should carry out in relation to share capital and reserves can be summarised as follows:

- check the opening balances with the previous year's financial statements
- review the statutory books for new shares issued in the relevant period
- ensure that the details have been properly disclosed in the financial statements
- review minutes of board meetings and the annual general meeting – this will provide information about dividend payments and share issues which the auditor can follow through to the final financial statements

The balances on reserves accounts can be audited by checking the opening balances to the previous year's audit file. Movements on reserves during the year, such as a movement on a share premium account, can be verified by reference to the statutory records and minute books. Movements on retained profits will relate to the profit earned in the year which can be checked to the audited profit and loss account.

Chapter Summary

- The auditors' task is to gather sufficient audit evidence to validate assertions about the existence, ownership (known as rights and obligations), valuation and correct recording (known as completeness) of all assets and liabilities shown on the balance sheet.

- Auditors will primarily use substantive testing procedures to verify balance sheet items, although when verifying current assets and liabilities, the results of compliance testing of system controls is also relevant.

- Fixed assets can be verified largely by substantive procedures where evidence is obtained through physical inspection and tests on original documents. In some cases it may be necessary to use independent experts where property or investments are being valued.

- Stock is a key figure in the accounts because it affects profits and net asset values. Audit tests on stock are therefore particularly important.

- The client will normally perform a stock take at the year end. The auditors must ensure that they always attend this.

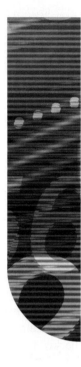

- The auditors' role is to observe the stock count and perform test counts on a sample of items.

- Cut-off procedures must be audited to ensure that both assets and liabilities are included in the correct accounting period.

- The auditor must ensure that stock and work in progress are valued in accordance with the principles laid down in IAS 2 (previously in SSAP 9).

- Debtors can be tested by sending a circularisation letter to a sample of customers who are asked to confirm the balance directly to the auditors.

- A confirmation letter should be sent to the client's bank(s) to request confirmation of bank balances, loans and securities held.

- Trade creditors can be verified by reconciling suppliers' statements to the purchase ledger balances.

- Share capital and reserves can be checked with the previous year's accounts and the statutory records.

Key Terms

audit risk	the risk of the auditors signing an incorrect audit report on the financial statements
compliance testing	testing of internal controls to ensure they are functioning correctly
substantive testing	all tests other than compliance tests, including analytical review
tangible fixed assets	assets which have a useful life of greater than one year and which physically exist, eg buildings
intangible assets	assets which have a useful life of greater than one year but which do not physically exist, eg patents
fixed assets register	a list of fixed assets recording all relevant details relating to the assets
stock take	a physical count of all stocks of raw materials, goods for resale, or finished goods which belong to the company
cut-off	a procedure to ensure that all aspects of a transaction are dealt with in the correct accounting period

third parties	in relation to the audit – parties other than the auditors and the client
net realisable value	the amount an item could be sold for on the open market
debtor circularisation	a form of audit testing where the auditors request a confirmation directly from the debtor of the amount outstanding at the year end
bank confirmation letter	a letter sent by the auditors to the client's bank(s) requesting confirmation of the client's bank balances and other details, including loans and overdraft facilities
bank reconciliation	a reconciliation of the balance of the bank account in the cash book with the balance on the bank statement
supplier statement reconciliation	a reconciliation between the amount shown in the purchase ledger and the balances on supplier statements
going concern	the assumption that the company will be able to continue to trade for the foreseeable future
statutory books	the records which have by law to be kept, and which record details of the ownership and management of the business
company secretary	the company official required to maintain the statutory books of the company

Student Activities

answers to the asterisked (*) questions are to be found in the Student Resources Section of www.osbornebooks.co.uk

6.1* The following statements have been found in a presentation to be given to some trainee auditors. Which of the statements are incorrect, and why?

(a) Only substantive testing techniques are used for checking the balance sheet.

(b) Suppliers' statement reconciliations are good audit evidence to verify the creditor figure in the balance sheet.

(c) If the compliance testing goes well there is no real need to test debtors and creditors.

(d) You do not need your client's permission to write to their bank.

(e) Auditors should ideally always attend the stock take.

(f) Do not bother with cash, it's usually not important.

(g) One way of verifying debtors is by circularising them.

(h) Cut-off means ensuring that transactions around the year end have been accounted for in the correct accounting period.

6.2* Your client, Bustas Ltd, has a year end of 30 November. The company manufactures pies, cakes and microwaveable foods for the catering industry.

The company accountant prepares a bank reconciliation every month. The reconciliation and the first bank statement for the next financial year are set out below. The bank balance per the cash book is £85,390.67 overdrawn.

Using this information:

(a) Audit the bank reconciliation, marking up the reconciliation to show the work that you have done.

(b) List three audit points that arise from the work you have done in (a) and, where necessary, explain what further audit work will be required.

Bustas Ltd: Bank Reconciliation: 30 November 200X

	£	£
Balance per bank statement		73,089.47 O/D
Add amounts not credited:		
29 November	12,067.45	
30 November	5,076.21	
		17,143.66
		55,945.81 O/D

Less:	£	£
Unpresented cheques		
Brought forward:		
March 200X	143.76	
June 200X	2,048.21	
September 200X	2,048.21	
December		
Cheque no.		
300823	12,374.87	
300824	7,539.02	
300825	423.00	
300826	1,874.90	
300828	2,983.89	
		29,425.86
Difference (not material)		19.00
Balance per cash book		85,390.67 O/D

Bank statement

OSBORNE BANK PLC

Customer Bustas Ltd – current account   Account number 289674539

Date	Details	Withdrawn	Paid in	Balance	
200X					
1 Dec	Brought fwd			73,098.47	O/D
2 Dec	Credit		12,067.45	61,031.02	O/D
2 Dec	300823	12,374.87		73,405.89	O/D
3 Dec	Credit		5,076.21	68,329.68	O/D
3 Dec	Credit		8,799.28	59,530.40	O/D
11 Dec	300824	7,539.02		67,069.42	O/D
14 Dec	300825	423.00		67,492.42	O/D
15 Dec	300834	28.90		67,521.32	O/D
18 Dec	300829	2,983.89		70,505.21	O/D
20 Dec	300826	1,874.90		72,380.11	O/D
22 Dec	300828	2,983.89		75,364.00	O/D
23 Dec	300331	289.45		75,653.45	O/D
24 Dec	Credit		4,086.39	71,567.06	O/D

6.3*   You are part of the audit team of Parsifal Ltd, a manufacturer of electronic equipment.

The company has supplied an analysis of creditors as follows:

Trade creditors	£
Purchase ledger balances	256,789
Accruals	
Rent	25,000
Light and heat	2,564
PAYE and NI	12,465
VAT	45,890
Property costs	3,457
Provisions	
Provision for product liability claim	120,000
Total	466,165

(a)   Set out at least three audit tests you could use to verify the trade creditors and accruals listed above. How would the materiality limit affect the testing work?

(b)   What additional evidence would you need in order to form an opinion as to the reasonableness of the provision for the product liability claim provision?

6.4* You are an audit senior on the audit of MaxiPaxi Ltd, a manufacturer of cartons and packaging solutions. Your audit junior has prepared a schedule of additions to fixed assets as follows:

Client: MaxiPaxi Ltd

Year end: 31 March 200X

Prepared by:

Reviewed by:

Additions to fixed assets – plant and machinery

Date	Description	Amount	Invoice seen
4 May	Schobel 437 cardboard folding machine	23,456.98	yes
12 June	Maxi Stitcher	4,385.87	yes
17 July	Parts for Stickit taper	2,386.13	
18 August	Dobro wrapper (including VAT)	12,800.00	yes
21 August	Installation Dobro wrapper	2,600.00	yes
6 November	Tools	175.00	
12 November	Tool holder	391.00	
4 December	Bigpush packager	36,900.00	yes
5 January	Replace cowl for Maxi Packer	5,100.00	yes
7 February	Desks	2,300.00	
7 February	Computer terminals	5,300.00	yes
5 March	Second hand walloper	8,730.00	yes
		104,524.98	

<u>Work carried out</u>

Invoices have been inspected for all marked items over £4,000.

All items marked were physically inspected and found to be in good working order except for the Maxi Stitcher which cannot currently process the correct size wrapping.

Information for this schedule was extracted from Nominal ledger account 2045.

<u>Conclusion</u>

The additions to plant and machinery are correctly stated as to existence, ownership, value and completeness.

You discover the following information:

■   Company policy is to only capitalise items over £2,500.

■   The Bigpush Packager actually cost £174,900. The balance is subject to a hire purchase agreement which has not been included in the accounts. The amount capitalised is the deposit.

You are to:

(a)   Prepare a list of review points for the audit junior who carried out this test.

(b)   Identify three possible adjustments which may be required as a result of the findings of this audit test.

6.5   You are the auditor of a fertilizer manufacturing company, Shooters Ltd, which makes a range of soil and peat based products and some liquid plant food under the 'Shootup' label.

The company buys raw materials such as soil, chemicals and other ingredients in bulk, mixes them in various different combinations and then bags them in printed plastic bags for sale to garden centres and shops.

Stock consists of:

■   bulk raw materials in sacks

■   tanks of liquid fertilizers

■   finished product in bags and bottles

The year end is 31 March. The company accountant is drafting the stock taking instructions for the year-end stock take and has asked you for help.

You are to:

List six key factors which will need to be incorporated into the instructions to ensure all the stock is counted properly.

6.6   You are carrying out the audit of the sales ledger debtors of your client Whistler Ltd, a motor parts dealer. The year end is 30th June 200X.

The terms of trade are that all invoices must be paid within 45 days. You decide that checking amounts received after the year end will be the best way to verify the balances, and all balances will be considered

Your audit junior has prepared the schedule below:

Client:	Whistler Ltd	Prepared by: *JO*
Year end:	30 June 200X	Reviewed by:

Sales ledger balances

Customer	Balance	Cash received to 31 August	Amounts still due
Macker	23,879.67	18,456.90	5,422.77
Doris	4,500.00	4,500.00	-
Hugo	12,875.90	10,000.00	2,875.90
Wilson	4,561.98	4,561.98	-
Abro	10,734.34	-	10,734.34
Caro	394.98	394.98	-
Simpson (in dispute)	3,850.89	3,000.00	850.89
Zouzou	1,984.90	-	1,984.90
	62,782.66	40,913.86	21,868.80

Using the above information, draft an audit working paper showing:

(a)   the objective of the test

(b)   any further work to be done on the balances outstanding before a conclusion is reached

7

Audit completion and audit reporting

This chapter examines the contents of the audit report and how it is affected when the auditors do not think that the financial statements of the organisation are true and fair. It also describes the report that the auditors produce for the management outlining the weaknesses in the client's internal control systems.

This chapter covers:

- dealing with 'subsequent events' – events after the year end
- 'going concern' – can the business carry on for the foreseeable future?
- 'management representations' – a letter from the client's management providing written confirmation of audit evidence they have provided
- final analytical procedures – overall review of the financial statements in comparison with previous years' results
- compliance review – compliance of the accounts with legislation and ISAs
- audit adjustments for errors and omissions
- auditors' reports to shareholders
- modified auditors' reports – reports with qualifications
- emphasis of matter – highlighting an issue in the accounts

PERFORMANCE CRITERIA COVERED

unit 17 IMPLEMENTING AUDITING PROCEDURES

element 17.1: contribute to the planning of an audit assignment

D   Record significant weaknesses in control correctly.

element 17.3 : prepare related draft reports

A   Prepare clear and concise draft reports relating to the audit assignment and submit them for review and approval in line with organisational procedures.

B   Draw valid conclusions and provide evidence to support them.

C   Make constructive and practicable recommendations.

D   Discuss and agree preliminary conclusions and recommendations with the audit supervisor.

E   Follow confidentiality and security procedures.

BACKGROUND TO THE REPORTING STAGE

We have now reached the last phase of the audit process – the audit report – but, before we examine this stage in detail, it is worth considering what we have covered so far. The audit processes can be summarised as follows:

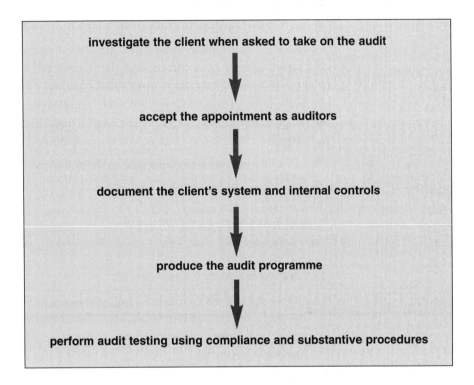

the report stage

The next and final stage – the report stage – has now been reached. By now the audit team have carried out their testing and recorded their findings. Any issues that have been found and any errors that have been identified will have been properly documented and highlighted to the senior members of the audit team.

It is at this point that the senior members of the team start to take a more active role in the audit. Before the auditors can give a final opinion on the financial statements, the **audit manager** and the **audit partner** must carry out the final reviews and procedures.

The last three steps to be carried out are:

- final audit review
- final review of financial statements using analytical review techniques
- final compliance review of the financial statements with the Companies Act 1985 and relevant Accounting Standards

FINAL AUDIT REVIEW

The main audit areas that need to be covered in this final review are:

- subsequent events review (events after the year end)
- going concern (whether the company is able to carry on trading)
- management representations (letters supporting audit evidence)

At this stage of the audit, these issues are often discussed at a senior level by the client's senior management and the partner and manager on the audit team. Discussions may cover issues that have not directly arisen from the audit work that has been carried out and will involve:

- an overview of the company's performance and discussions regarding its future
- a request for written confirmation from the management on difficult audit issues

SUBSEQUENT EVENTS REVIEW

ISA 560 'Subsequent Events' states:

> *'When the auditor becomes aware of events which materially affect the financial statements the auditor should consider whether such events are properly accounted for and adequately disclosed in the financial statements.'*

You will find that some of the points covered here link in with your studies for 'Drafting Financial Statements'.

During the course of their checking work, the auditors will have spent most of their time looking at events and transactions that occurred in the financial year being audited. A limited amount of their work will have involved them in looking beyond the year end. For example:

- reviewing payments received from debtors after the year end
- tracing uncleared cheques and uncredited lodgements from the bank reconciliation
- carrying out audit work on the client's cut-off procedures

post balance sheet events

During the period between the financial year end and the date that the auditor's report is signed, there may be events which shed new light on the financial statements. These are known as **post balance sheet events**.

Examples of post balance sheet events are:

■ insolvency of a debtor after the year end requiring an adjustment to the bad debt provision

■ adjustments to the valuation of stock or work in progress, for example where stock has proved unsaleable

■ a dispute arising over work carried out on a contract, meaning that the amounts receivable may not be paid to the client

■ significant changes to borrowing facilities from banks or other lenders which could affect the financial stability of the business, for example the company's bankers refusing to renew overdraft facilities

■ an issue of new share capital

■ a change in the way the business operates, for example a clothing retailer deciding to close all its high street shops and concentrate on selling over the internet

Some of these events will mean that the accounts must be amended to take account of them; others may simply require disclosing in the notes to the accounts or in the **Directors' Report**.

From the examples listed above the following events would provide additional information relating to conditions that existed at the balance sheet date, and so should be adjusted in the financial statements.

■ the insolvency of a debtor who owes a significant amount

■ writing down (reducing) the values of stock and work in progress by a significant amount

■ major changes in the financing of the business which could affect continued business operations

The following events, however, normally only require a mention in the notes to the accounts:

■ an issue of shares after the balance sheet date

■ a change in the way business is conducted

Note that while these events are informative and add to the general financial picture of the company, they do not relate to something which actually existed at the balance sheet date or happened within the financial period.

It is primarily the responsibility of the client's management to take these events into account when drafting the financial statements.

In some situations the auditors may disagree with the way in which the directors of a company decide to treat these events. In these cases, the auditors will have to consider how this will affect their audit report. We will discuss this in more detail later in the chapter.

audit tests for a subsequent events review

In order to satisfy themselves that all events after the year end have been appropriately dealt with and disclosed in the Financial Statements, the auditors should carry out certain audit tests. These will include:

- reading minutes of board meetings held since the balance sheet date
- reviewing management accounts and other information since the balance sheet date
- ensuring the adequacy of procedures that the client management has in place to identify such events
- asking management whether any significant issues have arisen since the year end

GOING CONCERN

ISA 570 'Going Concern' states:

'The auditors' responsibility is to consider the appropriateness of management's use of the going concern assumption in the preparation of the financial statements and consider whether there are material uncertainties about the entities ability to continue as a going concern that need to be disclosed in the financial statements.'

One of the fundamental accounting concepts is that the accounts of the company are assumed to be prepared on a **going concern** basis. What does this mean?

The assumption is that the business will carry on its activities in the same way for the 'foreseeable future'. In other words that:

- the management will be able to influence the way the business is run
- its products or services will continue to be bought by its customers
- suppliers will continue to supply the company
- it will have sufficient cash to fund its operations

The last point is probably the most important of all. Most businesses fail because they run out of cash and are unable to pay their bills. The 'foreseeable future' is a vague definition, but is usually taken to mean something between three and five years ahead.

the warning signs

How will the auditors be able to judge whether a business is a going concern? Various events and situations could indicate that a business may no longer be able to carry on for the foreseeable future:

- requested borrowing facilities have been turned down by the bank
- continuing negative cash flows (more cash out than in) from current activities with little prospect of improvement
- inability to pay creditors on the due dates
- loss of a major customer or key supplier
- fundamental changes in the market or in technology to which the company cannot respond
- changes in legislation which might adversely affect the business
- major legal claims against the company which cannot be met

It is the responsibility of the management to decide whether the company can continue as a going concern and to draft the financial statements accordingly.

If the auditors do not accept that this is the case because of over-optimism or a refusal to face reality by the management, the auditors may have to refer to this in their auditor's report. We will explain this later in the chapter.

You should be aware that any mention in the accounts or the auditor's report that the company is not a going concern is extremely serious and is not something that is undertaken lightly. In all probability it will mean that the company will have to cease to trade.

MANAGEMENT REPRESENTATIONS

ISA 580 'Management Representations' states:

'The auditor should obtain audit evidence that the management acknowledges its responsibility for the fair presentation of the financial statements in accordance with the ... financial reporting framework ...

The auditor should obtain written representations from management on matters material to the financial statements when other sufficient appropriate evidence cannot reasonably be expected to exist.'

In Chapters 4 to 6 we examined the ways in which the auditors gather evidence to come to a conclusion about the truth and fairness of the financial statements prepared by the directors.

Wherever possible the auditors will:

- generate their own evidence through compliance and substantive testing, attending stock takes, physically verifying assets
- obtain third party evidence, eg debtors circularisation, bank confirmation letters

However, during the course of the audit, there may be certain items for which the auditors are unable to find sufficient appropriate evidence and so require written assurance from the management, ie **management representations**. Examples of these items include:

- a provision has been made for a future loss on a major contract based on the opinion of the directors and for which there is no supporting documentation

- the directors state that a legal claim against the company has been settled and they anticipate no further claims for the issue involved

In each of these cases, there may be little evidence to substantiate the figures shown in the financial statements, and consequently the auditors are reliant on the word of the directors.

The auditors will request that the management provide them with a **management representation letter** to provide assurance of the information given to the auditors.

It is important to realise that this additional supporting evidence is not a substitute for audit testing.

The management representation letter should also contain an acknowledgment from the directors that it is their responsibility to prepare the financial statements in accordance with the Companies Act 1985 and the appropriate Accounting Standards.

A sample management representation letter is shown on the next page.

FINAL ANALYTICAL REVIEW

When the financial statements have been completed, the auditors should carry out final analytical review procedures on the accounts as a whole.

This will involve comparing the figures in the final accounts to the figures in the accounts for the previous year to assess their reasonableness. It will involve calculating selected ratios such as gross profit margin, net profit margin, return on capital employed, debtor days, creditor days and stock turnover. These ratios will be compared to the same ratios from previous years and also to appropriate industry averages if available.

The purpose of these procedures is to ensure that the financial statements as a whole make sense. Up until now, the auditors have been concerned with their detailed testing of the balances and systems and may have lost sight of the overall picture. Final analytical review will allow the auditors to stand back and take an objective look as to whether the final accounts are a true and fair view of the financial position of the business.

continued on page 206

WIBBLE LIMITED

GRUB STREET, NEWTOWN, NE3 4 TT

Messrs Tickett & Stampitt
Addit Road
Bigtown BG1 5ER

6 June 200X

Dear Sirs

We confirm to the best of our knowledge and belief, and after having made enquires of other directors and officials of the company, the following representations made to you in connection with your audit of the financial statements for the year ended 31 March 200X.

We acknowledge, as directors, our responsibilities under the **Companies Act 1985** for preparing the financial statements which show a true and fair view and for making accurate representations to you. We confirm that all the accounting records have been made available to you and all transactions made by the company have been recorded in those records. All other information and any related records, including minutes of directors' and management meetings have been made available to you.

The legal claim against us by Hugo Faster plc has been settled out of court by a payment of £250,000. No further claims have been received.

We confirm that the factory premises at Smalltown were properly valued by Messrs G Estimate & Co., Chartered Surveyors and Valuers, who are qualified to undertake this work. Their valuation of those premises on an open market existing use basis was £1.75 million, which has been properly reflected in the accounts.

The loan and overdraft facilities were renewed by the bank on 2 May 200X with no adjustments to the terms and conditions of the loans.

The fire at the offices in Grub Street is not expected to cause any detriment to the trading capability of the business.

There have been no events since the balance sheet date which would require any amendment to the financial statements or any notes.

Signed on behalf of Wibble Ltd

A Balir

G Bowen

Managing Director

Financial Director

Minuted by the board at their meeting on 6 June 200X

T Ricky

Company Secretary

a management representation letter

At this point in the audit process the auditors should also ensure that the figures in the final accounts agree to the figures that they have been auditing throughout the audit.

COMPLIANCE REVIEW

The auditors in their report are certifying that the accounts comply with the Companies Act 1985 and United Kingdom Generally Accepted Accounting Practice (GAAP). They will normally use a pre-prepared checklist to ensure that the accounts comply in all necessary respects.

AUDIT ADJUSTMENTS

When all the audit work has been completed, including the subsequent events review, the auditors prepare a summary of all the errors and omissions that they have found which would affect the profit and loss account and balance sheet. They will then have a meeting with the client management to discuss which, if any, of these items will be adjusted for in the financial statements.

Materiality is a key issue here. If the errors or omissions the auditors have found are not material (ie the accounts still give a true and fair view even if they are left out) then no further action needs to be taken. What the auditors have to remember is that each item on its own may not be material but they have to consider what happens when all the errors are taken together.

The following Case Study shows how audit adjustments might be presented.

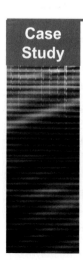

Case Study

CAPONE LTD: AUDIT ADJUSTMENTS

situation

The auditors have completed their work on the audit of their client Capone Ltd. They have found several errors and omissions which they want to bring to the attention of the directors. These items are:

- an under-provision for a possible bad debt from Bugsy Ltd of £10,350
- £5,260 worth of stock had been left out of the closing stock value
- the audit of the bank reconciliation showed that the bank figure shown in the cash book was £1,250 less than it should be
- the client had missed out an accrual for light and heat estimated to be £3,400

■ no provision had been made for a legal claim made by a large customer which could potentially cost the company £22,000

required

Prepare a schedule showing all the errors and omissions found and the effect they have on the financial statements.

solution

The auditors prepare a schedule showing all the necessary double-entry adjustments as follows:

Capone Ltd – year ended 31 March 200X

Schedule of unadjusted errors

	P & L Account		Balance sheet	
	Dr	Cr	Dr	Cr
Provision required for Bugsy Ltd debt	10,350			10,350
Closing stock undervalued		5,260	5,260	
Cash balance incorrectly stated		1,250	1,250	
Accrual omitted: light & heat	3,400			3,400
Provision for legal claim	22,000			22,000
	35,750	**6,510**	**6,510**	**35,750**

When they have prepared this schedule the auditors have to decide if these items are material and discuss any adjustments to the financial statements with the directors.

Obviously if the directors agree to amend the accounts then the auditors can issue a 'true and fair' audit report. If the directors decide not to amend the accounts the auditors will have to decide how material the adjustments are and what effect they might have on the readers of the financial statements.

If the auditors consider that without adjustment for the errors and omissions the accounts are misleading, they will have to issue some form of modified report. (Note: we will discuss this, in detail, later in the chapter, but first we will examine what is included in an unqualified auditor's report.)

AUDITOR'S REPORT TO SHAREHOLDERS

ISA 700 'The Auditor's Report on Financial Statements' states:

'The auditor's report should contain a clear written expression of opinion on the financial statements taken as a whole.'

As we stated at the beginning of this book, the auditors' primary task is to report to the shareholders on the truth and fairness of the financial statements prepared by the directors.

Having gathered all the necessary audit evidence and reviewed events since the balance sheet date, the auditors are now in a position to come to an opinion on the financial statements.

The audit opinion can either be:

■ an unqualified opinion

■ a modified opinion

In contrast to your own efforts to become 'qualified' as AAT technicians, the client is keen to receive an unqualified audit report. This means that, in the auditors' opinion, the accounts do give a true and fair view.

If the auditors' opinion is that the accounts do not give a true and fair view, or that something has prevented them from forming an opinion on all or part of the financial statements, the client will receive a **modified audit report**.

an important note on terminology

The term 'modified audit report' has been introduced by the requirements of international auditing standards, on which this book is based. The traditional term, based on the older UK standards, is **qualified audit report**.You will see this term commonly quoted and used by auditors. Remember:

qualified audit report = modified audit report

Note also that international auditing standards still refer to 'unqualified' audit reports.

unqualified audit reports

There are a number of different types of modified audit report that we will consider later, but first we will examine in detail the contents of an unqualified auditor's report.

For the purposes of your studies you will not be expected to write a full auditor's report but you should be familiar with:

■ what is contained in an unqualified report and what it looks like

■ when a modified audit report is appropriate and how it should be worded

contents of an auditor's report

The auditor's report to the shareholders is a detailed document which should leave the reader in no doubt as to the way in which the audit has been carried out. It should also give the reasoning behind the opinion that has been given.

The schedule below sets out what an unqualified report contains, together with the type of wording that would be used. The bold text sets out the items that should be included and the text in quotes is wording based on a suggested report issued by the Auditing Practices Board (www.apb.org.uk) This report contains all the key issues you will need for this Unit. You do not have to remember the precise form of words of an auditor's report, but you should be familiar with its contents.

CONTENTS OF THE AUDITOR'S REPORT

A clear heading including the word 'independent'

'Independent auditor's report'

It should be addressed to the shareholders

'to the shareholders of XYZ Ltd'

It should set out what is comprised in the financial statements, ie what has been audited

'We have audited the financial statements of XYZ Ltd for the year ended 31st December 200X which comprise the profit and loss account, the balance sheet the cash flow statement and the statement of recognised gains and losses and the related notes.'

It explains the basis on which the accounts have been prepared

'The accounts have been prepared under the accounting policies set out therein.'

The responsibilities of the directors should be set out

'The directors' responsibilities for preparing the Annual Report and the financial statements in accordance with applicable law and United Kingdom Accounting Standards are set out in the Statement of Directors' Responsibilities.'

It sets out the responsibilities of the auditors

'Our responsibility is to audit the financial statements in accordance with relevant legal and regulatory requirements and International Standards on Auditing.'

(Authors' note: the auditors might include a disclaimer here to the effect that they are only reporting to the shareholders and accept no responsibility towards any third party – see Chapter 2.)

It explains the primary purpose of the report

> 'We report to you as to whether the financial statements give a true and fair view and are properly prepared in accordance with the Companies Act 1985.'

and the secondary purpose of the report

> 'We also report to you if, in our opinion, the Directors' Report is not consistent with the financial statements, if the company has not kept proper accounting records, if we have not received all the information and explanations we require for our audit or if information specified by law regarding directors' remuneration and other transactions is not disclosed. '

It comments on the parts of the financial statements not covered by the audit and provides clear statement of where the auditors' responsibility ends

> 'We read other information contained in the Annual Report and considered whether it is consistent with the audited financial statements.' *(Followed by a statement of what the 'other information' is – see above.)*
>
> We consider the implications for our report if we become aware of any apparent misstatement or material inconsistencies with the financial statements.
>
> Our responsibilities do not extend to any other information.'

It sets out the basis of the audit opinion, ie how was the work carried out in order to provide evidence for the opinion

> 'We conducted our audit in accordance with International Standards on Auditing issued by the Auditing Practices Board.'
>
> 'An audit includes examination on a test basis of evidence relevant to the amounts and disclosures in the financial statements.'
>
> 'It also includes an assessment of the significant estimates and judgements made by the directors in the preparation of the financial statements and of whether the accounting policies are appropriate to the company's circumstances, consistently applied and adequately disclosed.'

It includes a statement about the level of evidence required, ie enough to give 'reasonable assurance'

> 'We planned and performed our audit so as to obtain all the information and explanations which we considered necessary in order to provide us with sufficient evidence to give reasonable assurance that the financial statements are free from material misstatement, whether caused by fraud or other irregularity or error. In forming our opinion we also evaluated the overall adequacy of the presentation of information in the financial statements.'

It gives the auditors' opinion (in this case an unqualified one)

'In our opinion the financial statements give a true and fair view, in accordance with United Kingdom Generally Accepted Accounting Practice, of the state of the company's affairs as at 31st December 200X and of its profit (or loss) for the year then ended, and ...

the financial statements have been properly prepared in accordance with the Companies Act 1985.'

It needs a name and a date

Tickett & Wrunne

Registered Auditors

I May 200X

Note that the wording above refers to the company's **Annual Report**, which includes, in addition to the financial statements and the auditor's report, some additional statements such as:

- a Chairman's Statement
- a five year review
- a trading review of the year

The auditors do not have to report on these items.

Examples of a full auditor's report is reproduced on the next two pages.

when is an unqualified report used?

As you have seen from the sample wording in the schedule above, an unqualified report states:

'*In our opinion ...*

the financial statements give a true and fair view, in accordance with United Kingdom Generally Accepted Accounting Practice, of the state of the company's affairs as at ... and of its profit (or loss) for the year then ended, and ...

the financial statements have been properly prepared in accordance with the Companies Act 1985.'

What this means is that:

- the auditors agree that proper accounting records have been kept and proper returns have been made from any branches they have not visited

continued on page 214

Example 3 - Non-publicly traded company incorporated in Great Britain - Auditor's report on individual company financial statements:

- Company DOES NOT prepare group financial statements.
- Company does not meet the Companies Act definition of a quoted company.
- UK GAAP used for individual company financial statements.
- Financial statements contain surround information other than the directors' report.

INDEPENDENT AUDITOR'S REPORT TO THE SHAREHOLDERS OF XYZ LIMITED

We have audited the financial statements of (name of entity) for the year ended ... which comprise [state the primary financial statements such as the Profit and Loss Account, the Balance Sheet, the Cash Flow Statement, the Statement of Total Recognised Gains and Losses] and the related notes. These financial statements have been prepared under the accounting policies set out therein.

Respective responsibilities of directors and auditors

The directors' responsibilities for preparing the Annual Report and the financial statements in accordance with applicable law and United Kingdom Accounting Standards are set out in the Statement of Directors' Responsibilities.

Our responsibility is to audit the financial statements in accordance with relevant legal and regulatory requirements and International Standards on Auditing (UK and Ireland).

We report to you our opinion as to whether the financial statements give a true and fair view and are properly prepared in accordance with the Companies Act 1985. We also report to you if, in our opinion, the Directors' Report is not consistent with the financial statements, if the company has not kept proper accounting records, if we have not received all the information and explanations we require for our audit, or if information specified by law regarding directors' remuneration and other transactions is not disclosed.

We read other information contained in the Annual Report, and consider whether it is consistent with the audited financial statements. This other information comprises only [the Directors' Report, the Chairman's Statement and the Operating and Financial Review]. We consider the implications for our report if we become aware of any apparent misstatements or material inconsistencies with the financial statements. Our responsibilities do not extend to any other information.

Basis of audit opinion

We conducted our audit in accordance with International Standards on Auditing (UK and Ireland) issued by the Auditing Practices Board. An audit includes examination, on a test basis, of evidence relevant to the amounts and disclosures in the financial statements. It also includes an assessment of the significant estimates and judgments made by the directors in the preparation of the financial statements, and of whether the accounting policies are appropriate to the company's circumstances, consistently applied and adequately disclosed.

We planned and performed our audit so as to obtain all the information and explanations which we considered necessary in order to provide us with sufficient evidence to give reasonable assurance that the financial statements are free from material misstatement, whether caused by fraud or other irregularity or error. In forming our opinion we also evaluated the overall adequacy of the presentation of information in the financial statements.

Opinion

In our opinion:
- the financial statements give a true and fair view, in accordance with United Kingdom Generally Accepted Accounting Practice, of the state of the company's affairs as at .... and of its profit [loss] for the year then ended; and
- the financial statements have been properly prepared in accordance with the Companies Act 1985.

Registered auditors   *Address*
Date

Sample unqualified Auditor's Report issued by the Auditing Practices Board

Independent auditors' report to the members of Tesco PLC

We have audited the financial statements which comprise the Group profit and loss account, the balance sheets, the cash flow statement, the statement of total recognised gains and losses and the related notes which have been prepared under the historical cost convention and the accounting policies set out in the statement of accounting policies. We have also audited the disclosures required by Part 3 of Schedule 7A to the Companies Act 1985 contained in the Directors' remuneration report ('the auditable part').

Respective responsibilities of directors and auditors
The Directors' responsibilities for preparing the annual report and the financial statements in accordance with applicable United Kingdom law and accounting standards are set out in the statement of Directors' responsibilities. The Directors are also responsible for preparing the Directors' remuneration report.

Our responsibility is to audit the financial statements and the auditable part of the Directors' remuneration report in accordance with relevant legal and regulatory requirements and United Kingdom Auditing Standards issued by the Auditing Practices Board. This report, including the opinion, has been prepared for and only for the company's members as a body in accordance with Section 235 of the Companies Act 1985 and for no other purpose. We do not, in giving this opinion, accept or assume responsibility for any other purpose or to any other person to whom this report is shown or in to whose hands it may come save where expressly agreed by our prior consent in writing.

We report to you our opinion as to whether the financial statements give a true and fair view and whether the financial statements and the auditable part of the Directors' remuneration report have been properly prepared in accordance with the Companies Act 1985. We also report to you if, in our opinion, the Directors' report is not consistent with the financial statements, if the company has not kept proper accounting records, if we have not received all the information and explanations we require for our audit, or if information specified by law regarding Directors' remuneration and transactions is not disclosed.

We read the other information contained in the annual report and consider the implications for our report if we become aware of any apparent misstatements or material inconsistencies with the financial statements. The other information comprises only the Directors' report, the unaudited part of the Directors' remuneration report, the Chairman's statement, the operating and financial review and the corporate governance statement.

We review whether the corporate governance statement reflects the company's compliance with the nine provisions of the 2003 FRC Combined Code specified for our review by the Listing Rules of the Financial Services Authority, and we report if it does not. We are not required to consider whether the Board's statements on internal control cover all risks and controls, or to form an opinion on the effectiveness of the company's or Group's corporate governance procedures or its risk and control procedures.

Basis of audit opinion We conducted our audit in accordance with auditing standards issued by the Auditing Practices Board. An audit includes examination, on a test basis, of evidence relevant to the amounts and disclosures in the financial statements and the auditable part of the Directors' remuneration report. It also includes an assessment of the significant estimates and judgements made by the Directors in the preparation of the financial statements, and of whether the accounting policies are appropriate to the company's circumstances, consistently applied and adequately disclosed.

We planned and performed our audit so as to obtain all the information and explanations which we considered necessary in order to provide us with sufficient evidence to give reasonable assurance that the financial statements and the auditable part of the Directors' remuneration report are free from material misstatement, whether caused by fraud or other irregularity or error. In forming our opinion we also evaluated the overall adequacy of the presentation of information in the financial statements.

Opinion In our opinion:

- the financial statements give a true and fair view of the state of affairs of the company and the Group at 26 February 2005 and of the profit and cash flows of the Group for the period then ended;

- the financial statements have been properly prepared in accordance with the Companies Act 1985; and

- those parts of the Directors' remuneration report required by Part 3 of Schedule 7A to the Companies Act 1985 have been properly prepared in accordance with the Companies Act 1985.

PricewaterhouseCoopers LLP
Chartered Accountants and Registered Auditors
London 11 April 2005

Auditor's Report of Tesco PLC

■ the financial statements agree with the underlying accounting records and returns

■ all information and explanations they needed have been received from the staff and the directors and managers

■ the auditors have had unrestricted access to the books and records

■ details of all transactions involving the directors have been correctly disclosed

■ there are no material misstatements in the accounts

In other words, the audit has been completed satisfactorily and the auditors have been able to gather all the evidence they need to support their unqualified opinion.

If, however, there is a difference of opinion between the directors and the auditors about something in the financial statements, or the auditors have had problems gathering the evidence they need, they may have to issue a modified audit report.

MODIFIED AUDIT REPORTS

Remember: 'modified' = 'qualified'.

ISA 700 'The auditor's report on financial statements' states:

'the auditor's report is considered to be modified in the following situations ...

a qualified opinion

a disclaimer of opinion

an adverse opinion'

ISA 700 also includes suggested wording and phrases which can be used in a range of different situations.

It is unlikely that you will be asked to draft an audit report in your assessment for this Unit. However, you may have to produce an extract from a modified report. We have included some sample wording to illustrate how a modified audit report might be drafted (see page 217).

Firstly, it is important that you understand that auditors do not have the power to insist that the financial statements are amended for any errors or omissions that have been found during the course of the audit. The financial statements are the responsibility of the directors and the auditors have no authority to overrule them when it comes to the content.

What the auditors can do is use their auditor's report to tell the shareholders of the company what they have discovered and to express their opinion as to whether this affects the truth and fairness of the financial statements.

effect of a modified audit report

Auditors generally consider that modifying their report is a last resort.

In practice they will discuss the 'problem' issues with the client's management at some length in order to avoid having to issue a modified report. In most cases the directors will be prepared to adjust the financial statements for errors and omissions which the auditors have brought to their attention, as they are keen for the accounts to be accurate.

They will also be aware that a modified report can have serious consequences for the company:

■ it could affect the shareholders' confidence in the company and its management

■ it could discourage potential investors

■ it could affect the willingness of lenders to continue offering a borrowing facility to the company

■ it could affect the company's creditworthiness with its suppliers

However, if the auditors consider that a modified opinion is appropriate, they must be able to justify the basis for their decision and explain it fully in the audit report.

issuing modified audit reports

If the auditors have serious doubts about the truth and fairness of the financial statements, or have been prevented from carrying out their work to its full extent they must consider issuing a modified audit report.

The auditors must use their professional judgement to decide how serious the issues involved are. This will then influence precisely which form of modification will be included in the audit report.

The three situations which give rise to the types of qualification above are:

■ **qualified 'except for' opinion**

The issue is material but not to the extent that the financial statements no longer give a true and fair view, ie the auditors agree that the accounts give a true and fair view 'except for' the issue in question.

■ **disclaimer of opinion**

The auditors' work has been limited, either by the management preventing them from performing the work they needed to do, or by other factors preventing them from gathering all the evidence they require – this is known as a 'limitation of scope'.

■ **adverse opinion**

The issue is so material, that it affects the truth and the fairness of the financial statements as a whole – a situation described in ISA 700 as being 'pervasive'.

Note: it is also possible for the auditors to be faced with a minor limitation of scope. In this case the auditors would also use an 'except for' opinion.

To make this clearer we will provide some examples of situations where each type of report might be issued.

USE OF DIFFERENT TYPES OF MODIFIED REPORT

'Except for' – issues are material but not pervasive (minor limitation of scope)

Inadequate provision for doubtful debts.

Disagreement over the value of some part of stocks, eg obsolete stocks that are still valued at cost instead of scrap value.

Non-disclosure in the accounts of going concern problems.

Except for – limitation of scope

Client maintained limited record of cash purchases.

Some cash sales records lost due to accidental flooding at the client's premises.

Cash flow statements only prepared for nine months after the year end, so full consideration of going concern issues not possible.

Disclaimer of opinion – limitation of scope

Auditors appointed after the year end and so unable to attend stock taking where stock is a material item.

Directors deny the auditors access to information regarding significant legal claims against the company.

No cash flow forecasts or cash budgets prepared so the going concern situation cannot be considered.

Adverse opinion

Failure to comply with Companies Act 1985, accounting standards or UK GAAP without an acceptable reason.

Significant uncertainties regarding the existence, ownership, valuation or recording of material assets and liabilities, eg failure to provide for material probable losses on long-term contracts.

The company's accounts have been prepared on a going concern basis despite significant concerns on the part of the auditors about the company's ability to continue as a going concern.

THE WORDING OF MODIFIED AUDITORS' REPORTS

The wording of modified auditors' reports must be as clear and precise as possible, ensuring that the reader is in no doubt as to why a qualification has been necessary.

Whatever the basis of their qualification the auditors should always:

- explain the facts of the disagreement
- detail the implications to the financial statements
- quantify the financial effect where possible

As stated earlier, ISA 700 offers a range of alternative reports, but for simplicity we have only included the most common example of each type of qualification so that you can see how auditors formally word these qualifications in their auditor's report.

In each of the reports below we have extracted the wording from some sample auditor's reports to illustrate the different types of qualification. Key words and phrases have been underlined to make them clearer.

'except for' qualifications

If the issue is material but not pervasive the auditors will use an 'except for' qualification. This means that the auditors are saying that the financial statements give a true and fair view, except for the matters in dispute.

1 **an example of an 'except for' qualification caused by a disagreement which is material but not pervasive**

The auditors agree that the accounts still give a true and fair view 'except for' the disagreement in question.

INDEPENDENT AUDITOR'S REPORT TO THE MEMBERS OF ALPHA LIMITED (EXTRACT)

Basis of audit opinion

We planned and performed our audit so as to obtain all the information and explanations which we considered necessary in order to provide us with sufficient evidence to give reasonable assurance that the financial statements are free from material misstatement, whether caused by fraud or other irregularity or error. In forming our opinion we also evaluated the overall adequacy of the presentation of information in the financial statements.

Included in debtors is an amount of £1 million due from a company which has ceased trading. In our opinion the company is unlikely to receive any payment and full provision should have been made for this debt, reducing the profit before taxation and net assets by that amount.

> **Qualified opinion arising from disagreement about accounting treatment**
>
> <u>Except for</u> the absence of this provision in our opinion:
>
> ■ the financial statements give a true and fair view, in accordance with United Kingdom Generally Accepted Accounting Practice, of the state of the company's affairs as at 31 December 200X and of its profit (or loss) for the year then ended, and
>
> ■ the financial statements have been properly prepared in accordance with the Companies Act 1985
>
> Herbert Norman & Co, Registered Auditors
>
> Address, Date

2 an example of an 'except for' qualification caused by limitation of scope

The auditors agree that the accounts still give a true and fair view 'except for' the area where their investigations were limited by lack of documentation and/or suitable audit evidence.

> **INDEPENDENT AUDITOR'S REPORT TO THE MEMBERS OF BETA LIMITED (EXTRACT)**
>
> **Basis of audit opinion**
>
> We conducted our audit in accordance with International Standards on auditing issued by the Auditing Practices Board, <u>except the scope of our audit work was limited, as explained below.</u>
>
> An audit includes examination on a test basis of evidence relevant to the amounts and disclosures in the financial statements.
>
> It also includes an assessment of the significant estimates and judgements made by the directors in the preparation of the financial statements and of whether the accounting policies are appropriate to the company's circumstances, consistently applied and adequately disclosed.
>
> 'We planned _(note the words 'and performed' have been deleted)_ our audit so as to obtain all the information and explanations which we considered necessary in order to provide us with sufficient evidence to give reasonable assurance that the financial statements are free from material misstatement, whether caused by fraud or other irregularity or error.
>
> <u>However the evidence available to us was limited because £120,000 of the company's purchases of string was paid for in cash without adequate</u>

documentation. There was no system of control over these payments on which we could rely for the purposes of our audit. There were no audit procedures we could adopt to confirm that these purchases were properly recorded.

In forming our opinion we also evaluated the overall adequacy of the presentation of information in the financial statements.

Qualified opinion arising from limitation in audit scope

Except for the financial effects of any adjustments as might have been necessary had we been able to obtain sufficient evidence concerning these purchases in our opinion:

■ the financial statements give a true and fair view, in accordance with United Kingdom Generally Accepted Accounting Practice, of the state of the company's affairs as at 31 December 200X and of its profit (or loss) for the year then ended, and

■ the financial statements have been properly prepared in accordance with the Companies Act 1985

Herbert Norman & Co, Registered Auditors

Address, Date

3 disclaimer of opinion

If the scope of the auditors work has been so limited that they have not been able to carry out enough audit testing to allow them to form a view on the financial statements they must issue a disclaimer of opinion.

This basically says 'we cannot express an opinion because the scope of our work has been so restricted'.

INDEPENDENT AUDITOR'S REPORT TO THE MEMBERS OF GAMMA LIMITED (EXTRACT)

Basis of audit opinion

We conducted our audit in accordance with International Standards on Auditing issued by the Auditing Practices Board, except the scope of our audit work was limited, as explained below.

An audit includes examination on a test basis of evidence relevant to the amounts and disclosures in the financial statements.

It also includes an assessment of the significant estimates and judgements made by the directors in the preparation of the financial statements and of whether the accounting policies are appropriate to the company's circumstances, consistently applied and adequately disclosed.

We planned _(note the words 'and performed' have been deleted)_ our audit so as to obtain all the information and explanations which we considered necessary in order to provide us with sufficient evidence to give reasonable assurance that the financial statements are free from material misstatement, whether caused by fraud or other irregularity or error.

However the evidence available to us was limited because we were not able to observe all physical stock and confirm trade debtors due to limitations placed on our work by the company. As a result of this and in the absence of any satisfactory alternative procedures we have been unable to perform our necessary audit procedures on both physical stock and trade debtors. Because of the significance of these items we have been unable to form a view on the financial statements.

In forming our opinion we also evaluated the overall adequacy of the presentation of information in the financial statements.

Opinion: disclaimer on view given by financial statements:

Because of the possible effect of the limitation in evidence available to us we are unable to form an opinion as to whether:

- the financial statements give a true and fair view, in accordance with United Kingdom Generally Accepted Accounting Practice, of the state of the company's affairs as at 31 December 200X and of its profit (or loss) for the year then ended , and

- the financial statements have been properly prepared in accordance with the Companies Act 1985

In respect alone of the limitation of our work referred to above:

- we have not obtained all the information and explanations that we considered necessary for the purpose of our audit

- we were unable to determine whether proper accounting records were maintained

Herbert Norman & Co, Registered Auditors

Address, Date

In this case the auditors has an issue with two aspects of the accounts, which, together, were so significant, or **pervasive**, that they affected the audit opinion on the accounts as a whole.

4   adverse opinion

If the auditors consider that the items they are disputing with the directors are so serious that as a result the financial statements are misleading, they must issue an **adverse opinion**. This basically states that 'the financial statements do **not** give a true and fair view'.

INDEPENDENT AUDITOR'S REPORT TO THE MEMBERS OF DELTA LIMITED (EXTRACT)

Basis of audit opinion

We planned and performed our audit so as to obtain all the information and explanations which we considered necessary in order to provide us with sufficient evidence to give reasonable assurance that the financial statements are free from material misstatement, whether caused by fraud or other irregularity or error. In forming our opinion we also evaluated the overall adequacy of the presentation of information in the financial statements.

As explained in Note 13 no provision has been made for losses expected to arise on certain long term contracts currently in progress. In our opinion provision should be made for foreseeable losses on individual contracts. If a provision for such losses had been made the effect would have been to reduce the profit before taxation and the net assets by £10 million.

Should the losses on these contracts materialise there is significant doubt as to whether the company will be able to continue as a going concern in the foreseeable future. This issue has not been addressed by the directors and the financial statements have been prepared on a going concern basis which may not be appropriate.

Adverse opinion

In view of the failure to provide for losses referred to above and to consider the effects of those losses on the future position of the company , in our opinion the financial statements do not give a true and fair view , in accordance with United Kingdom Generally Accepted Accounting Practice, of the state of the company's affairs as at 31 December 200X and of its profit (loss) for the year then ended.

In all other respects, in our opinion the financial statements have been properly prepared in accordance with the Companies Act 1985.

Herbert Norman & Co, Registered Auditors

Address, Date

As you can see from this last example, although the auditors only had an issue with one aspect of the accounts they decided that the effect it had on the financial statements was so significant that not mentioning it would completely mislead anyone reading them.

Now read the following Case Study which illustrates the principles of modified reports and refers back to the examples just given.

Case Study

AUDITOR'S REPORTS: HATCHES, MATCHES AND DESPATCHES

situation

You are the audit manager of Tickett & Co, registered auditors, and you are reviewing the audit files of three clients, all of whom have 31 December year ends. The three clients are Hatches Ltd, Matches Ltd and Despatches Ltd.

Hatches Ltd

Hatches is an old-established audit client which manufactures pine furniture in a factory in the town. It is a family company, owned by the directors.

The following information has been extracted from the audit file.

Most of Hatches' sales are to credit customers. Unfortunately at the year end their offices were flooded and many of the company's records were damaged. The main problem with respect to the audit was that the sales records for May to August were completely lost. The audit team were able to carry out audit work on the sales records for the other months of the year. At the year end there were no other significant audit points to report.

Matches Ltd

Matches has only been in business for two years and has never made a profit. It operates as a nationwide internet-based dating agency and operates from offices in the city centre. It is owned and run by Mike Match and his brother Roy.

The business is financed by Mike and Roy and members of their family. They also have a start-up loan from Venture Bank plc.

The latest accounts show another loss and a post balance sheet review has revealed the following points:

■ The budget prepared by the company shows that the business is due to make a profit within the next three months and its cash flow projection indicates that it will start to generate enough cash to pay off its loans within the next twelve to eighteen months. The audit senior who reviewed the budget and cash flow forecast thinks they are very optimistic and does not think that they show a realistic picture.

■ The auditors have reviewed a letter to Matches from Venture Bank reminding them that the start-up loan must be repaid within the next twelve months. It also says that, unless there is a major improvement in the company's financial performance, they will not continue lending money to the business.

Despatches Ltd

Despatches is a cash and carry warehouse which buys tinned, packaged and frozen food, drinks and tobacco from manufacturers and importers and sells it to shops, cafes and restaurants.

It does not accept credit cards and most of its transactions are by cash or cheque. It does not give credit.

The net profit for the year is £220,000 and the net asset value of the business is £3 million.

This is the first year your firm has been the auditors for Despatches. The audit file reveals the following:

■ Controls over cash sales are very poor. Customers are given a receipt when they pay at the till. The tills are emptied at the end of the day by the directors who also bank the cash. The following weaknesses have been identified by the auditors:

- The directors do not always reconcile the till takings with the till rolls.

- The directors often pay wages and other bills out of the cash takings.

- The directors only record in the cash book what was banked.

■ The biggest item on the balance sheet is the stock which is valued at over £1 million. The company carries out a rolling stock check but did not do a year-end one because of pressure of work and the forthcoming public holiday. The audit team carried out some sample tests during the course of the audit which did not reveal any problems.

required

You have been asked to make a recommendation to the audit partner as to the type of audit report that should be prepared for each of these three clients.

solution

Hatches Ltd

The audit work was generally satisfactory and no real problems were revealed. However the auditors could not examine the sales records from May to August because these had been destroyed.

The scope of the audit work has been limited, but only partially, so the report should contain:

an 'except for' opinion arising from a limitation of scope.

Study the example wording on pages 218-219.

Matches Ltd

The company seems to have a major going concern problem. They have produced some optimistic forecasts but these are of very limited value. Also, the bank has indicated that they will not continue to support the business in the future without a major improvement in its fortunes. At the moment this does not look likely.

A realistic prediction might be that the company cannot survive. It might be possible for Matches to find alternative forms of financing, but as it has yet to make a profit and as the future is still uncertain, this is unlikely.

The way in which the accounts have been prepared means that the audit report will include an

adverse opinion because the accounts have been prepared on a going concern basis which is not appropriate.

The accounts do not show a 'true and fair view' of the company's financial position.

Study the example wording on page 221.

Despatches Ltd

The auditors have been faced by two serious issues.

They have had problems gathering evidence about cash sales as the system is so poor and they were not able to verify stock by attending the stock take because it did not take place!

This casts doubt as to whether the auditors have been able to gather any meaningful evidence about two of the key figures – cash sales and stock – in the financial statements. The scope of their audit work has been limited to such an extent that they cannot express an opinion.

The audit opinion should, therefore, be a

disclaimer caused by a limitation of scope.

Study the example wording on pages 219-220.

EMPHASIS OF MATTER

There is one final situation which the auditors may have to consider when drawing up their auditor's report. This is where they wish to draw the attention of the shareholders to a significant matter in the accounts. In other words, they want to **emphasise** a certain **matter** which they consider important.

Although there is no disagreement between the auditors and the management as to how the matter has been treated in the accounts, the auditors consider that it should be highlighted to the shareholders in the auditor's report. The auditors would expect the client to discuss the issue in more detail in a note to the financial statements.

The auditors are therefore *not* qualifying their report in relation to this matter but *are* drawing attention to its disclosure in the accounts.

An example of this kind of situation is the outcome of legal proceedings between a company and another party where there are claims and counterclaims on both sides and the question of liability cannot easily be settled.

Set out below is an example of the wording of an emphasis of matter based on that type of situation. The wording is placed as a note at the end of the 'opinion' section which appears at the end of each report illustrated earlier in this chapter. It is underlined in this example (although not in practice!).

---

opinion

In our opinion

■ the financial statements give a true and fair view, in accordance with United Kingdom Generally Accepted Accounting Practice, of the state of the company's affairs as at 31 December 200X and of its profit (or loss) for the year then ended, and

■ the financial statements have been properly prepared in accordance with the Companies Act 1985'

<u>Without qualifying our opinion we draw attention to Note 6 to the financial statements. The company is defendant in legal proceedings alleging infringement of certain patent rights and claiming royalties and punitive damages. The company has filed a counter claim and preliminary hearings on both actions are in progress. The ultimate outcome of the matter cannot presently be determined and no provision for any liability that may result has been made in the financial statements.</u>

Herbert Norman & Co, Registered Auditors

Address, Date

REPORTING TO MANAGEMENT

In the course of their audit the auditors have:

■ carried out a review of the accounting systems
■ reviewed and tested the internal controls
■ examined the way the client records assets and liabilities

During this detailed work the auditors will have seen all aspects of the client's business and the systems that it operates. It is likely that this work will highlight possible areas for improvement to the client's systems that would strengthen the internal control procedures and the control environment within which they operate.

The auditors should report these points to the management in the form of a **letter of weakness**.

letter of weakness

The main purpose of this letter is to ensure that the management are aware of these weaknesses and the implications that they could have on the company if action is not taken. The auditors will also make recommendations as to how these controls could be improved.

The auditors must ensure that the points that are included in the letter of weakness are:

■ systems weaknesses – 'one off' events which should only be reported if they indicate an underlying weakness in the system

■ material – the management are unlikely to take seriously any weaknesses which they consider to be immaterial or insignificant

■ capable of being improved – if it is not possible to improve the system there is little point in mentioning it

The auditors should try to ensure that the management see the letter of weakness as being useful to them. The management is responsible for operating the financial systems and so will only be prepared to change the way in which these systems work if they see the suggestions as valid and useful.

Management will be reluctant to make changes if:

■ the points made are fine in theory but in practice are too difficult or complicated to operate easily

■ the suggestions have been tried before and do not work, despite the auditors believing that they will

■ the cost of introducing new controls outweighs any possible losses if the system was to remain as it is

Experienced auditors will always aim to 'add value' with their letter of weakness. Whether the management agree or not, the auditors should ask that they reply to each point individually. The letter of weakness and the management's responses should then be filed on the permanent file.

When the next audit commences the audit team should then check that the management have acted on what they agreed to do to rectify the weaknesses. Study the example on the next page.

contents of a letter of weakness

There is no standard layout for a letter of weakness, but the table below and on the following two pages shows what it can contain.

The letter of weakness would be sent with a covering letter addressed to the directors of the client company.

To the Directors

The following points arose from the audit for the year ended 31 March 200X.

Please note that this is not a comprehensive statement of all weaknesses which may exist or of all improvements which could be made. We set out below those matters which we consider to be of fundamental importance.

Tickett & Wrunne, Registered Auditors.

WEAKNESS	IMPLICATION	RECOMMENDATION
INTERNAL CONTROL – GENERAL POINTS **Budgeting** At the moment we understand that you prepare an annual budget prior to the commencement of the financial year and submit it to the bank to support the application for the renewal of your overdraft. Budgeting is a useful management tool and it would greatly assist the management of your business if the budget was used to monitor the progress of the business.	As the budget does not appear to be used other than to support the finance application, an opportunity is being lost to improve the management's control of the business. It is preferable for management to respond positively at the time problems or opportunities appear rather than have to rely on historical data which may be several months old by the time they see it.	A budgetary control system should be introduced comprising a monthly budget and management accounts and an explanation of significant variances. This should be produced in a timely manner each month and presented to the board for discussion.

WEAKNESS	IMPLICATION	RECOMMENDATION
Internal control – computer accounting system The computer software currently being used is obsolete. You are using Version 3. The latest issue is Version 8. Whilst it continues to support the basic accounting system, that is the day books and ledger, it has no facility for stock control nor has it any facility for recording costing information.	Use of outdated software is a missed opportunity to enhance the speed, accuracy and flexibility of financial reporting. The additional features provided by the upgraded software will improve managers control of business activities and provide the information on which they could base business decisions.	The computer software should be upgraded to Version 8. The cost of doing this is likely to be outweighed by increased efficiencies in the system and the reduction in the current paper based systems. For example, improved stock control might serve to reduce current stock holding levels and free up cash for use in the business.
INTERNAL CONTROL – DETAILED POINTS **Internal control – payroll** There is no evidence of review of the payroll. There is no independent evidence of authorisation of recruitment of new staff. At present the new employee form is signed by the wages clerk.	The payroll may contain unauthorised or fictitious employees or payments at incorrect or unauthorised rates. Fictitious employees might be introduced to the payroll. Details for new employees may be entered incorrectly on the new employee form as the wages clerk may not be aware of all the information required.	The payroll should be reviewed and signed by the production manager each week. New employee forms should be authorised by the personnel manager and countersigned by the production manager.

WEAKNESS	IMPLICATION	RECOMMENDATION
Internal control – debtors An aged debtor analysis is only produced quarterly. Slow paying customers are often not identified until well after their terms of trade have expired.	Poor credit control means that slow paying customers are not identified quickly enough so that steps could then be taken to collect money due. This means that the working capital requirement is greater than it otherwise could be. As this is presently financed by overdraft facilities the company is currently incurring excess interest cost because of slow paying debtors.	Aged debtor reports should be prepared monthly. The acquisition of new computer software should enable this to be done automatically. All customer should be reminded of the terms of trade and credit control procedures introduced to collect overdue debts.

Now read the Case Study which follows. It illustrates the issues that can be raised in a letter of weakness.

Case Study

LETTER OF WEAKNESS: MEGASTORES LTD

situation

Megastores Ltd is a small chain of three local supermarkets operating in Hightown, Lowtown and Toptown.

All the stores are roughly the same size and operate from high street premises selling a range of groceries, fresh fruit and vegetables, alcohol, tobacco and newspapers. They open seven days a week from 8am to 10pm (except Sundays when they open at 10 am) and they only close on 25 December.

Together they employ about 40 full time staff in the stores plus another ten part-time staff at weekends.

Each store has its own small warehouse attached which is replenished daily by deliveries from a central depot in Toptown. Store managers re-order by email every day from the central stores.

A significant part of their takings are in cash.

Takings in each store are counted and banked locally by store managers and they are responsible for reconciling the takings from each till every day to the internal till rolls. They submit a weekly cash sheet to the head office, which is in Toptown, recording the cash takings, the till roll totals and noting any discrepancies.

If store managers are away from the store or on holiday each store has a designated assistant manager who will carry out these duties. This is usually an experienced member of staff who does not receive any extra pay for carrying out these duties.

Head office is responsible for ordering goods into the central warehouse, maintaining the accounting records and preparing the payroll.

During the audit the following points were established:

The person who was the designated assistant manager at the Lowtown store had left the company early in the financial year. Since she left, three different people had been involved in dealing with cash takings and re-ordering at weekends. The most recent one has only been with the company two months. The manager takes every weekend off.

Managers were allowed to recruit casual workers for temporary posts and pay them from takings in the store, provided they entered this on the cash sheet. No other information was required by head office and these workers were not included on the payroll. Investigations revealed the manager at Lowtown had employed 27 casual workers during the year paying them approximately £100 each for 'weekend cover'.

The computer system does not have a stock control facility and it is the warehouse manager at the central warehouse who is responsible for re-ordering.

There was a year-end stock take at each store and the central warehouse. The stock records at the central warehouse, which are maintained on a card index file, were found to be completely out of date. The stores did not maintain any stock records so the staff just counted what was on the shelves and did not agree what they had counted back to any stock records.

The stores and the warehouse were closed when the year-end stock count was undertaken, as it was done late at night. The auditors were happy with the actual count and the year-end stock figure.

When the cash sheets from the stores were received in the accounts department the information about sales, bankings and any payments were taken from the sheets by the accounts staff and the sheets filed in the accounts office. No other checking or review of them was carried out.

required

Prepare the necessary points to be included in a letter of weakness to be sent to the management of Megastores Ltd.

solution

The letter should contain the points set out below. Note the alternative presentation to the tabular format shown on pages 227-229.

TAKINGS AT LOWTOWN

weaknesses
Cash takings at the weekend at the Lowtown store are currently counted and banked by an inexperienced member of staff. There is no formal review of any reconciliations performed between the till and the cash takings.

implications
Takings might be incorrectly recorded and reconciliations with till rolls might be incorrectly carried out.

It may not be sensible to assume that the new member of staff is trustworthy.

recommendation
Ask the manager to work weekends and have other days off in the week. Cover the manager's days off with staff seconded from another store until a more experienced person can be recruited or transferred from another store permanently.

CASUAL WORKERS

weaknesses
Managers are permitted to recruit temporary staff without them being included on the payroll.

Casual workers are paid out of cash takings.

implications
There is no verification that the casual staff actually worked or to whom the money was paid.

HM Revenue & Customs procedures for employment of casual workers have not been followed – penalties could be incurred.

The practice of making payments out of takings could mean that takings are incorrectly recorded.

recommendation
Employment of all casual staff should be authorised by head office.

HM Revenue & Customs procedures should be followed for all casual staff.

Takings should be recorded and banked intact. A petty cash float on an imprest basis should be introduced into each store so that no money needs to be taken from the till.

STOCK CONTROL

weaknesses
There is no stock control at the central warehouse because the card index system does not work.

The computer system has no stock recording facility.

There is no stock control in place at individual stores.

implications
The lack of control over stock levels has several implications:

1   Lack of control over stock levels could mean the company is holding excessive stock which is not efficient use of working capital.

2   Slow moving or deteriorating stocks cannot be identified quickly. This is important where perishable items such as food are concerned.

3   Lack of control between warehouse and stores could result in theft of stock going unnoticed.

4   Lack of stock control at stores means that stock losses due to pilfering, breakages, short deliveries etc, cannot be established.

5   The results from individual stores might be unreliable if stock levels are not properly accounted for.

recommendation   A computerised stock control system should be introduced at head office.

If funds permit, this could be linked to an Electronic Point of Sale (EPOS) system installed at each store to monitor stock being sold at each store.

A system of recording deliveries from the central warehouse to individual stores should be established.

Regular stock takes should be performed at the central warehouse and the stores on a rolling basis. Results should be reconciled to the stock recording system and any differences should be investigated.

CASH SHEETS

weaknesses   The cash sheets are not used for any other purpose apart from as a basis for extracting information about takings.

implications   The company is only recording takings and expenses and is missing the opportunity to use the cash sheets as a basis for analysing the performance of each store.

recommendation   The cash sheets should be used to assess the performance of each store by making comparison to previous weeks and other stores.

Note

You may notice that not everything mentioned in the audit file is included in the letter of weakness.

For example, managers can be permitted to re-order stock, even though, in the absence of a proper stock control system, this could be considered an area of weakness. For the auditors to suggest a bureaucratic stock ordering procedure, or to imply managers are dishonest in the absence of any firm evidence will devalue the report.

The auditors' role is to highlight systems weaknesses, point out the implications and come up with suggested improvements.

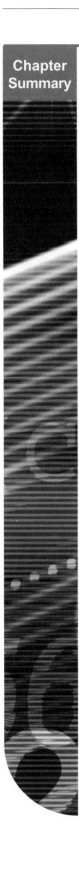

Chapter Summary

- Before the auditors sign their report, they should review 'subsequent' events from the balance sheet date up to the date of signing their report. They have to consider the effect that events since the balance sheet date have on the financial statements and decide if they are significant enough to require the financial statements to be amended.

- If events after the balance sheet date do not relate to conditions which existed at the balance sheet date then the financial statements do not require amendment, but a note to the accounts might be needed to explain the situation to readers.

- Auditors have to review the viability of the business to ensure that the business can continue as a going concern for the foreseeable future.

- The auditors should obtain representations from the management in respect of matters for which there is a limited amount of evidence or where knowledge is confined to senior management. Management should also acknowledge responsibility for preparation of the financial statements.

- Auditors should summarise the errors and omissions that they have found during the audit and discuss them with management to identify any changes needed to be made to the accounts.

- If the auditors are happy that the accounts give a true and fair view they can sign an unqualified report. Otherwise they will have to sign a modified report.

- If the scope of the audit has been limited, auditors must either issue an 'except for' opinion or a disclaimer of opinion depending on to what extent their work has been limited, and how material that limitation is to the accounts.

- If the auditors disagree with the accounting treatment or disclosures they can issue either an 'except for' opinion, or an 'adverse' opinion if the disagreement is material and pervasive, and the auditors consider the financial statements do not give a true and fair view.

- Auditors may include an emphasis of matter paragraph in their report if they want to draw the shareholders' attention to a particular matter included in the notes to the accounts.

- A letter of weakness is used to report to management any weaknesses that the auditors have found during their audit work on the financial systems. The letter will contain recommendations for improvement of the systems.

- Management should respond to each of the points in the letter of weakness so that over time the internal control environment can be improved.

audit manager	person responsible for the day-to-day running of the audit
audit partner	person responsible for the audit and for signing the auditor's report
post balance sheet events	events arising after the balance sheet date but before the date of signing the auditor's report
directors report	a report required by the Companies Act 1985 which includes details of directors and their opinion of the performance of the company during the financial year
going concern	the ability of the company to carry on its activities in the same way for the foreseeable future
management representation letter	a letter from the management used as additional audit evidence for items which cannot be fully substantiated by independent evidence or of which only the management have knowledge
unqualified audit report	an audit report which gives a 'true and fair' audit opinion without any qualification
modified auditor's report	a report in which the auditors express doubts about or disagree with certain amounts in the financial statements or with the financial statements as a whole
limitation of scope	where the auditors have been prevented from carrying out all the audit work required to gather the evidence they need
annual report	the annual report to the shareholders, prepared within the company, which includes not only the financial statements but various management reports and summaries which do not have to be audited
chairman's statement	a report to the shareholders from the chairman of the board presenting the company's performance in the financial year
pervasive	an event which is fundamental to a full understanding of the financial position of the company
letter of weakness	a report to management which identifies systems and control weaknesses and their implications and which makes recommendations to rectify them

answers to the asterisked (*) questions are to be found in the Student Resources Section of www.osbornebooks.co.uk

Student Activities

7.1* You have been asked to mark some student exercises. Set out below is a selection of the comments that have been made. Which of these are incorrect, and why?

(a)   Management representation letters place responsibility for providing the audit evidence with the management not the auditors.

(b)   Disclaiming an opinion means that the auditors' scope of work was so limited that they could not carry out a proper audit.

(c)   A letter of weakness should highlight management failings in running the business.

(d)   Modified (previously known as qualified) audit reports are issued when there is a disagreement between the auditors and the directors or when auditors are unable to gather the audit evidence that they require.

(e)   'Except for' reporting means all is well apart from items specifically mentioned.

(f)   Auditors should only insist on the accounts being adjusted for something that is material.

(g)   Events that happen after the balance sheet date can be ignored until the next year's audit.

7.2* You are the audit manager at Tickett & Co a firm of registered auditors and are reviewing audit files on Bodgers, a storage and distribution company, prior to signing them off.

When you review the fixed assets section you discover the following:

■   the company does not maintain a fixed assets register

■   all invoices for additions to fixed assets are filed in a separate file – unfortunately the office junior by accident threw away the one relating to the year being audited during an office reorganisation

■   the computer system only records invoice reference numbers and amounts in the nominal ledger, so whilst there is a record of amounts debited to the relevant fixed assets accounts there is no record of what the invoices were actually for

■   because of the points above, the audit team was only able to carry out work on disposals of fixed asset and arithmetical calculations

The financial statements have been drafted with an unqualified audit report, but fixed assets is a material figure in the accounts.

Following your review, what would your recommendation be to the audit partner in this case?

7.3* You are reviewing the final accounts of a client Sallyforth Ltd, a manufacturer of children's clothes. The summarised balance sheet, with prior year figures, is as follows:

	This year (£'000's)		Last year (£'000's)	
Fixed assets		1,562		1,893
Current assets				
Stock	59		85	
Debtors	87		53	
Bank balances	-		11	
	146		149	
Creditors				
Trade creditors	95		61	
Bank overdraft	72		-	
	167		61	
Net current liabilities/assets		(21)		88
Long-term loan		(300)		(350)
		1,241		1,631
Share capital		500		500
Reserves		741		1,131
		1,241		1,631

A subsequent events review and conversations with the company accountant reveal the following:

■ machinery in one of the client's factories had been repossessed by a leasing company because of payment defaults

■ the company has exceeded its overdraft limit three times in the last two months; the bank granted a temporary extension, but has told the company that this will expire in three months' time and will not be renewed

■ the company is currently negotiating with another bank for a refinancing package, but this has not been agreed; provisional indications are that the current poor trading performance of Sallyforth is putting off the new lenders

■ the directors have approached one of their competitors with an offer for them to buy Sallyforth, but the competitor declined

Until this point, the audit had gone well and no problems had been encountered. You have recommended an unqualified audit report. How will these issues change your view of the company's financial situation and what form of audit report might you now recommend? Use appropriate analytical review techniques when drafting your answer.

7.4   You have been asked to carry out a subsequent events review as part of the audit of Muchado Ltd which is a company specialising in the manufacture and sale of agricultural machinery.

The profit for the year was £120,000 and the net asset value was £12 million.

The company holds regular monthly directors' meetings which are minuted by the Company Secretary. At these monthly meetings the directors all receive a pack which includes management accounts comparing actual results to budget and providing explanations for major variances.

You ask the Company Secretary for the minutes of all the directors meetings since the year end and also for copies of the latest management accounts.

Your review of these documents reveals the following:

- Two months after the year end the company made a rights issue of shares to raise finance to repay borrowings.

- Sales of the Model 7 Swirling Machine had declined dramatically because of competition from an overseas competitor. Consequently Muchado was considering dropping the machine from its range and selling the stock off cheaply. At the year end there were twelve finished machines in stock and seventeen part-completed, all of which were valued at cost.

- Digga's, one of the company's main agents in Scotland had gone into liquidation owing Muchado £40,000. Total debtors at the year end were £2,350,000.

- There had been a fire in part of the factory which had damaged one of the production units. The company was fully insured for all the damage.

- The company's bankers had written requesting a meeting with Muchado as they were concerned that at some point in each month Muchado was always at the full extent of its overdraft facility.

(a)   Decide which of these items might require an adjustment to the financial statements.

(b)   List any other points that you feel that audit partner may wish to clarify with the senior management of Muchado.

7.5   You are an audit senior on the audit of Luckyboy Ltd – a company which runs a large nightclub and bar in Moretown. On Friday and Saturday nights takings regularly exceed £10,000 and are mostly in cash. However, during the rest of the week the average nightly takings are about a quarter of this.

During the audit the following notes have been made:

Business operations

The company employs two bar managers on a full time basis one of whom is on the premises at all times when the club is open.

They also employ four full-time bar staff. The rest of the staff are casual workers who are mostly employed on Friday and Saturday nights. On a busy night Luckyboy may employ up to twenty additional casual workers in the bar and nightclub. Bar managers are responsible for hiring both full-time and casual bar staff.

Casual staff are paid in cash at the end of the night by the bar managers and are not required to sign for their wages.

Only the bar managers have a key to the cellar and the stock room. You have been in to Luckyboys on a Saturday evening when it was busy and have seen the bar manager hand the key over to another member of staff to get stock when it was urgently needed.

Takings

The tills at Luckyboy are electronic and contain a sealed till roll. At the end of each shift, the bar manager on duty counts the cash in the tills and reconciles it to the total on the till roll. There is often a difference, the largest to date being £100. This was put down to staff incorrectly ringing up amounts on the till.

Supplies

All supplies are purchased from the brewery and other suppliers on credit. Deliveries are made during the day. If no one is available to receive deliveries because the club is closed, all items except for beers, wines and spirits, are left at the back of the premises. On two occasions boxes containing glasses and other items have gone missing. The supplier claimed to have delivered them but they were never traced.

Payroll

Full-time staff are paid by direct credit into their bank accounts. Bar managers are paid a basic salary plus an additional hourly rate for overtime. They submit a time sheet each Monday. Bar staff have a similar arrangement but their time sheets are authorised by the bar manager.

There is an office at the back of the club, where all personnel and accounting records are kept on a small computer network of three computers which run Sage software. The office is used by Mrs Harrison, the bookkeeper, the bar managers and other staff who sometimes use the computers to carry out internet searches, write letters and to e-mail DJs. There is no password restriction on the computer except for the payroll which is kept by Mrs Harrison. She has sole responsibility for the payroll which she prepares on a weekly basis before providing Mr Jackson, the club director, with a BACS credit transfer form to sign for bar staff and bar managers.

Based on the information set out above, prepare a schedule of weaknesses in the systems which you believe should be included in the management letter for Luckyboy Ltd.

You should present your findings in a table in the format shown below.

Weakness	Implication	Recommendation

7.6 You are the audit manager on the audit of Flintov Ltd. and have recommended to the audit partner that an unqualified audit opinion should be given.

A junior member of the audit team has queried this decision pointing out that:

- Errors discovered during the audit would have reduced pre-tax profit by £12,500 had the client amended the accounts. The pre-tax profit of Flintov Ltd is £275,000 and the balance sheet total is £7.3M.

- The client refused permission for a circularisation of debtors' balances, so the auditors had to use alternative procedures to verify debtor balances.

- After the year end, the company had to withdraw one of its products and issue a free replacement due to a manufacturing fault. Flintov Ltd held no stocks of the product at the year end. The total costs to Flintov to withdraw and replace this product were estimated to be £190,000.

(a) Taking into account the points made above, how would you explain the basis of your decision to the junior member of the audit team?

(b) Explain the implications to the junior member of the audit team of the three possible modifications to the audit opinion – ie 'except for', a disclaimer of opinion and an adverse opinion.

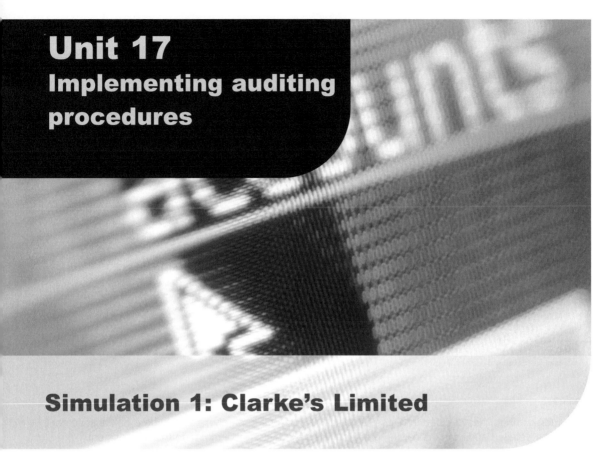

Unit 17
Implementing auditing procedures

Simulation 1: Clarke's Limited

Element coverage

17.1   contribute to the planning of an audit assignment
17.2   contribute to the conduct of an audit assignment
17.3   prepare related draft reports

Scenario and contents

This Simulation is based on Clarke's Limited, a private company which operates a car dealership in the North of England. The tasks include:

- assessment of inherent risk
- identification of control weaknesses in the accounting system and recommendations for improvements
- audit tests: tests of control, transactions tests, analytical procedures
- analytical review of financial results
- audit treatment of fixed assets
- reconciliation of credit sales debtors
- identification of issues arising from the stock take
- dealing with client staff
- audit of payroll system
- appreciating the need for confidentiality
- management representations and modified audit reports

Suggested time allocation: four hours

SIMULATION 1
CLARKE'S LIMITED

SITUATION

You are the audit senior of a firm of accountants and registered auditors. You are part of the team for the audit of Clarke's, a large motor dealership in the North of England. The year end is 31 March 2005

The tasks you have been set by the audit manager are set out below.

TASKS

Task 1

The audit manager has decided that, as part of the audit procedures, there should be a risk assessment before the detailed audit work is carried out. She has asked you to contribute to this assessment.

Based on the information on pages 246, highlight the areas of inherent risk which relate to this business. Use page 254 for your answer.

You should allow 15 minutes to complete this task.

Task 2

Review the accounting system notes on pages 246 to 248.

Using the proforma provided on pages 255-256, set out four control weaknesses which are present in the system.

(a)   For each weakness state what error or irregularity might occur as a result.

(b)   For each weakness recommend a system improvement which you could bring to management's attention.

You should allow 30 minutes to complete this task

Task 3

You have been asked to prepare an audit programme for:

■   sales of new cars

■   shop sales

The objective of the audit testing is to ensure that all sales are recorded (completeness) at the correct amounts (accuracy).

(a)   Using the proforma on pages 257 to 258, show the tests that may be performed to evidence the assertions above using:

- tests of control

- transactions test

- analytical procedures

(b)   On page 258 detail any limitations you consider there may be in obtaining sufficient reliable evidence from the tests.

You should allow 30 minutes to complete this task.

Task 4

The audit manager has asked you to carry out some preliminary analytical procedures to help identify areas where the audit work might need to be concentrated.

(a)   On page 259 explain how analytical procedures can be used at each of the three stages of the audit, ie planning, testing and completion.

(b)   Using the extracts from the financial data set out on page 249, identify any unusual trends or relationships between the figures given and explain what issues they might raise. Use page 259 for your answer.

You should allow 20 minutes to complete this task

Task 5

A junior member of staff has prepared the analysis of repairs and renewals shown on page 249.

It is company policy to capitalise expenditure on fixed assets in excess of £500.

(a)   On the schedule on page 260 indicate the items that should be transferred to fixed assets,

(b)   Describe on pages 260 and 261 the additional audit tests you would perform to test the assertions that fixed assets are complete and accurate and that they exist.

You should allow 20 minutes to complete this task.

Task 6

You have decided to carry out a reconciliation of credit sales debtors.

You circularised twenty of the sales ledger accounts and received ten replies. The information that you need to complete this task is set out on pages 250 to 251. Using this data:

(a)   Complete the table on page 261.

(b)   Using pages 262 and 263, set out:

- the objective of the test

- the results of your work, including any reconciliations that you have performed

- details of any further work that is required before a conclusion can be reached

You should allow 25 minutes to complete this task

Task 7

A member of your firm attended the stock take on 31 March. Her report is set out on pages 252 and 253. Several audit issues appear to have arisen as a result of that visit.

You obtain an analysis of stock as follows:

	£
New car stock	563,900
Used car stock	172,400
Parts	13,456
Petrol and diesel	3,845
Garage stock	1,250
Total	754,851

(a) List three good points which have arisen from the stock taking attendance report (use page 264).

(b) Describe the audit issues which have emerged from the report (use page 264).

You should allow 30 minutes to complete this task.

Task 8

Your audit manager was the senior on the previous year's audit of Clarke's. He has explained that to you that he had a major disagreement with Pat Hindle who views the audit as an unnecessary interruption to her busy schedule. He is keen for things to go as smoothly as possible this year and has asked you to brief the audit junior on how to deal with Ms Hindle.

Using page 265, set out a short memo to your junior explaining how audit staff should deal with members of the client staff.

You should allow 15 minutes to complete this task

Task 9

As part of the audit you have to carry out some testing on the payroll system. Details of the payroll system are given in the extracts from the accounting systems notes on page 247.

Using pages 266 to 267:

(a) State what the audit objectives would be when testing payroll to ensure that the key assertions of occurrence, completeness, accuracy, cut-off and classification are covered.

(b) With reference to the objectives identified in (a), suggest one audit test to cover each of the assertions for payroll.

(c) Suggest two ways in which internal control within the payroll system could be improved.

You should allow 20 minutes to complete this task

Task 10

One of your colleagues, Grace Quirrell, approaches you. She is an audit senior on the audit of Motas 4 U a rapidly rising competitor of Clarke's. She claims she is new to auditing motor dealerships and needs some help.

She asks if she can borrow your audit files overnight and bring them back the next day so that she can see how the audit should be done.

What would be your response to Ms Quirrell?

Use page 268 for this task.

You should allow 15 minutes to complete this task.

Task 11

As part of your role as audit senior you are responsible for training the audit junior. She has asked you a number of questions regarding the final stages of the audit which are detailed below.

(a)   As the audit partner left the room for a meeting with the senior management of Clarke's, he mentioned that he needed to discuss the management representation letter. This is something she has never heard of before and is unclear what it is and what it is for.

(b)   The audit manager has suggested that, in view of the problems with stock verification, an 'except for' report would be appropriate. The junior does not understand the implications of this report and has asked you to explain the reasons for an 'except for' qualification in the report.

Use page 268 for your explanations of (a) and (b).

You should allow 20 minutes to complete this task.

CLARKE'S LIMITED: BACKGROUND INFORMATION

Clarke's is a motor dealership which has expanded very quickly in the last few years following the arrival of a new managing director Julian Gold. Mr Gold replaced the last of the family directors, Simon Clarke, who retired from the business.

The business is still owned by the Clarke family, but none of them takes an active part in the business. In addition to Mr Gold there are two other directors

Sales director – Susan Harries

Financial Director – James Waters

Before the arrival of Julian Gold, the business was tied to one manufacturer and sold their range of cars only. Mr Gold ended this arrangement and the company is now a dealership for three manufacturers. Its main new car sales are concentrated on 4x4 off road vehicles and sports cars.

The company also sells second-hand cars, some of which have been traded in against new cars, and some of which are bought at auction specifically for resale.

Clarke's also offers servicing, parts and petrol and has a garage shop which sells a range of groceries, confectionery, newspapers and magazines.

CLARKE'S LIMITED: EXTRACTS FROM ACCOUNTING SYSTEMS NOTES

In addition to the financial director, Mr Waters, there is a company accountant, Pat Hindle and two clerical assistants.

The company uses Sage software for bookkeeping and payroll

All other duties are shared between the office staff. There is a small computer network of four machines but there are no passwords or restrictions, except for access to the payroll programme

The accounts office is in an area of the building between the main showroom and the service bays; sales and repair staff often pass through it

Sales

In addition to Susan Harries there are two full-time sales staff and a part-time person who works on Saturdays and Sundays, which are the busiest days for car sales. All three earn a fixed salary plus a commission based on the value of the cars they sell.

All sales of cars are invoiced. All documentation is passed through to the accounts office, although a copy of the sales invoice is retained in the sales office.

These invoices are used by Ms Harries to calculate the sales team's commission.

In the workshop all repairs and service details are recorded on job cards. These record the parts used and the time spent by the mechanic, charged out at a standard rate of £20 per hour.

When the work on the vehicles is completed, the job cards are taken to the office where the details form the basis of the sales invoice to the customer. The job cards are filed in the accounts office.

A high proportion of the petrol and shop sales are for cash; the remainder are on credit and debit cards.

Most of the sales of parts and servicing are paid for by credit or debit cards, although there are some twenty local businesses which operate credit accounts which are settled monthly.

Susan Harries is responsible for the service department but usually delegates most of the day-to-day running of that department to the service manager, Mr Johnstone, who is her brother.

There are very few cheque transactions.

Receipts from debit and credit cards are credited to the company's bank account automatically. Cash takings are banked daily by Ms Hindle. She generally tops up the petty cash from the takings. There is no set float – she just takes as much cash out as she thinks is needed and puts it in a tin in the office.

Purchases and creditors

New and second-hand car stock is controlled by the sales director, Susan Harries, who places orders with manufacturers. She also buys cars at auction. From time to time she will take cash with her to buy cars.

Parts are ordered by Joe Spanner the head mechanic. He is responsible for the stores of parts which are kept in a storeroom by the side of the workshop or on shelves in the workshop.

The storeroom is never locked as mechanics need access to it at all times. When parts stocks run low, Joe places an order with the local motor parts suppliers. He or Mr Johnstone the service manager are allowed to sign these orders.

Stock for the garage shop and petrol is ordered by Ms Hindle. Orders for these items have to be authorised by Mr Waters, but if he is not available Ms Hindle can authorise them herself and Mr Waters countersigns them later.

All purchase documentation is sent through to the accounts office, where the accounts staff match the invoices received with orders and goods received notes, as far as possible.

Payroll

Mr Waters is responsible for preparing the payroll. All staff except three mechanics and the part-time staff who work in the garage shop are paid monthly. The others are paid weekly in cash.

The mechanics fill in a time sheet which details what hours they have worked and also which cars they have been working on. They complete their time sheets on Monday mornings and hand them in to the accounts office. These sheets are not seen by any of the managers.

Part-time staff also complete a time sheet. This is checked to the staffing rota by Ms Hindle and any discrepancies are investigated. Ms Hindle authorises the time sheets for casual staff in the shop.

Mr Waters has sole access to the Sage Payroll programme and also keeps the personnel files.

The total number of employees has remained largely unchanged for the last five years.

Monthly accounts

Mr Waters produces monthly management accounts which show the turnover and direct expenses for the main departments. These are:

- new and used car sales
- forecourt and shop
- repairs and servicing

Administration and other costs which relate to the business as a whole, including marketing, light and heat, building repairs, property costs and directors salaries are classed as general overheads and not allocated to departments.

The actual costs are matched against a budget and explanations sought for major variances.

Fixed assets

The company owns its own freehold land and buildings. It moved into its present premises in 1996.

Fixed assets are shown in the books at original cost less depreciation. The company depreciates land and buildings.

The company is constantly improving its workshop facilities and often buys new equipment. This is ordered by Julian Gold who is not very good at writing the details on the orders. The office staff have a policy of posting these costs to repairs and renewals if they are not sure what they are for.

DATA FOR TASK 4 (b)

Extracts from draft financial statements and previous years' accounts

	2002 £000	2003 £000	2004 £000	2005 £000
Sales	8,280	8,450	8,800	8,220
Cost of Sales	5,810	5,900	6,160	6,080
Gross Profit	2,470	2,550	2,640	2,140
Net Profit	1,400	1,450	1,510	1,420
Payroll costs	480	515	540	620

DATA FOR TASK 5 (a)

Analysis of repairs	£
Replacement Guttering	1,254.78
New drilling machine	234.67
Window repairs	564.98
Insurance recovery	(364.98)
Ramp	3,876.90
Painting of the accounts office	455.90
Roof leak	287.56
Loose tools	45.87
Pump repairs	87.54
Compressor repairs	487.00
Welding machine	580.00
Welding supplies	145.98
Spraying booth replacement curtains	873.98
Air hose	98.65
Refurbish canteen	1,763.90
painting -showroom	3,452.90
Replace carpet tiles	675.00
Printer/photocopier	789.00
	15,309.63

Data For Task 6

Debtors' circularisation responses – text of replies received which indicated a discrepancy

---

Client name: ANIMAL PARK

According to our client's records the balance of their account with you at 31 March 2005 was £2,340.00.

Reply:

Should be £1964.09

Client name: DASHERS DELIVERIES

According to our client's records the balance of their account with you at 31 March 2005 was £940.45

Reply:

According to our agreement you should have cancelled this invoice after the appalling job you carried out. We have agreed this with Mr Gold and any further demands for money will be referred to our solicitors.

Client name: KALL KWICK TAXIS

According to our client's records the balance of their account with you at 31 March 2005 was £1,023.56.

Reply:

£200 paid 31 March

Client name: PETER REMOVALS

According to our client's records the balance of their account with you at 31 March 2005 was £187.34

Reply:

According to us it's £123.67 – have you missed something ??!!

Client name: ROLAND

According to our client's records the balance of their account with you at 31 March 2005 was £ 2,865.09

Reply:

Balance should be £2,565.09 – see below.

		£
Invoice 2356	Feb	1,567. 36
Invoice 2834	Mar	1,783.89
Paid	Jan	(786.16)
Balance		2,565.09

Clarke's sales ledger balances

Animal Park			
	Dr	*Cr*	*Balance*
B/fwd	1,987.45		1,987.45
01.03.05 CB67		1,987.45	nil
02 03 05 2765	674.87		674.87
16 03 05 2793	754.23		1,429.10
23.05.05 2834	534.99		1,964.09
31.03.05 2845	375.91		2,340.00

Dashers Deliveries			
	Dr	*Cr*	*Balance*
16.03.05 2788	940.45		940.45

Kall Kwick Taxis			
	Dr	*Cr*	*Balance*
B/fwd	345.87		345.87
03.03.05 2773	376.67		722.54
10.03.05 2790	127.45		849.99
16.03.05 2813	95.71		945.70
23.03.05 2845	77.86		1,023.56

Peter Removals			
	Dr	*Cr*	*Balance*
B/fwd	63.67		63.67
10.03.05 2791	62.45		126.12
17.03.05 2829	61.22		187.34

Roland			
	Dr	*Cr*	*Balance*
B/fwd	1,567.36		1,567.36
03.03.05 CB69		486.16	1,081.20
05.03.05	597.32		1,678.52
15.03.05	598.67		2,277.19
23.03.05	587.90		2,865.09

DATA FOR TASK 7

CLARKE'S LTD: ATTENDANCE AT STOCK TAKING – 31 MARCH 2005

I attended the stock taking at Clarke's on 31 March 2005.

The stock to be counted was:

> New Cars
>
> Used cars
>
> Petrol and diesel
>
> Oils and greases
>
> Motor parts
>
> Garage stock

The company issued a full set of stock taking instructions, a copy of which is enclosed *(not needed for this exercise)*. They also briefed all the staff undertaking the count before the count started.

Stock was counted on pre-numbered rough stock sheets. The last sheet number used was 56.

The last delivery into the stores was the day before and the last delivery note number was 6875.

The garage was closed for the period of the stock taking except for the forecourt.

New and used cars

New and used car stock was counted by the Financial Director, Mr Waters and his assistant Ms Wallace. All cars were accounted for except two used cars – registration numbers:

> V768 YWS – cost £3,500
>
> AH 03 TNU – cost £4,000

Ms Harries, the Sales Director, said she did not know where they were and promised to investigate. This needs to be followed up at the year end audit.

Petrol and diesel

It was not possible to close the forecourt for the stock take

Mr Waters took readings from the pump meters at about 5.30 p m and said that it would be possible to calculate the stock from those readings. They were:

Unleaded pump 1	73098
Unleaded pump 2	84011
Diesel pump 3	64092
Diesel pump 4	58098

Mr Waters stated that any movement in petrol stock in one day was immaterial. He told the cashier to total up the till and book all sales after 5.30 as the next day on the sales sheets.

He said that what was not in stock would go into sales the next day so the cut-off would be OK. This needs considering at the year end.

Parts stock

I carried out a test count on parts stock with Ms Wallace. The results of the count are attached (*schedule not required for this task*). We could not agree any of the actual parts stock with the computer stock record.

This needs following up at the year end.

Oils and greases

We counted the bottles of oil and tins of grease. There were no book stock records so we counted what was in the stores and on the shelf and that is the stock.

Garage stock

Mr Waters said he hadn't time to count the garage stock as he had to go. He said the stock level remained fairly constant and wasn't material so he would ask the garage manager to count it and give us a copy of the stock sheets.

As the company staff had all left I went home too.

Susan Wintergreen

Susan Wintergreen

2 April 2005

ANSWER PAGES

Task 1

Client ....   **Prepared by** ....

Accounting date ....   **Date** ....

Reviewed by ....

Date ....

Task 2

Client ....   Prepared by ....

Accounting date ....   Date ....

Reviewed by ....

Date ....

This table shows the key control weaknesses and suggestions for improving the system.

control weakness	error or irregularity	suggested improvement

Task 2 (continued)

control weakness	error or irregularity	suggested improvement

Task 3 (a)

Client ....   **Prepared by** ....

Accounting date ....   **Date** ....

                                                          Reviewed by ....

                                                          Date ....

SALES AUDIT PROGRAMME

tests of control	transaction tests	analytical procedures

Task 3 (a) continued

tests of control	transaction tests	analytical procedures

Task 3 (b)

Task 4 (a)

Client ....   **Prepared by** ....

Accounting date ....   **Date** ....

Reviewed by ....

Date ....

Task 4 (b)

Task 5 (a)

Client ....
Prepared by ....

Accounting date ....
Date ....

Reviewed by ....

Date ....

ANALYSIS OF REPAIRS	£	transfer to fixed assets *(please tick as appropriate)*
Replacement Guttering	1,254.78	
New drilling machine	234.67	
Window repairs	564.98	
Insurance recovery	(364.98)	
Ramp	3,876.90	
Painting of the accounts office	455.90	
Roof leak	287.56	
Loose tools	45.87	
Pump repairs	87.54	
Compressor repairs	487.00	
Welding machine	580.00	
Welding supplies	145.98	
Spraying booth replacement curtains	873.98	
Air hose	98.65	
Refurbish canteen	1,763.90	
Painting showroom	3,452.90	
Replace carpet tiles	675.00	
Printer/photocopier	789.00	
	15,309.63	

Task 5 (b)

Task 5 (b) continued

Task 6 (a)

Client ....   Prepared by ....

Accounting date ....   Date ....

Reviewed by ....

Date ....

Client	Per reply £	Per sales ledger £	Agreed	Reconciled
Animal Park	1,964.09	2,340.00		
Berties Brushes	126.40	126.40		
Dashers Deliveries	Nil	940.45		
Kall Kwick Taxis	823.56	1,023.56		
Lemon & Lime Fruiterers	23.80	23.80		
Maxis taxis	647.00	647.00		
Nellie Dean Bakery	738.90	738.90		
Peter Removals	123.67	187.34		
Roland	2,565.09	2,865.09		
Salad Daze	358.90	358.90		

Task 6 (b)

Objective

Workings (including reconciliations)

Further work required

Task 7 (a)

Client ....
Accounting date ....

Prepared by ....
Date ....
Reviewed by ....
Date ....

Task 7 (b)

Task 8

Client ....

Accounting date ....

Prepared by ....

Date ....

Reviewed by ....

Date ....

MEMORANDUM

Task 9

Client ....   **Prepared by** ....

Accounting date ....   **Date** ....

                                                     Reviewed by ....

                                                     Date ....

(a) audit objectives

(b) suggested tests for each assertion

Occurrence

Completeness

Accuracy

Cut-off

Classification

(c) improvements to internal control

Task 10

Task 11

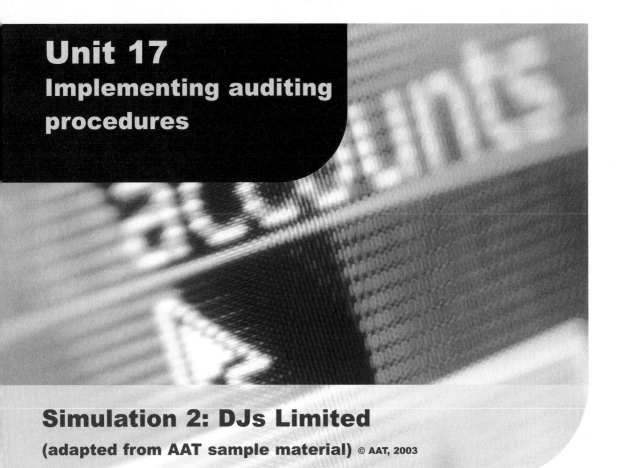

Unit 17
Implementing auditing procedures

Simulation 2: DJs Limited
(adapted from AAT sample material) © AAT, 2003

Element coverage

17.1   contribute to the planning of an audit assignment

17.2   contribute to the conduct of an audit assignment

17.3   prepare related draft reports

Scenario and contents

This Simulation is based on DJs Limited, a private company which owns a large restaurant complex on the East Coast of England. The tasks include:

■   assessment of inherent risk

■   identification of weaknesses in the accounting system and their consequences

■   audit testing and its limitations

■   setting up of a sampling system

■   creditors' statement reconciliation

■   classification of fixed assets and repairs and renewals

■   confidentiality of the audit

■   audit testing and its limitations

■   assessment of the risks of theft or fraud

■   drafting audit reports

Suggested time allocation: four hours

SIMULATION 2
DJS LIMITED

SITUATION

You are employed as an audit senior by a firm of accountants and registered auditors. You are helping with the audit of DJs Ltd, a private company which owns a large restaurant complex on the East Coast of England. The year end is 31 December 2002.

The tasks that your manager would like you to complete are set out below.

TASKS

Task 1

It has been decided that the audit will concentrate on the following areas:

■ sales

■ purchases and creditors

■ payroll

■ fixed assets

Read the background information on page 273 and for each of the above areas explain why you think they should have been selected for particular attention.

Use pages 279-280 for your answers.

Note: consider inherent risk only; do not refer to accounting systems at this stage.

Allow 20 minutes for this task.

Task 2

Review the accounting systems notes on page 274.

Using the table on pages 281-282, set out four weaknesses that are present in the system. For each weakness state what error or irregularity may occur as a result.

Allow 20 minutes for this task.

Task 3

You have been asked to prepare the audit programme for sales.

1 Complete the tables on pages 283-285 to show the tests within the following categories that may be performed to achieve the objectives shown at the top of each table:

■ the tests of control

■ the transactions test

■ the analytical procedures

2 State the limitations in the evidence from each of the above types of test. Use page 286.

Allow 30 minutes for this task.

Task 4

You are deciding on the sample selection for the testing of creditors.

Using page 287:

1 State three factors you would take into account in determining your sample size.

2 Suggest, with reasons, the most appropriate population from which to select your sample when testing creditors for understatement.

Allow 15 minutes for this task.

Task 5

You are leading the audit of the purchases and creditors section. Your junior has prepared the working paper set out on page 275 and has given it to you to review.

The planning notes for this work state that the objective of this purchase test is to ensure that purchases are accurately recorded, and are not overstated.

The sample size has been set at 15, and it has been decided that the sample should be selected on a systematic basis.

Use pages 288-289 to set out the review points.

Allow 25 minutes for this task.

Task 6

You are performing a creditors' statement reconciliation.

The creditors to be tested are set out on page 290. The balances that have been agreed to the statement have already been noted on the working paper. The information to complete this task is given on pages 276 - 278.

Complete the working paper on page 290.

Using pages 290-291, set out:

■ the objective of the test

■ the results of your work (you should show any reconciliations)

■ any further work that is required before a conclusion can be reached

Allow 40 minutes for this task.

Task 7

Your junior has prepared a schedule of the items included in the repairs and renewals account which he thinks may be fixed assets. It is the company's policy to capitalise amounts over £100. The schedule is on page 292.

1   On the schedule on page 292, show which items should be treated as fixed assets by placing a tick in the column headed 'transfer to fixed assets'.

2   On pages 292-293, set out what additional audit tests you would perform to confirm that fixed assets are complete and accurate and that they exist.

Allow 25 minutes for this task.

Task 8

A friend of yours has a job as a waitress in the restaurant. She has seen you in the restaurant and knows that you are performing the audit. She has asked you out for a drink and has said that she wants to hear all the inside information that you have access to. She is particularly interested in what her colleagues get paid.

Use page 294 to set out how you would deal with this situation.

Allow 15 minutes for this task.

Task 9

The client has asked for advice on how their systems can be improved. They specifically want to ensure that they are not losing money through theft or fraud.

Use pages 295-296 to set out four weaknesses in the current system which may lead to theft or fraud, and make recommendations for improvement.

Allow 30 minutes for this task.

Task 10

The results of the sales testing seem to be inconclusive. The analytical procedures have shown that there are unexplained differences between actual and expected sales, and that the differences between the takings sheets and the tills have not been properly explained.

Overall you feel that you cannot conclude on the sales work. However, although this is a material matter, it is unlikely to make the financial statements misleading.

On pages 297-298:

1   State the type of audit report which should be given as a result of this.

2   Draft the opinion paragraph of the audit report.

Allow 20 minutes for this task.

DJS LTD: BACKGROUND INFORMATION

DJs Ltd is a private limited company which owns a large restaurant plus a café and takeaway. The owners of the company are David Golding and John Selwood who are old friends and have run the business together for 5 years. They have 50% of the share capital each and they are both directors of the company.

David is responsible for the financial side of the business and is 'front of house' whereas John is more involved with the day-to-day running of the business. However they have recently appointed two managers who are allowing David and John to spend less time in the restaurant.

The trade is very seasonal with high turnover and profits in the summer months. However the restaurant remains open for the whole year and gains from weekenders and Christmas holiday makers. It also has an increasing local clientele.

During the summer months a large number of casual workers are taken on. Some only last a few days and are never seen again. Many are at school or college and are taking a holiday job. During the rest of the year there are around 15 people on the payroll. Most of these have been there for at least two years and that element of the workforce is fairly stable.

Many of the sales are cash sales, particularly in the café and takeaway.

Purchases are bought on credit from a number of different suppliers.

The company owns the premises from which the business is run.

DJS LTD: EXTRACTS FROM ACCOUNTING SYSTEMS NOTES

Monthly accounts and payroll

The company employs a bookkeeper for a few hours a month to prepare monthly accounts and the payroll. Both are prepared using Sage software. There is no password protection over the software.

The computer is kept in the office at the back of the restaurant; this is also used as a rest room for staff.

Sales

Customers can pay by cash, cheque or credit card. There is an automatic link for credit card payments so the amount is automatically transferred into the company's bank account.

A large amount of sales are paid for in cash.

At the end of each day the tills are totalled and the money in each till is counted by one of the newly appointed managers. Sales are recorded on a daily takings sheet. A comparison is made between the amount in the tills and the amount per the till rolls. However, although differences are noted, there is little or no follow up unless there is a very large difference.

On most days money from the tills is used to pay for small items. Receipts are sometimes attached to the daily sheet for these but there is no real discipline over this.

The cheques are paid into the bank on the following day. Cash is kept in a safe in the office and is used to pay for purchases and wages as much as possible. It is kept in the house which David and John share.

Purchases and creditors

Food orders are made by the head chef. He is also responsible for checking deliveries, to ensure that items are in good condition and that the delivery matches the order.

David pays the invoices in the month following the date of the invoice. He matches the invoices to the statements received and clips them together. He notes the amount paid on the statement and states whether the payment was made by cash or cheque, giving the cheque number as appropriate.

The creditors at any one time are therefore usually one month's worth of purchases and expenses.

Payroll

Wages are paid on a fortnightly basis and are calculated from the hour sheets which the staff complete for themselves. Payments are made in cash when possible. The bookkeeper uses Sage payroll to calculate the wages but has problems in obtaining P45s, P46s, addresses, NI numbers, dates of birth etc for the staff in the summer months.

Once the bookkeeper has calculated the wages she counts out the cash and puts it in envelopes for the staff.

Fixed assets

These are purchased by David and John as required. The bookkeeper is not very reliable at posting them to the correct account and is more likely to post fixed assets to the repairs and renewals account.

DATA FOR TASK 5

Client	....	Prepared by	....
Accounting date	....	Date	....
		Reviewed by	....
		Date	....

PURCHASES

TEST TO ENSURE THAT PURCHASES ARE CORRECT AND ARE NOT OVERSTATED

	Purchase invoice no DJs ref	Supplier	Description	£	Included in purchases
1	22272	Nice Ice	Ice Cream	185.60	✔
2	22273	Boozers	Wine	250.25	✔
3	22275	The Meat Co	Ham	132.43	✔
4	22280	The Pet Shop	Dog food	155.45	✔
5	22379	Olivers Ltd	Cooking oil	45.00	✔
6	22481	The Veg shop	Vegetables	38.70	✔
7	22511	Nice Ice	Ice cream	123.56	✔
8	22570	Foodies	Desserts	189.00	✔
9	22692	Not found	replaced by 22693		✕
	22693	Boozers	Beer	354.67	✔
10	22733	Heatons Ltd	Ingredients	65.54	✔
11	22815	The News	Christmas advert	87.50	✔
12	22896	Coffee Club	Coffee	67.89	✔

Conclusion

Purchases are correctly recorded.

Suppliers' statements

OLIVER'S LTD   Statement
Cooking oil for the catering trade
2 The Industrial Estate, Highestoft, Suffolk

Customer name	DJs Ltd
Address	2 The Sea Front, Suffolk

	debit	credit	balance
	£	£	£
Brought forward			540.50
14/10/02 inv. 30741	100.00		640.50
21/10/02 inv. 30814	176.60		817.10
28/10/02 inv. 30902	108.10		925.20
31/10/02 payment – thank you		817.10	108.10
06/11/02 inv. 31102	180.60		288.70
13/11/02 inv. 31198	131.80		420.50
20/11/02 inv. 31281	308.60		729.10
28/11/02 inv. 31350	141.70		870.80
30/11/02 payment – thank you		420.50	450.30
02/12/02 inv. 31423	109.00		559.30
12/12/02 inv. 31534	218.00		777.30
20/12/02 inv. 31678	196.20		973.50
Balance due at 31/12/02			973.50

Data For Task 6

```
THE VEG SHOP
1 HIGH STREET
SUFFOLK

THE FOLLOWING INVOICES ARE OUTSTANDING:

No 1127  15/12/02      £120.70
No 1842  22/12/01      £ 99.64
Total                  £220.34

Please pay immediately
```

BOOZERS					STATEMENT
17 WINES WAY INDUSTRIAL ESTATE, IPSFORD, SUFFOLK					31 DECEMBER 2002

Date	Transaction			Amount £	Balance £
30/11/02	Balance forward				5,202.67
06/12/02	Invoice DJ125			75.65	5,278.32
12/12/02	Invoice DJ187			608.40	5,886.72
27/12/02	Invoice DJ254			84.70	5,971.42

Current	1-30 days	31-60 days	61-90 days	Over 90 days	Amount due
768.75	3,385.51	1,817.16	-	-	5,971.42

DATA FOR TASK 6

Creditors ledgers

Boozers

Tp	Date	Ref	Details	Balance
Balance				5,202.67
PI	06/12/02	22873	DJ125	75.65
PI	12/12/02	22901	DJ187	608.40
PA	30/12/02			-1,817.16
			Total	4,069.56

Olivers Ltd

Tp	Date	Ref	Details	Balance
PI	28/10/02	22604	30902	108.10
PI	06/11/02	22636	31102	180.60
PI	13/11/02	22741	31198	131.80
PI	20/11/02	22793	31281	308.60
PI	28/11/02	22801	31350	141.70
PA	28/11/02		payment	-420.50
PI	02/12/02	22852	31423	109.00
PI	12/12/02	22871	31534	281.00
PI	20/12/02	22915	31678	196.20
			Total	1,036.50

The Veg Shop

Tp	Date	Ref	Details	Balance
PI	08/12/02	22864	1011	140.20
PC	08/12/02	c103	credit note	-10.24
PA	10/12/02	22858	payment	-140.20
PI	15/12/02	22901	1127	120.70
PI	22/12/02	22928	1842	99.64
			Total	210.10

ANSWER PAGES

Task 1

Client ....

Accounting date ....

Prepared by ....

Date ....

Reviewed by ....

Date ....

Task 1 (continued)

Task 2

Client ....

Prepared by ....

Accounting date ....

Date ....

Reviewed by ....

Date ....

weakness	error or irregularity

Task 2 (continued)

weakness	error or irregularity

Task 3

Client ....

Prepared by ....

Accounting date ....

Date ....

Reviewed by ....

Date ....

Audit objectives:
- all sales are recorded
- sales have been recorded accurately

TESTS OF CONTROL

Task 3 (continued)

Audit objectives:
- all sales are recorded
- sales have been recorded accurately

TRANSACTIONS TESTS

Task 3 (continued)

Audit objectives:
- all sales are recorded
- sales have been recorded accurately

ANALYTICAL PROCEDURES

Task 3 (continued)

LIMITATIONS OF AUDIT EVIDENCE
Tests of control
Transactions tests
Analytical procedures

Task 4

Client ....   **Prepared by** ....
Accounting date ....   **Date** ....
                                                                                                Reviewed by ....
                                                                                                Date ....

Task 5

Client ....

Accounting date ....

Prepared by ....

Date ....

Reviewed by ....

Date ....

Task 5 (continued)

Task 6

Client ....   Prepared by ....

Accounting date ....   Date ....

Reviewed by ....

Date ....

Creditors statement reconciliation - working paper				
Creditor	**Balance per client (£)**	**Balance per statement (£)**	**Agrees to statement**	**Reconciled**
Boozers	4,069.56	5,971.42		
Jo Bakers	425.35	425.35	✔	
Coffee Club	1,287.10	Not available		
Foodies	3,924.50	3,924.50	✔	
Heatons	1,008.18	Not available		
The Meat Club	2,478.64	2,478.64	✔	
Olivers Ltd	1,036.50	973.50		
The Veg Shop	210.10	220.34		

Task 6 (continued)

Task 7

Client ....   **Prepared by** ....

Accounting date ....   **Date** ....

                                                        Reviewed by ....

                                                        Date ....

FIXED ASSETS: REVIEW OF REPAIRS AND RENEWALS

	£	Transfer to fixed assets
Replacement Plates	1,670	
Maintenance of tills	400	
Computer software	150	
New chairs for outside	2,500	
Paper napkins	357	
Repair of fridge	125	
Coffee making machine	4,500	
Decorator: wall papering restaurant	500	
Annual maintenance of security system	200	
Grass cutting: weekly	500	
Repair of dishwasher	97	
Replacement dishwasher	980	
Picture hanging	125	
Mural painted on restaurant wall	900	
Plant care	3,000	
New cutlery	5,000	
Tea towels	200	
Sign writing for outside	350	

Task 7 (continued)

Task 8

Client ....

Accounting date ....

Prepared by ....

Date ....

Reviewed by ....

Date ....

Task 9

Client ....

Accounting date ....

Prepared by ....

Date ....

Reviewed by ....

Date ....

OBJECTIVE: TO ENSURE MONEY IS NOT LOST THROUGH THEFT OR FRAUD

current situation	recommendation for improvement

Task 9 (continued)

Client ....   Prepared by ....

Accounting date ....   Date ....

Reviewed by ....

Date ....

OBJECTIVE: TO ENSURE MONEY IS NOT LOST THROUGH THEFT OR FRAUD

current situation	recommendation for improvement

Task 10

Client ....

Accounting date ....

Prepared by ....

Date ....

Reviewed by ....

Date ....

Task 10 (continued)

Appendix

MAPPING OF ISAs to SASs

The **International Standards on Auditing** (ISAs) which have been developed by the International Auditing and Assurance Standards Board (IAASB) are replacing the **Statement of Auditing Standards** (SASs) which have traditionally regulated the auditing profession.

Their relevance to the study of Unit 17 is explained on pages 25-26 of this book.

The message to students is that you do not need to memorise this set of Standards or be able to quote their texts or reference numbers, but you do have to be aware of the way in which they provide a regulatory framework. You could compare the situation with speeding offences in the UK: you do not have to know the name of the Road Traffic Acts, but you do have to know what to do if you see the number 30 in a red circle on a roadside sign!

The mapping below supplements the explanation of ISAs in Chapter 2, and should prove useful both to tutors and also to students who may be familiar with SASs from previous studies or in their day-to-day work.

The mapping is carried out on an element-by-element basis and therefore contains some duplications.

The full texts of ISAs can be downloaded from www.apb.org.uk

Element 17.1 Contribute to the planning of an audit assignment

SAS	Replacement ISA
SAS 200 – 'Planning'	ISA – '300 Planning the Audit'
SAS 210 – 'Knowledge of the business'	ISA 315 – 'Obtaining an understanding of the entity and its environment and assessing the risks of material misstatement'
SAS 220 – 'Materiality and the audit'	ISA 320 – 'Audit materiality'
SAS 230 – 'Working papers'	ISA 230 – 'Documentation'
SAS 240 – 'Quality control for audit work'	ISA 220 – 'Quality control for audits of historical financial information'
SAS 300 – Accounting and internal control systems and audit risk assessment	ISA 315 – 'Obtaining an understanding of the entity and its environment and assessing the risks of material misstatement'
SAS 410 – 'Analytical procedures'	ISA 520 – 'Analytical procedures'
SAS 430 – 'Audit sampling'	ISA 530 – 'Audit sampling and other selective testing procedures'

Element 17.2 Contribute to the conduct of an audit assignment

SAS	Replacement ISA
SAS 400 – 'Audit evidence'	ISA 500 – 'Audit evidence'
	ISA 501 – 'Audit evidence – additional considerations for specific items'
SAS 410 – 'Analytical procedures'	ISA 520 – 'Analytical procedures'
SAS 420 – 'Audit of accounting estimates'	ISA 540 – 'Audit of accounting estimates'
SAS 430 – 'Audit sampling'	ISA 530 – 'Audit sampling and other selective testing procedures'
SAS 440 – 'Management representations'	ISA 580 – 'Management representations'
SAS 450 – 'Opening balances and comparatives'	ISA 510 – 'Initial engagements – opening balances'
SAS 460 – 'Related parties'	ISA 550 – 'Related parties'
SAS 470 – 'Overall review of the financial statements'	ISA 520 – 'Analytical procedures'
SAS 500 – 'Considering the work of internal audit'	ISA 610 – 'Considering the work of internal audit'
SAS 510 – 'The relationship between principal auditors and other auditors'	ISA 600 – 'Using the work of another auditor'
SAS 520 – 'Using the work of an expert'	ISA 620 – 'Using the work of an expert'

Element 17.3 Prepare related draft reports

SAS	Replacement ISA
SAS 600 – 'Auditors' reports on financial statements'	ISA 700 – 'The Independent auditor's report on a complete set of general purpose financial statements'
	ISA 701 – 'Modifications to the independent auditors report'
SAS 610 – 'Communication of audit matters to those charged with governance'	ISA 260 – 'Communication of audit matters with those charged with governance'

SAMPLE PERMANENT AUDIT FILE INDEX

CONTENTS OF FILE	
Section Heading	*Information provided*
1 **Memorandum & articles of association**	'Objects' clause Minimum share capital Rights and duties of directors Voting rights
2 **Background and history of client**	Nature and history of business Ownership Registered office Nature of business/trade Management structure Directors Key staff other than directors Position in industry Premises details Key products Major suppliers Customers (details of major customers)
3 **Systems**	Flow charts Systems notes Location of records Computer system details Specimen documents Code list

4	**Legal documents/minutes**	Contract details
		Finance agreements
		Leases
		Title deeds
		Company books (including minutes)
5	**Group structure**	Subsidiary companies
		Associated undertakings
6	**Taxation**	Tax district and reference
		VAT information
7	**Other advisors**	Bankers
		Solicitors
		Valuers
		Other auditors (if any)
8	**Rotational visits**	Branches to be visited
9	**Reporting**	Copies of previous year management letters
10	**Administration**	Letters of authority
		Letter of engagement
11	**Any other relevant points**	

SAMPLE CURRENT AUDIT FILE INDEX

Section	Heading	Information
1	**Draft and final accounts**	Copies of draft and final signed accounts
2	**Letters and reports**	Letter of representation Management letter Points to carry forward
3	**Checklists**	Directors' Report disclosure Financial accounts disclosure Audit file review checklist
4	**Balance sheet**	Lead schedules and audit verification details, including verification letters Items covered: Fixed assets Intangible assets Stock and work in progress Debtors Bank balances Cash balances Short-term creditors Long-term creditors Loans Share capital Reserves
5	**Income statement**	Lead schedules and audit verification details, including verification letters

6	**Cash Flow statement**	Lead schedules and audit verification details, including verification letters
7	**Systems audit**	Audit programs Control tests Walk through tests Queries and notes Weaknesses – letter of weakness
8	**Trial balance**	Copy of extended trial balance
9	**Statutory audit**	Extracts from minutes Details of changes Rotation of directors
10	**Analytical review and data**	Ratio analysis Comparison with Planning Memorandum Five year summary
11	**Any other points**	Notes and points relevant to the audit but not leading to material adjustments

SAMPLE ENGAGEMENT LETTER

> **important note**
>
> This is a working document which includes instructions (*in italics*) to the staff of the auditing firm drawing up the document. It can be amended where indicated to suit the circumstances of the auditor/client relationship.

LIMITED COMPANY: AUDIT

This letter deals solely with the audit requirements of a company under the Companies Act 1985. Other services such as accounts preparation or completion of tax returns should be dealt with in a separate letter or by adding paragraphs as appropriate from the Limited Company — other services letter.

* Delete or amend, as appropriate.

The board*/committee of management*/trustees*/governors*.....................*(title of governing body)*
.... *(name of entity)*

Dear Sirs,

We are pleased to accept/continue* the appointment as your auditors and are writing to confirm the matters discussed at our meeting (with you/Mr....................................) on.................................... .

The purpose of this letter and the attached Standard Terms of Business is to set out the basis on which we are to act as auditors and to clarify our respective responsibilities in respect of the audit. A separate letter will be issued to cover all other work undertaken.

We are bound by the ethical guidelines of *[Name of Professional Body]*, and accept instructions to act for you on the basis that we will act in accordance with those ethical guidelines.

1   Your responsibilities as directors

1.1   As directors of the company, you are required to prepare financial statements for each financial year that give a true and fair view of the state of affairs of the company and of the profit or loss of the company for that period. In preparing those financial statements, you are required to:

        (a)   select suitable accounting policies and then apply them consistently;

        (b)   make judgements and estimates that are reasonable and prudent; and

        (c)   prepare the financial statements on the going concern basis unless it is inappropriate to presume that the company will continue in business.

1.2   You are responsible for keeping proper accounting records which disclose with reasonable accuracy at any time the financial position of the company and to enable them to ensure that the financial statements comply with the Companies Act 1985 (the Act).

1.3   You are responsible for safeguarding the assets of the company and hence for taking reasonable steps to ensure the company's activities are conducted honestly and for the prevention and detection of fraud and other irregularities.

1.4 You are responsible for ensuring that the company complies with laws and regulations applicable to its activities, and for establishing arrangements designed to prevent any non-compliance with laws and regulations and to detect any that occur.

1.5 Where audited information is published on the company's website or by other electronic means, it is your responsibility to advise us of any intended electronic publication before it occurs and to ensure that any such publication properly presents the financial information and auditor's report. We reserve the right to withhold consent to the electronic publication of our report if it or the financial statements are to be published in an inappropriate manner.

1.6 It is your responsibility to ensure there are controls in place to prevent or detect quickly any changes to that information. We are not required to review such controls nor to carry out ongoing reviews of the information after it is first published. The maintenance and integrity of the company's website is your responsibility and we accept no responsibility for changes made to audited information after it is first posted.

2 Our responsibilities as auditors

2.1 Our legal and professional duty is to make a report to the members stating whether, in our opinion, the financial statements of the company which we have audited give a true and fair view of the state of the company's affairs, and of the profit or loss for the year, and whether they have been properly prepared in accordance with the Companies Act 1985. In arriving at our opinion we are required by law to consider the following matters, and to report on any in respect of which we are not satisfied:

(a) whether proper accounting records have been kept by the company and proper returns adequate for our audit have been received from branches not visited by us;

(b) whether the company's balance sheet and profit and loss account are in agreement with the accounting records and returns;

(c) whether we have obtained all the information and explanations which we think necessary for the purpose of our audit; and

(d) whether the information in the directors' report is consistent with that in the audited financial statements.

2.2 As noted above, our report will be made solely to the company's members, as a body, in accordance with Section 235 of the Companies Act 1985. Our audit work will be undertaken so that we might state to the company's members those matters we are required to state to them in an auditor's report and for no other purpose. In those circumstances, to the fullest extent permitted by law, we will not accept or assume responsibility to anyone other than the company and the company's members as a body, for our audit work, for the audit report, or for the opinions we form.

2.3 There are certain other matters, which according to the circumstances, may need to be dealt with in our report. For example, where the financial statements do not give details of directors' remuneration or of their transactions with the company, the Companies Act 1985 requires us to disclose such matters in our report.

2.4 In addition, we have a professional duty to report if the financial statements do not comply in any material respect with Financial Reporting Standards or Statements of Standard Accounting

Practice, unless in our opinion non-compliance is justified in the circumstances. In determining whether or not any departure is justified we will consider:

(a) whether the departure is required in order for the financial statements to give a true and fair view; and

(b) whether adequate disclosure has been made concerning the departure.

2.5 Our professional duties also include:

(a) incorporating in our report a description of the directors' responsibilities for the financial statements, where the financial statements or accompanying information do not include such description, and

(b) considering whether other information in documentation containing the financial statements is consistent with the audited financial statements.

3 Scope of audit

3.1 Our auditing procedures will be carried out in accordance with the Statements of Auditing Standards issued by the Auditing Practices Board, and will include such tests of transactions and of the existence, ownership and valuation of assets and liabilities as we consider necessary.

3.2 We will ascertain the accounting systems in order to assess their adequacy as a basis for the preparation of the financial statements and to establish whether the company has maintained proper accounting records. We will need to obtain relevant and reliable evidence sufficient to enable us to draw reasonable conclusions therefrom.

3.3 The nature and extent of our tests will vary according to our assessment of the company's accounting and internal control systems, and may cover any aspects of the business's operations. We shall report to the management any significant weaknesses in, or observations on, the company's systems that come to our attention of which we believe the directors should be made aware. Any such report may not be provided to any third party without our prior written consent. Such consent will only be granted on the basis that such reports are not prepared with the interests of any party other than the members in mind and that we therefore neither have nor accept any duty or responsibility to any other party as concerns the reports.

3.4 The responsibility for safeguarding the assets of the company and for the prevention and detection of fraud, error and non-compliance with law or regulations rests with the management. However, we will plan our audit so that we have a reasonable expectation of detecting material misstatements in the financial statements resulting from irregularities, fraud or non-compliance with law or regulations, but our examination should not be relied upon to disclose all such material misstatements or frauds, errors or instances of non-compliance that might exist.

3.5 As part of our normal audit procedures, we may request you to provide formal representations concerning certain information and explanations we receive from you during the course of our audit. In particular, where we bring misstatements in the financial statements to your attention that are not adjusted, we shall require written representation of your reasons. In connection with representations and the supply of information to us generally, we draw your attention to section 389A of the Companies Act 1985 under which it is an offence for an officer of the company to mislead the auditors.

3.6　To enable us to conduct a review of your financial statements, which constitutes part of our audit, we will request sight of any documents or statements, which will be issued with the financial statements.

3.7　Once we have issued our report we will have no further direct responsibility in relation to the financial statements for that financial year. However, we expect that you will inform us of any material event occurring between the date of our report and that of the annual general meeting which may affect the financial statements. We are entitled to attend all general meetings of the company, and to receive notice of all such meetings.

And if applicable

3.8　We appreciate that the present size of your business renders it uneconomic to create a system of internal control based on the segregation of duties for different functions within each area of the business. In the running of your company we understand that the director(s) is/(are) closely involved with the control of the company's transactions. In planning and performing our audit work we shall take account of this supervision.

4　Communication

4.1　In order to ensure that there is effective two-way communication between us we set out below the expected form and timing of such communications.

- We shall contact .... by telephone prior to each year-end for preliminary discussions concerning the audit. We will confirm in writing the matters discussed and any agreed action.

- We will arrange a meeting to discuss the forthcoming audit prior to the expected start date. Again we will confirm in writing the matters discussed and any agreed action.

- We will arrange a meeting to discuss any matters arising from the audit after completion of the detailed work. Again we will confirm in writing the matters discussed and any agreed action.

4.2　The formal communications set out above are the minimum required to comply with auditing standards. We shall of course contact you on a more frequent and regular basis regarding both audit and other matters.

The above paragraphs are a suggestion only. It is important that the wording is tailored to the procedures in your practice and for the client concerned. The letter of engagement is a contract between you and the client. You should not include procedures that will not be performed.

5　Other services

5.1　We have also agreed to *[insert as appropriate]*

5.2　However, there are many other areas where we can be of assistance and we shall be pleased to discuss any matters with you. These other services include:

(a)　reports in support of returns or claims, eg, insurance company certificates, government claims, etc.;*

(b)　advice on financial matters;*

(c)   management accounting, including such matters as cash flow statements, costing systems, etc., and advice on management;*

(d)   advice on the selection and implementation of computer systems;*

(e)   investigations for special purposes, eg, acquisitions of other businesses, or examination of specific aspects of your business; and*

(f)   advice on the selection and recruitment of staff.*

Only include services not already shown.

5.3   *[We enclose a copy of our brochure which explains more fully the services that we can provide.]*

6   Agreement of terms

6.1   The terms set out in this letter and our attached Standard Terms of Business (last revised *[insert date]*) shall take effect immediately upon your countersigning this letter and returning it to us or upon the commencement of the audit,* accounts,* and tax return* for the accounting period ended [.....], whichever is the earlier.

6.2   [These terms will also apply to any matter dealt with in respect of periods prior to the period ended [.....], namely period(s) ended [...] to [...], *[complete as appropriate]*.] [We will not be responsible for earlier periods. Your previous advisers, [...] *[insert name of previous advisers]*, will deal with the audit,* accounts,* and outstanding returns,* assessments,* and other matters* relating to earlier periods and will agree the position with the relevant authorities.] *[Delete/amend as appropriate.]*

6.3   Once it has been agreed, this letter and the attached Standard Terms of Business will remain effective until they are replaced. We shall be grateful if you could confirm your agreement to these terms by signing the enclosed copy of this letter and returning it to us immediately.

Yours faithfully,

I/We* confirm that I/we* have read and understood the contents of this letter and the attached Standard Terms of Business and agree that they accurately reflect the services that I/we* have instructed you to provide.

Signed   ....   Dated   ....

Signed   ....*   Dated   ....*

For and on behalf of *[Insert name of company]*

Index